Basic Economics

Basic Economics

Alvina Cuoco

Larsen & Keller
www.larsen-keller.com

Basic Economics
Alvina Cuoco
ISBN: 978-1-64172-451-7 (Hardback)

Larsen & Keller
Published by Larsen and Keller Education,
5 Penn Plaza,
19th Floor,
New York, NY 10001, USA

Cataloging-in-Publication Data

Basic economics / Alvina Cuoco.
p. cm.
Includes bibliographical references and index.
ISBN 978-1-64172-451-7
1. Economics. 2. Economics--Methodology. I. Cuoco, Alvina.
HB171 .B37 2020
330--dc23

Printed and bound in China.

For more information regarding Larsen and Keller Education and its products, please visit the publisher's website www.larsen-keller.com

Table of Contents

Preface

The social science that deals with the study of the production, distribution, and consumption of goods and services is known as economics. It observes the behavior and interactions of economic agents and the working of economies. Economics is broadly divided into two parts, microeconomics and macroeconomics. Microeconomics deals with the basic elements in the economy such as markets and individual agents like households, firms, sellers, etc. It also deals with the interactions between them and the outcomes of their interactions. Macroeconomics is involved in the study of the entire economy that consists aggregated production, consumption, saving and investment. It also deals with the issues affecting the economies such as unemployment of resources, inflation, economic growth and the public policies, which deal with these issues. This textbook provides comprehensive insights into the field of economics. Some of the diverse topics covered in this book address the varied branches that fall under this category. It will serve as a valuable source of reference for those interested in this field.

To facilitate a deeper understanding of the contents of this book a short introduction of every chapter is written below:

Chapter 1- Economics is the branch of social science that deals with the study of production, distribution and consumption of goods and services. Economics is categorized into two major types - microeconomics and macroeconomics. This is an introductory chapter which will briefly introduce all the significant aspects of economics and its types.

Chapter 2- Market is any structure that facilitates trade and allows the exchange of goods and services for buyers and sellers. A few fundamentals of market and firm are theory of production, market forms, market equilibrium, market failure, etc. This chapter has been carefully written to provide an easy understanding of these fundamentals of market and firm.

Chapter 3- Consumer equilibrium refers to the balance between the expenditure of income on goods and services and maximum satisfaction achieved from the spending on consumption. Supply and demand refers to the amount of goods and services that are available for people to buy compared to the amount of goods and services that people want to buy. All the aspects of consumer equilibrium, demand and supply have been carefully analyzed in this chapter.

Chapter 4- Income refers to the revenue earned from selling of the goods and services. Employment is defined as the relationship between employer and employee that are involved in the production, distribution and supply of goods and services. The topics elaborated in this chapter will help in gaining a better perspective about the aspects related to income and employment.

Chapter 5- Aggregate demand refers to the final goods and services that are demanded in an economy at a particular period of time. Inflation is defined as the rise in the price of goods and services. Defla¬tion is defined as the fall in the price of goods and services. This chapter discusses in detail about aggregate demand, inflation and deflation.

Chapter 6- Government budget is an annual financial statement that estimates government expenditure and revenue for the coming financial year. The policy that falls under the domain of taxation, money supply, government budgets, labor market, etc. is termed as economic policy. This chapter closely examines the concepts of government budget and economic policy to provide an extensive understanding of the subject.

Chapter 7- International economics deals with the study of economic and political issues between international economies in relation with trade and finance. Some of its aspects include international monetary system, international trade, exchange rates, foreign exchange, foreign direct investment, etc. All these aspects of international economics have been carefully analyzed in this chapter.

I owe the completion of this book to the never-ending support of my family, who supported me throughout the project.

Alvina Cuoco

1

Introduction to Economics

Economics is the branch of social science that deals with the study of production, distribution and consumption of goods and services. Economics is categorized into two major types - microeconomics and macroeconomics. This is an introductory chapter which will briefly introduce all the significant aspects of economics and its types.

Economy

An economy is the large set of inter-related production and consumption activities that aid in determining how scarce resources are allocated. The production and consumption of goods and services are used to fulfil the needs of those living and operating within the economy, which is also referred to as an economic system.

An economy encompasses all activity related to production, consumption, and trade of goods and services in an area. An economy applies to everyone from individuals to entities such as corporations and governments. The economy of a particular region or country is governed by its culture, laws, history, and geography, among other factors, and it evolves due to necessity. For this reason, no two economies are identical.

Types of Economies

Market-based economies allow goods to flow freely through the market, according to supply and demand. The United States is considered a market economy where consumers and producers determine what's sold and produced. Producers own what they make and decide their own prices, while consumers own what they buy and decide how much they're willing to pay.

However, the law of supply and demand can impact prices and production. If consumer demand for a specific good increases and there's a resulting supply shortage, prices tend to rise as consumers are willing to pay more for that good. In turn, production tends to increase to satisfy the demand since produces are driven by profit. As a result, a market economy has a tendency to naturally balance itself. As the prices in one sector for an industry rise due to demand, the money, and labor necessary to fill that demand shift to those places where they're needed.

Pure market economies rarely exist since there's usually some government intervention or central planning. Even the United States could be considered a mixed economy. Regulations, public education, social security benefits are provided by the government to fill in the gaps from a market economy and help to create balance. As a result, the term market economy refers to an economy that is more market-oriented in general.

Command-based economies are dependent on a central political agent, which controls the price and distribution of goods. Supply and demand cannot play out naturally in this system because it is centrally planned, so imbalances are common.

Green economies depend on renewable, sustainable forms of energy. These systems operate with the end goal of cutting carbon emissions, restoring biodiversity, relying on alternative energy sources and generally preserving the environment. Green economies tend to focus on technological innovations that increase energy efficiencies. The goal of green economies is to provide consumption and production while reducing or eliminating any adverse impacts on the earth and its resources.

Studying Economies

The study of economies and the factors affecting economies is called economics. The discipline of economics can be broken into two major areas of focus, microeconomics, and macroeconomics.

Microeconomics studies the behavior of individuals and firms in order to understand why they make the economic decisions they do and how these decisions affect the larger economic system. Microeconomics studies why various goods have different values and how individuals coordinate and cooperate with each other. Microeconomics tends to focus on economic tendencies, such as how individual choices and actions impact changes in production.

Macroeconomics, on the other hand, studies the entire economy, focusing on large-scale decisions and issues. Macroeconomics includes the study of economy-wide factors such as the effect of rising prices or inflation on the economy. Macroeconomics also focuses on the rate of economic growth or gross domestic product (GDP), which represents the total amount of goods and services produced in an economy. Changes in unemployment and national income are also studied. In short, macroeconomics studies how the aggregate economy behaves.

Economics

Economics is the scientific study of the *ownership, use, and exchange of scarce resources* - often shortened to the *science of scarcity*. Economics is regarded as a social science because it uses scientific methods to build theories that can help explain the behaviour of individuals, groups and organisations. Economics attempts to explain *economic* behaviour, which arises when scarce resources are exchanged.

In terms of methodology, economists, like other social scientists, are not able to undertake controlled experiments in the way that chemists and biologists are. Hence, economists have to employ different methods, based primarily on observation and deduction and the construction of abstract models.

As the social sciences have evolved over the last 100 years, they have become increasingly specialised. This is true for economics, as witnessed by the development of many different strands of investigation including micro and macro economics, pure and applied economics, and industrial and financial economics. What links them all is the attempt to understand how and why exchange takes place, and how exchange creates benefits and costs for the participants.

The Study of Economics

The study of economics involves three related investigations.

- Why scarce resources are exchanged?
- How consumers and producers behave as they interact with each other in markets, in their attempt to achieve mutually beneficial exchange?
- The role of government in compensating for the limitations of markets in achieving mutually beneficial exchange?

Methods

Economists use scientific observation and deduction in their investigations. To achieve this they:

Describe and Measure the Exchanges they Observe

Economists describe changes in economic variables, and measure these changes over time. For example, economists describe and measure how interaction in markets determines the prices of such diverse products as motor cars, houses, haircuts, and computer software. Measurement in economics can take many forms, including measuring absolute and relative quantities and values. When measuring relative values it is common to use index numbers.

Explain how Interactions Arise and Create Costs and Benefits

Economists try to explain the effects, or results, of economic transactions. For example, economists can explain why, despite bubbles and crashes, the long-run trend in house prices in the UK has been upwards over the last 30 years, and can identify those who have been affected positively and negatively by this increase. Of course, economists also try to explain the short-term movements in prices, and how they also have costs and benefits.

Propose Hypotheses, Construct and Apply 'Models' to Test these Hypotheses

Like all scientists, economists develop hypotheses to explain why economic behaviour takes place, and then construct models to test these hypotheses. For example, economists may propose that price rises are caused by excess demand, and then attempt to construct a model of price that explains how excess demand can raise price. Economists frequently use versions of the demand and supply model to help explain events such as house price trends and movements. Economic models usually employ graphical and mathematical analysis to help explain and illustrate such economic processes.

Gather Data to Put into the Model

Models must be tested against the real world, which means gathering statistical data about real events. In this way, a model can be improved and revised when necessary.

Predict Behaviour Based on these Models

The ultimate goal of the economist is to predict future behaviour. For example, by using a demand and supply model and by inputting real data about the housing market, economists can show that even a small fall in bank lending can trigger behaviour that leads to a significant fall in house prices in the short run. The ultimate value of an economic model is that it can accurately predict the onset and the effect of an economic event. The better the model is, the more useful it is in helping economists make predictions.

Economists assume that economic events and phenomena do not occur at random, but are determined by underlying and understandable causes. Unlike the pure scientist, economists cannot undertake controlled experiments, so they must test their models in different ways. Statistical analysis of actual economic data can provide a flow of information from which to build models and test hypotheses. For example, by gathering data about changes in house prices it is possible to deduce factors that cause house prices to go up or down, and by how much. Economists use index numbers to help make comparisons between countries and over time.

Correlation analysis can help determine the strength of particular causal relationships so that strong and weak relationships can be identified. For example, it might be possible to demonstrate that, of all the factors that have contributed to falling house prices, the reduced availability of credit is the single biggest factor.

The Role of the Professional Economist

Professional economists apply their skills of description, analysis, model building, and prediction to generate knowledge and, from this, provide advice to private firms, to governments and other organisations.

Providing Knowledge

- The first function of the economist is to provide information, called economic intelligence, from which decisions can be made. For firms to survive and succeed, they need to take many decisions, but each decision carries with it a risk. The professional economist can help reduce such risks by gathering and analysing economic intelligence. This economic intelligence is only useful when it can be put into an economic model, and then applied to the decisions that need to be taken.

- The second function of the professional economist is to interpret the data that has been gathered and provide informed advice to firms, organisations, and governments about the likely costs and benefits of the decisions they make.

In providing advice, the economist will always make an assessment of the other options that could have been chosen. For example, a large petrol refiner and retailer may be faced with a significant rise in the costs of crude oil – should it now raise price? After having made an assessment of all the pricing options, and having taken account of the likely response of rivals, the firm's chief economist may advise it to hold price constant – perhaps the least 'common sense' answer.

Positive and Normative Economics

As a social science, economics attempts to use the principles and methods of science to explain economic behaviour. This involves making *positive statements* about the economic world.

Positive statements are those that can be verified, and are factual, such as:

'House prices have fallen by 15% over the last year.'

In contrast, *normative statements* are based on opinion and *value judgement*. Statements suggesting that something 'ought to' happen, or that something is 'unfair', are normative because they are matters of opinion.

For example, *'the recent fall in house prices is unfair to the rich'*.

This statement cannot be tested because it not based on anything testable. If there is an agreed definition of fairness, and it can be measured, then it might be possible to test the effect of the change in house prices on the degree of fairness experienced by a certain identifiable group of people defined as *rich*. Therefore, this statement is normative, impossible to verify, and based on opinion rather than fact.

The Ceteris Paribus Rule

Economics is a social science, and, unlike the physical sciences, cannot engage in controlled experimentation to demonstrate how variables are connected.

In the real world, economic variables such as *price* and *income*, are constantly changing, and this creates a problem in demonstrating the relationship between variables. For example, a fall in price is likely to lead to a rise in consumer demand if we assume nothing else changes.

Of course, for independent reasons, income could also fall while demand does not rise. The fall in price could have been counteracted by a fall in income. The ceteris paribus rule, that *all other things remain the same,* is used whenever attempting to demonstrate the link between economic variables. Without this assumption, positive economics is impossible.

The Evolving Role of the Economist

Over time the role of the professional economist has broadened. In recent years much interest has been shown in the interconnections between economics and psychology, and there has been a considerable increase in the popularity of behavioural economics. This is both in terms of the number of Universities offering courses in behavioural economics, and in terms of how public policy makers have turned to this branch of economics, especially in the wake of the financial crisis. While it has its critics, behavioural economics has captured the imagination of a new breed of economists looking for answers in an increasingly uncertain and unpredictable world, and to what generally appear to be the failings of some traditional 'micro' economic theory. In terms of 'macro' economic theory, events can challenge existing assumptions and lead to a requirement to modify existing models, or completely replace them. For example, the financial crash of a 20 years ago led to a thorough re-thinking of the nature of financial risk, and to the establishment of better ways to understand why banking systems can fail, as well as develop more effective ways to regulate them. Similarly, the emergence of cryptocurrencies, such as Bitcoin, have forced economists to reassess the nature of money in a globalised world. Trading relationships between countries, and theories to explain them, have also been put under the spotlight as a result of Brexit.

Economic System

An economic system is a means by which societies or governments organize and distribute available resources, services, and goods across a geographic region or country. Economic systems regulate factors of production, including capital, labor, physical resources, and entrepreneurs. An economic system encompasses many institutions, agencies, and other entities.

Types of Economic Systems

There are many economies around the world. Each has its own distinguishing characteristics, although they all share some basic features. Each economy functions based on a unique set of conditions and assumptions. Economic systems can be categorized into four main types: traditional economies, command economies, mixed economies, and market economies.

Traditional Economic System

The traditional economic system is based on goods, services, and work, all of which follow certain established trends. It relies a lot on people, and there is very little division of labor or specialization. In essence, the traditional economy is very basic and the most ancient of the four types.

Some parts of the world still function with a traditional economic system. It is commonly found in rural settings in second- and third-world nations, where economic activities are predominantly farming or other traditional income-generating activities.

There are usually very few resources to share in communities with traditional economic systems. Either few resources occur naturally in the region or access to them is restricted in some way. Thus, the traditional system, unlike the other three, lacks the potential to generate a surplus. Nevertheless, precisely because of its primitive nature, the traditional economic system is highly sustainable. In addition, due to its small output, there is very little wastage as compared to the other three systems.

Command Economic System

In a command system, there is a dominant, centralized authority – usually the government – that controls a significant portion of the economic structure. Also known as a planned system, the command economic system is common in communist societies since production decisions are the preserve of the government.

If an economy enjoys access to many resources, chances are that it may lean towards a command economic structure. In such a case, the government comes in and exercises control over the resources. Ideally, centralized control covers valuable resources such as gold or oil. The people regulate other less important sectors of the economy, such as agriculture.

In theory, the command system works very well as long as the central authority exercises control with the general population's best interests in mind. However, that rarely seems to be the case. Command economies are rigid compared to other systems. They react slowly to change because power is centralized. That makes them vulnerable to economic crises or emergencies, as they cannot quickly adjust to changed conditions.

Market Economic System

Market economic systems are based on the concept of free markets. In other words, there is very little government interference. The government exercises little control over resources, and it does not interfere with important segments of the economy. Instead, regulation comes from the people and the relationship between supply and demand.

The market economic system is mostly theoretical. That is to say, a pure market system doesn't really exist. Why? Well, all economic systems are subject to some kind of interference from a central authority. For instance, most governments enact laws that regulate fair trade and monopolies.

From a theoretical point of view, a market economy facilitates substantial growth. Arguably, growth is highest under a market economic system.

A market economy's greatest downside is that it allows private entities to amass a lot of economic power, particularly those who own resources of great value. The distribution of resources is not equitable because those who succeed economically control most of them.

Mixed System

Mixed systems combine the characteristics of the market and command economic systems. For this reason, mixed systems are also known as dual systems. Sometimes the term is used to describe a market system under strict regulatory control.

Many countries in the west follow a mixed system. Most industries are private, while the rest, comprised primarily of public services, are under the control of the government.

Mixed systems are the norm globally. Supposedly, a mixed system combines the best features of market and command systems. However, practically speaking, mixed economies face the challenge of finding the right balance between free markets and government control. Governments tend to exert much more control than is necessary.

Economic systems are grouped into traditional, command, market, and mixed systems. Traditional systems focus on the basics of goods, services, and work, and they are influenced by traditions and beliefs. A centralized authority influences command systems, while a market system is under the control of forces of demand and supply. Lastly, mixed economies are a combination of command and market systems.

Economic Models

An economic model is a simplified description of reality, designed to yield hypotheses about economic behavior that can be tested.

Economic modeling is at the heart of economic theory. Modeling provides a logical, abstract template to help organize the analyst's thoughts. The model helps the economist logically isolate and sort out complicated chains of cause and effect and influence between the numerous interacting elements in an economy. Through the use of a model, the economist can experiment, at least logically, producing different scenarios, attempting to evaluate the effect of alternative policy options, or weighing the logical integrity of arguments presented in prose.

Certain types of models are extremely useful for presenting visually the essence of economic arguments. No student of economics has sat through a class for very long before a picture is drawn on a chalkboard. The visual appeal of a model clarifies the exposition.

Types of Models

There are four types of models used in economic analysis, visual models, mathematical models, empirical models, and simulation models.

Visual Models

Visual models are simply pictures of an abstract economy; graphs with lines and curves that tell an economic story. They are primarily used in textbooks and teaching, and the reader who has had any exposure to economics at all has probably seen dozens, if not hundreds of them.

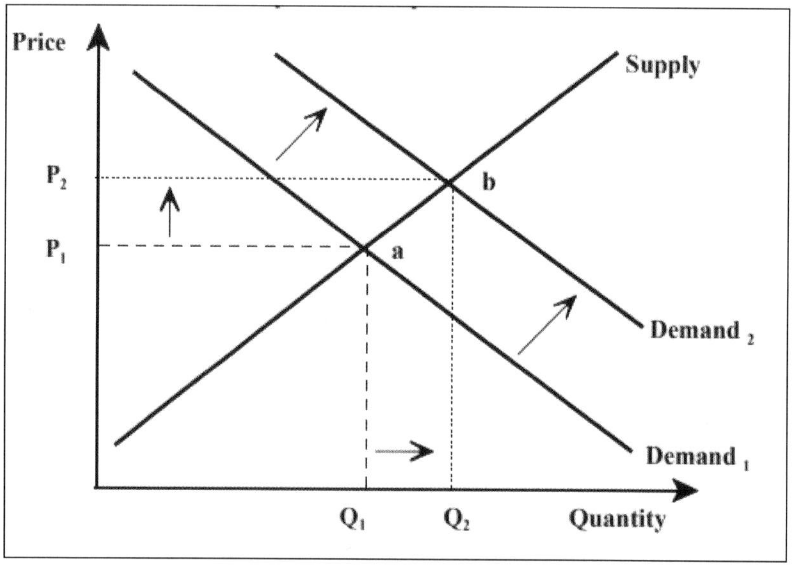

An example of a visual economic model.

Some visual models are merely diagrammatic, such as those which show the flow of income through the economy from one sector to another. In other words, they employ a visual device to present a very general economic concept. Most visual models, though, are visual extensions of mathematical models. Implicit in their structure is an underlying mathematical model. Sometimes when they are presented the mathematics are explained, sometimes they are not. The models do not normally require a knowledge of mathematics, but still allow the presentation of complex relationships between economic variables. These models are relatively easy to understand, but are somewhat limited in their scope.

The common supply-and-demand model that most economics students see in their first exposure to economics. This model will be discussed in more detail at the end of the chapter. The example is meant to show the effect of inflationary expectations upon price and output. In this application, an increase in inflationary expectations causes demand to shift, raising prices and output.

The Elementary Supply and Demand Model with Inflationary Expectations,

- The first demand curve represents demand prior to the formation of inflationary expectations.
- The second demand curve represents the effects of inflationary expectations upon demand.
- Prices and output finally settle at P_2 and Q_2 higher in both cases.

Mathematical Models

The most formal and abstract of the economic models are the purely mathematical models.

These are systems of simultaneous equations with an equal or greater number of economic variables. Some of these models can be quite large. Even the smallest will have five or six equations and as many unknown variables. The manipulation and use of these models require a good knowledge of algebra or calculus.

For example, a very simple microeconomics model would include a supply function (explaining the behavior of producers, or those who supply commodities to the market), a demand curve (explaining the behavior of purchasers) and an equilibrium equation, specifying the simple conditions that must be met if the model's equilibrium is to be satisfied.

The variables in a model like this represent a type of economic activity (such as demand) or data (information) that either determines or is determined by that activity (such as a price or interest rate).

Variables can usually be classified as *endogenous* or *exogenous*. An endogenous variable is one that is determined within the model, or by the model's solution. Its value becomes known when the model is solved. For example, if the final level of demand is determined by the model's solution, demand is an endogenous variable. On the other hand, if the value of a variable comes from outside the model, if its value is preset, it is an exogenous variable. In macroeconomics, many policy variables, such as the income tax rate or money supply growth rate, are treated as exogenous. For example, the money supply growth rate is regarded as exogenous because it is set by policy-makers rather than determined by the dynamics of the model.

An example of a very elementary mathematical model. It is the mathematical version of the visual model shown in previous figure. The reader might recognize it as a variation of the simple supply-and-demand model taught in microeconomics, where the purpose is to determine equilibrium price and quantity in a market.

The model has three equations; a supply equation $S = a + bP$, a demand equation $D = c - dP + eIE$, and an equilibrium identity $S = D = Q^0$, which declares that at equilibrium supply will equal demand (and is represented by 'Q', for "quantity"). There are three endogenous variables with unknown values; price, quantity supplied, and quantity demanded. There is one exogenous value, inflationary expectations (IE) in the demand equation, the value of which would have to be provided before the model could be solved. The values a, b, c, d, and **e** are called coefficients or parameters.

The solution values for price and quantity are shown in equations and. This simple model is provided merely for illustration. Obviously, reliable macroeconomic mathematical models are much larger and more complex than this.

Sometimes the purely mathematical model is simply solved, to see what result is produced. Often, however, the analyst merely tries to evaluate the sensitivity of one variable to another. For example, the analyst might only want to evaluate the sensitivity of investment to income, essen- tially asking a question like, "What will happen to investment if income rises one percent?" Using calculus, these questions can usually be answered without actually solving the model (deriving a general solution for the model's variables). Numerical values do not even necessarily have to be assigned to the model's variables to do this.

Example: The Elementary Supply and Demand Model with Inflationary Expectations,

$$S = a + bP$$

$$D = c - dP + eIE$$

$$S = D = Q^0$$

$$P^0 = \frac{(c + eIE - a)}{(B + d)}$$

$$Q^0 = a + bP^0$$

This model is the mathematical version of the model that was in the shown in the figure above. The model has three endogenous variables; S, representing the quantity supplied, D, representing the quantity demanded and P, representing price. These variables are determined by the solution of the model. The value Q simply represents quantity, and reflects the fact that at the solution equilibrium, quantity supplied and quantity demanded are equal.

The model has one exogenous variable, IE, representing inflationary expectations. The value for this variable comes from outside the model and a solution for the endogenous variables cannot be obtained unless the value is known.

The value a, b, c, d and e are called coefficients or parameters. These are behavioral variables that reflect the reaction of producers (supply) and buyers (demand) to price.

Equation ($S = a + bP$) is the supply function and equation ($D = c - dP + eIE$) is the demand equation, which includes the variable for inflationary expectations. Equation ($S = D = Q^0$) tells us that at equilibrium supply will equal demand. By solving these three equations for P through substitution, we obtain the solution for price in equation ($P^0 = \frac{(c + eIE - a)}{(B + d)}$) and quantity in equation ($Q^0 = a + bP^0$).

Empirical Models

Empirical models are mathematical models designed to be used with data. The funda- mental model is mathematical, exactly as described above. With an empirical model, however, data is gathered for the variables, and using accepted statistical techniques, the data are used to provide estimates of the model's values. For example, suppose in an economic study the following question is asked: "What will happen to investment if income rises one percent?" The purely mathematical model might only allow the analyst to say, "Logically, it should rise". The user of the empirical model, on the other hand, using actual historical data for investment, income, and the other variables in the model, might be able to say, "By my best estimate, investment should rise by about two percent".

For example, after manipulating the simple supply-and-demand model shown above in figure and represented mathematically in figure and supposing this to represent an actual market for a commodity like an automobile, with data available, the econometrician might estimate that if inflationary expectations were to rise by ten percent, demand for the auto would shift and the price of this product would rise by six percent.

Empirical models are advanced and cannot be understood unless the student has an introductory background in statistics. They will not be discussed in this text but are mentioned because they are important for more advanced research and are largely built from mathematical models.

Simulation Models

Simulation models, which must be used with computers, embody the very best features of mathematical models without requiring that the user be proficient in mathematics. The models are fundamentally mathematical (the equations of the model are programmed in a programming language like Pascal or C++) but the mathematical complexity is transparent to the user. The simulation model usually starts with initial or "default" values assigned by the program or the user, then certain variables are changed or initialized, then a computer simulation is done. The simulation, of course, is a solution of the model's equations. The user can usually alter a whole range of variables at will.

The computerized simulation model can show the interaction of numerous variables all at once, including hidden feedback and secondary effects that are not so apparent in purely mathematical or visual models. With such simulations, the careful user, especially if guided by a good text or instructor, can reason through the complicated chains of influence without necessarily understanding the underlying mathematics. Such models are therefore quite useful in classroom instruction.

Static and Dynamic Models

Most of the models used in economics are comparative statics models. Some of the more sophisticated models in macroeconomics and business cycle analysis are dynamic models. There are some fundamental differences between these models and how they are used.

Comparative Statics Models

A good example of a comparative statics model was provided by the elementary supply- and-demand model shown in above Figures. Most models used in economics and virtually all used in economics textbooks are comparative statics models.

These models try to show what happens over time (or as time passes), but time itself is not represented or embodied directly in the model. The model usually begins with an equilibrium condition identified, then a "shock" to the model is presumed (the value of one or more of the coefficients or variables are changed), then the new equilibrium condition is identified without an exposition of what happened in the transition from one equilibrium to another.

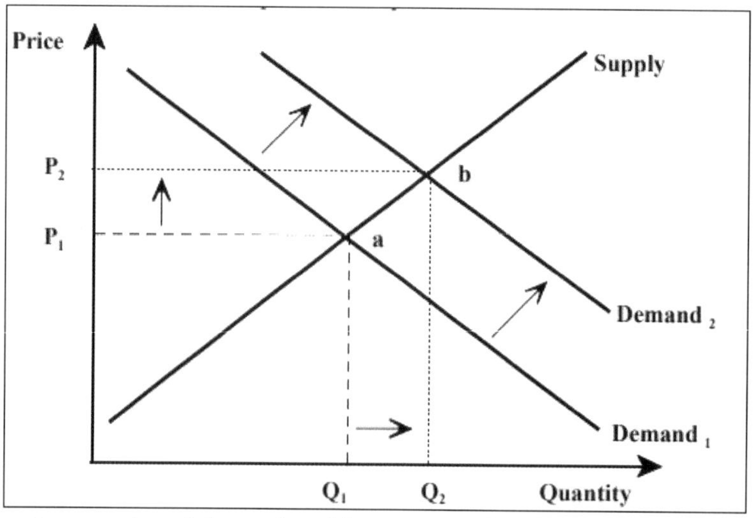

The elementary supply and demand model as an example of a comparative statics model.

This is the same model as was shown in the figure above. Equilibrium point a shows the initial condition - the first "snapshot" of the model. Equilibrium point b shows the second and final snapshot, the revised equilibrium after the "shock," which in this case was the sudden appearance of inflationary expectations. The analyst can see that prices and quantity have risen. It is presumed that some time has passed, but what has happened in the interim is not shown. The explanation, however, can be told as a story on the side.

Given some presumed level of inflationary expectations, the initial equilibrium (point 'a') identifies theprice and level of output that would obtain, given assumptions about supply and demand and the level of inflationary expectations. Then the model is shocked by introducing a higher level of expectations, demonstrating a new equilibrium at point 'b'. Obviously this movement in equilibria and the shift in the model's solution happened over time, but neither the visual model nor its mathematical counterpart can demonstrate what happened in the interim. The model shows only the starting point and the ending point.

The comparative statics approach is roughly analogous to using snapshots from a camera to record developments during a dynamic event. With each snapshot a static but informative picture is presented. Imagine, for example, taking a picture at the beginning of a horse race, ten shots throughout the race, and one at the finish. The developed film would constitute a "comparative statics" record of a very dynamic race. As such it would have very useful information about the race, but probably not as much as a video record.

In a comparative statics economic model, each equilibrium solution is like a snapshot of the economy at one point in time.

A difference equation from a dynamic economic model.

$$I_t = a + b\,(y_{t-1} - Y_{t-2})$$

This investment equation, drawn from a larger model of similar equations, is an example of a difference equation used in a dynamic model. Here discrete time is embodied directly into the model.

This equation can be interpreted to say that investment (I) at any time (t) is determined by the level of income in the previous period (t-1) less the level of income the period before (t-2).

More generally, if this time period is defined to be months, this equation says that investment this month depends upon the change in income last month (which is equal to the difference between income last month and the month before).

Dynamic Models

Dynamic models, in contrast, directly incorporate time into their structure. This is usually done in economic modeling by using mathematical systems of difference or differential equations. In this example, which uses a difference equation from a business cycle model, investment now depends upon changes in income in the past. Time is incorporated into the model through subscripts.

Dynamic models, when they can be used, sometimes better represent the subtleties of business cycles, because certainly lags in behavioral response and timing strongly shape the character of a cycle. For example, if there is a delay between the time income is received and when it is spent, a model that can capture the delay is likely to have higher integrity than a model that cannot.

Why comparative statics models are usually used:

One might ask, therefore, why comparative status models are usually used in business cycle theory. The answer is simple - comparative statics models are much easier to solve. Any student of calculus knows the difficulty of solving systems of difference or (especially) differential equations. The latter, as soon as they achieve any complexity, are sometimes impossible to solve. Therefore dynamic models must be kept extremely simple and are therefore so elementary that more is lost than gained.

Simple dynamic models, nonetheless, often provide valuable insights into the complex interactions between variables over time. They can capture remarkably subtle feedback effects that are easily missed by static models.

It should be noted that dynamic models are much easier to simulate on computers than they are to solve outright. The user can experiment with an endless variety of values and assumptions to see whether results obtained are realistic or insightful.5 Since computers are now powerful and cheaper, the importance of dynamic simulation models should gradually grow in importance.

Expectations-enhanced Models

Economic models often incorporate economic expectations, such as inflationary expectations. Such models are called expectations-enhanced models. The elementary supply- and-demand model, which incorporated inflationary expectations, was an example of such a model.

Generally, expectations-enhanced models include one or more variables based upon economic expectations about future values. For example, if consumers, for whatever reason, expect the inflation rate to be much higher next year than this year, they are said to have formed inflationary expectations. If numerical values are being used in a model and the current inflation rate is nine percent, if they expect inflation to be higher next year, the variable for inflationary expectations might be given a value of twelve percent. Normally, though, general models used for instruction or analysis merely assume an expectation value to be "high", where it will have an impact on the model's result, or "low" or "non-existent" where it will have no impact. In the simple supply-and-demand model presented earlier, inflationary expectations were "high", shifting the equilibrium and causing higher prices and output.

There are many types of expectations found in economics. In addition to inflationary expectations, economists might consider interest rate expectations, income expectations, and wealth expectations. This list is hardly exhaustive. For virtually any variable that might be included in a model, a corresponding expectations variable is logically possible.

Expectations matter because they have such a profound impact upon economic behavior. Consumers, for example, base their purchasing decisions not only upon their present income but also whether they expect that income to rise or fall (hence, expected income). In this age of consumer credit, readily available, consumers are less tied to direct income as a source of purchasing. If they expect a surge in income or wealth, many are inclined to use credit to buy now and pay later. As another example, business investment, or the new purchase of expensive plant and equipment or real estate, probably depends as much upon expected future profits as upon current profits. Therefore, changes in expectations about the future cause changes or fluctuations in current spending behavior. Given that business cycle theory investigates the causes of fluctuations in economic activity, the importance of expectations and expectations-enhanced models is evident.

There are two general approaches to theories explaining the development of expectations, the theory of adaptive expectations and the theory of rational expectations. Because these theories are fundamentally different and both are used in economic models, they are distinguished here.

Adaptive Expectations

The theory of adaptive expectations presumes that expectations are primarily learned from experience. For example, the theory of adaptive expectations would say that if consumers begin to actually see prices rising, say from three percent to five percent to seven percent, over a period of, say, two years, they will begin to form robust expectations of inflationary expectations - perhaps even expectations of double-digit inflation. The same theory might claim that consumers will expect an economic recovery to begin only after ample evidence that the turning point has been passed.

Adaptive expectations imply, therefore, that economic agents learn from recent experience, or begin to see trends emerge that they expect to continue. The theory of adaptive expectations implies, therefore, that expectations are relatively slow to form. This feature of adaptive expectations - the relatively long lag in the formation of expectation, becomes a critical issue in the timing of such phenomena as business cycles.

Rational Expectations

The theory of rational expectations presumes that expectations are formed when economic agents see new developments in the economy and they logically deduce expectations based upon the information they have. For example, if the Federal Reserve System were to suddenly increase the money supply, according to the theory of rational expectations, consumers would immediately form inflationary expectations, not because prices are actually rising, but because they deduce that excessive money supply growth is likely to cause inflation.

The theory of rational expectations emphasizes the effects of changes in economic policy upon expectations, although the theory is not restricted to policy decisions alone.

Obviously, the theory of rational expectations presumes a relatively high degree of economic sophistication among those who make economic decisions. It also presumes that people have access to (or even care about) information on the economy, such as the money supply growth rate, the rate of taxation, etc.

With rational expectations there is normally a much shorter lag in response time between the initial stimulus and the formation of expectations. Sometimes rational expectations are formed immediately, whereas adaptive expectations may take months or even years to form.

Consider as an example the issue involving the money supply growth rate, discussed above. With rational expectations, virtually the moment it becomes known that the money supply has dramatically increased, inflationary expectations begin to form. Assuming adaptive expecta- tions, the picture is more complex. Suppose the high money supply growth rate does eventually cause inflation.6 This may not happen until many months have passed. Only then, when inflation is actually experienced, are adaptive inflationary expectations (of more inflation) formed.

Which Theory is Appropriate?

When describing the economic activity of consumers in general or even certain types of business decisions the theory of adaptive expectations is probably most suitable. Rational expectations implies a degree of economic knowledge and sophistication among ordinary citizens that they probably don't have. The theory was developed by economists and seems to imply that most people think like economists. They probably don't.

When describing an environment, however, where the decision-makers are likely to be sophisticated and well-informed and where their decisions involve high stakes, the theory of rational expectations is more suitable. The activities of traders in the finance markets provide a good example. Institutional traders of financial assets, managing huge portfolios, watch and respond to new economic information virtually every moment of their working day. The markets respond instantly to even the most subtle shifts in Federal Reserve Policy, anticipating the impact of such policy on interest rates, for example.

The choice of the theory of expectations, therefore, depends upon context. Models incorporating both theories will be developed and used.

How Models are Used

Students sometimes have the mistaken impression that the economic models found in textbooks are devices that are directly used by people making economic decisions, such as managers of a business firm. Students think they are learning an algorithm or tool that can be directly applied to a management decision. For example, a student learning the elementary supply-and-demand model used earlier in first figure might get the mistaken impression that managers in an industry might actually, from data, draw supply and demand curves (or solve the equations behind them) to help them set the actual market price they should be using.

Economic models are almost never used directly in this way. These models are not applied models. They are meant to merely represent a type of consistent economic behavior either visually or mathematically. They provide a "picture" of that behavior.

Typically in a market economy economic decisions, and alterations to those decisions, are determined by market incentives, a series of rewards and penalties, that alter behavior in a way that it is forced to loosely conform to conditions described by the model. Models that identify a market equilibrium are not used by business managers to set price and quantity but instead repre- sent the theory that rational market incentives will force the market to eventually move to the equilibrium.

The Limitations of Models

Even when used as a template or for instruction, models have limitations which reduce their reliability.

Improper Assumptions

Models have high integrity because they are mathematical and, hence, conform to the rigorous standards of logic inherent in mathematics. Nonetheless, mathematical models must begin with precise assumptions about economic activity. In great measure, the conclusions and insights offered by the model are restricted or even determined by the initial assumptions. There- fore, if the initial assumptions are wrong or misleading, or even if they are incomplete, despite the logical integrity of the model, the model's conclusions will be as much in error as the initial assumptions. A model can be logically consistent internally, and still yield bad results.

As an example, the theories of public policy, one economist might assume that elected officials are motivated to act on behalf of the interests of their constituency, performing a public duty. Other economists might assume that the same officials act on behalf of their own self- interest, formulating policy merely for the purpose of maximizing votes in an election, even if it is to the ultimate detriment of the voters. The former model might specify an objective function that is "socially optimal" (a mathematical equation that optimizes net social satisfaction, benefit, or gain), whereas the latter might specify an objective function which maximizes some measure of the individual politicians's personal gain. The contrary results from such different beginnings are hardly surprising. The first model will tend to promote the idea that interventionist government policy is advisable if not indispensable. The second will, in contrast, suggest that intervention is corruptly expedient and counter-productive.

Which model would be right? In part, this will depend upon the validity of the assumptions.

Oversimplification

Macroeconomic models are widely used because they allow the analyst to simplify a situation. A real economy is a virtual porridge of interaction and data. To make some sense of this recondite chaos, the analyst will pull out those key variables which seem to have the most importance and fit only them into a logical scheme, omitting the others. Likewise, composites of individual human economic behavior are aggregated in macroeconomic models, and as such are simplified. A rational consumption function with all of its arguments (e.g. consumption depends upon income, wealth, expected income and wealth, the rate of inflation, etc.), for example, makes the useful simplifying assumption that individual consumers are fairly consistent and similar in their economic behavior, allowing for a generalization of the aggregate behavior.

Such simplifications are not only expedient but necessary. Nonetheless, the model in its simplicity is different than the real economy (or segment of the real economy) that it is designed to replicate. The omitted variables often do matter in the real economy. Likewise some generalizations end up being too crude to produce precise or accurate results.

Mathematical Intractability

Models that are mathematical, directly or implicitly, are also limited because they must be tractable, which is to say, they are useless unless they can be solved or manipulated to produce insightful results. This poses serious mathematical problems that have nothing to do with economics. Macroeconomic models, such as those used in business cycle analysis, usually have a large number of equations and variables. All of these must be reduced to a solution if the model is to be of any value. Because of the difficulties in solving large mathematical systems, sometimes the underlying equations must either be linear, or easily converted to linear, such as exponential or log-linear.

But real economic behavior doesn't necessarily exhibit patterns that are "linear", or even represented well by orderly equations that are non-linear and that can still be used in a large model. The "math of reality", if a term like that can be indulged for the moment, is remarkably complex, and cannot be faithfully duplicated in abstract model of human design.

Models are therefore quite useful, in fact indispensable, in economic analysis, but they do have their limitations. Again, they help us guide our thoughts, organize our thinking and, in exposition, explain our theories. But as abstractions, they are somewhat if not substantially different from the reality they purport to represent. They provide guidance and insight, but not the final word.

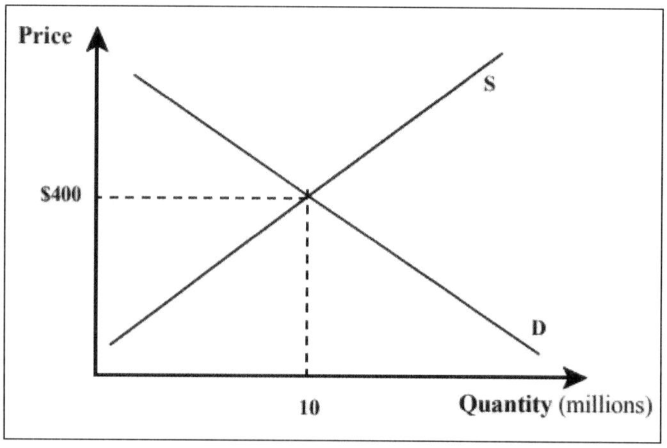

The microeconomic supply and demand model: digital video players (DVPs).

The supply curve (**S**) represents the production decisions of microcomputer manufactures of the Digital Video Player (DVP), which plays digital video disks and competes with VCRs and other consumer video output devices. The curve implies that the higher the price, the more of these machines will be manufactured.

The demand curve (D) represents the purchasing intentions of the potential buyers of the Digital Video Player. Obviously the lower the price, the higher the level of sales (demand).

The market-clearing equilibrium price, when the level of production (supply) equals the level of sales (demand) is $400 per machine. At this price 10 million machines would be produced and sold.

The Microeconomic Supply-and-demand Model Formally Presented

The visual microeconomic supply-and-demand model is shown in above Figure. In order to make the example realistic, it is presumed that the market represented is for Digital Video Players (hereafter DVPs), a relatively new technology offered to consumers by a large number of manufacturers.

In this model, the supply curve (**S**) represents the quantity of DVPs that would be manufactured and supplied at various prices. Generally, the higher the price the higher the level of production. The demand curve (D) shows that the lower the price the greater will be the quantity demand by consumers.

There is a single market-clearing equilibrium price, '**e**', of $400 where the level of production (supply) will equal the level of sales (demand). At any other price, higher of lower, there will be a disequilibrium where production will exceed sales or sales will exceed production.

The Tendency Toward Equilibrium

This type of model is not a tool used by the manufacturers of digital video players to set their prices. It is not a management device. The numerous manufacturers of these computers don't have enough information on potential consumer responses to a full range of prices to even construct a demand curve. Since the supply curve represents the aggregate response of all competing manufacturers of DVPs, a reliable supply curve would be impossible to construct.

Instead, the model represents an equilibrium price towards which the market automatically tends to converge. Although the location of the demand curve may not be known, the relationship described by the demand curve certainly exists, and at some given price only a certain quantity of machines will be sold. At a higher price fewer will be sold, at a lower price more will be sold. The demand curve is like a "ghost", invisible, but nonetheless acting as a constraint upon producer pricing decisions.

The best way to illustrate this is to consider a disequilibrium condition and to see what happens when such a condition persists. Refer to the above Figure. Suppose the price of digital video players is too high, at $600 instead of the market-clearing price of $400. What would happen? The supply curve demonstrates that producers will manufacture more computers than are desired by consumers at that high price. At a price of $600 per unit, consumers only want 8 million units, whereas manufacturers are making 14 million. Because the market is not clearing (production exceeds sales, or supply is greater than demand), this is a disequilibrium condition.

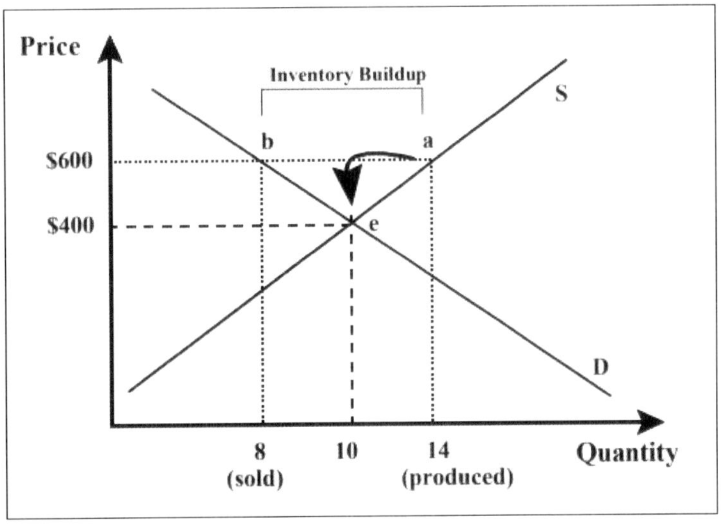

The tendency toward equilibrium from a disequilibrium condition in the market for digital video players.

The appropriate market clearing price is $400. Suppose the actual price was $600. At this price, the quantity of DVPs manufactured would be 14 million (see point a). The quantity sold, however, would only be 8 million (see point b). This would cause an inventory buildup of 6 million digital video players over the production period. Manufacturers, seeing slow sales and rising inventory, must respond by cutting back on production and reducing prices. This moves them closer to the equilibrium price and level of output described by point e.

Producers do not have supply and demand curves to tell them that this disequilibrium exists. They don't need them. They know they have problems because they are seeing disappointing sales and because they have an inventory buildup of unsold DVPs. This inventory buildup is represented by the distance between point 'a' and 'b' in figure and, in this example, is equal to 6 million DVPs.

An unwanted inventory buildup is expensive for two reasons. First, the cost of manufactures still must be paid and yet revenues for sales are not being realized, and, second, the company (or retailers for the product) must pay storage and financing costs for maintaining the inventory.

The manufactures, therefore, have no choice but to cut back on production and reduce prices until such time as sales levels and production are at least roughly matched and inventory balances are reconciled. This reaction to the disequilibrium condition is indicated by the arrow in Figure, which demonstrates the tendency of the producer to move prices and production levels back into the general area of the equilibrium point '**e**'.

In the event that prices are too low (not shown), sales would exceed the level of production (i.e. demand would exceed supply), inventories would be depleted, and producers would have the incentive to raise prices and output, again moving them in the direction of equilibrium point '**e**'.

The model, in its purity, merely identifies the market-clearing equilibrium and does not suggest that the manufacturers will immediately and precisely move to the equilibrium. Instead, there would be an automatic tendency to move gradually into the vicinity of the equilibrium.

Because in reality both supply and demand conditions are constantly changing, the actual equilibrium is actually shifting around. Producers are dynamically "chasing" that equilibrium by always monitoring inventory and adjusting both prices and levels of production.

The Model as an "Image" of Economic Activity

Two important points are being made here:

- This model, like most in economies, is not an applied model, where anyone actually uses it to determine appropriate prices and levels of production. (To be more specific, it is not an applied management model; corporations don't use these models to make pricing decisions). Instead, the model represents a type of consistent behavior that economists see in the market place, and it presents an image of that behavior. It allows an economist to both ask and answer the question, "What would we expect to happen in a market where prices are too high or too low? What kind of adjustment would take place, and why?"
- The market reactions of the economic decision-makers are not undertaken by virtue of their use of this model or any other, but is instead motivated by their necessary response to market signals that tell them that they must alter their decisions. In the example above, the primary signals were poor sales and an unwanted inventory build-up. The model, therefore, simply captures their responses to a series of market signals.

The price variable here is the automatic market-adjusted "clearing mechanism" that keeps production roughly matched to the level of sales. It is the "invisible hand" that regulates the market, as described by Adam Smith more than 200 years ago.

Generally, modeling economic behavior presumes that people consistently respond to the mix of market signals, adjusting their behavior as the incentives change.

Models like the one described here normally imply a more fluid case than is likely to be seen in a real market. Students of economic theory are always told that price movements are sometimes very "sticky" - especially price movements downward and that response times are often long. Likewise, the less competitive an industry, the less likely it is to be well represented by this model. Nonetheless, the model provides a reasonable approximation of economic behavior in competitive markets.

Using a Comparative-statics Model

The elementary supply-and-demand model has not so far been used for very much. The model becomes interesting and useful when supply or demand is "shocked" or disturbed by some economic variable. When this happens, the supply or demand curve shifts (or both shift) and the model's equilibrium is changed. It is this change in equilibrium that can lead to important economic insights.

Table: Variables that Effect Supply and Demand Curves.

Factors that Effect Demand		Factors that Effect Supply	
1. Price	(–)	1. Price	(+)
2. Income	(+)	2. Labor Costs	(-)
3. Wealth	(+)	3. Resource Costs	(-)
4. Population	(+)	4. Advertising Costs	(-)
5. Advertising	(+)		
6. Substitute Prices	(+)		
7. Inflationary Expectations	(+)		

(+) Shift curve right (–) Shift curve left

These are some of the variables that will effect supply and demand. The price variables are reflected in the slopes of the supply and demand curves. The other variables, when they change, will cause the appropriate curve to shift to the right or left. The direction of the shift is shown by the sign in the parenthesis: a (+) implies a shift right, a (–) implies a shift left.

Although the supply and demand curves look rather simple, embodied in their structure is a complex relationship to many other economic variables. Refer to the table in Figure.

Shown in that table are a list of variables that will influence supply and demand curves. The list is not exhaustive; it is meant to be illustrative. These variables represent the fact that the demand and supply curves implicitly reflect demand and supply functions in all of these variables. In other words, to list the factors that effect demand is merely another way of saying that "the quantity demanded is a function of the price of the product, consumer income, consumer wealth, etc.

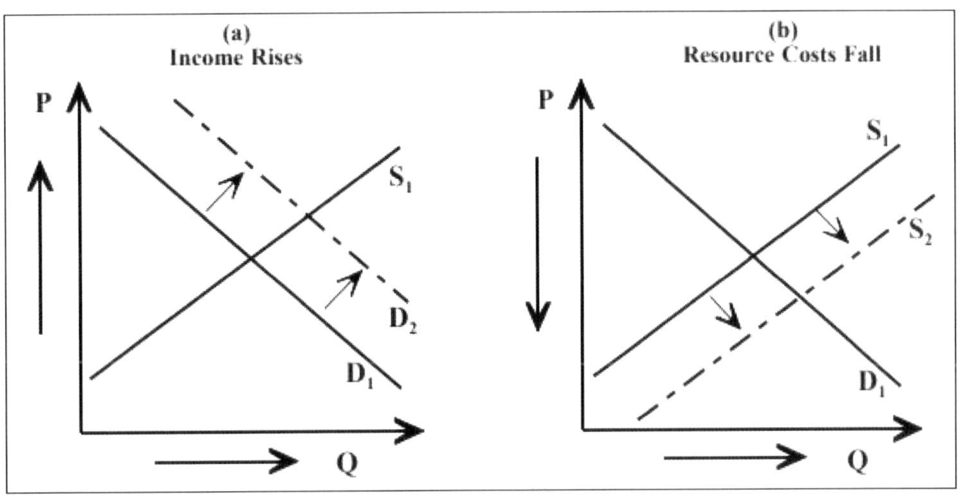

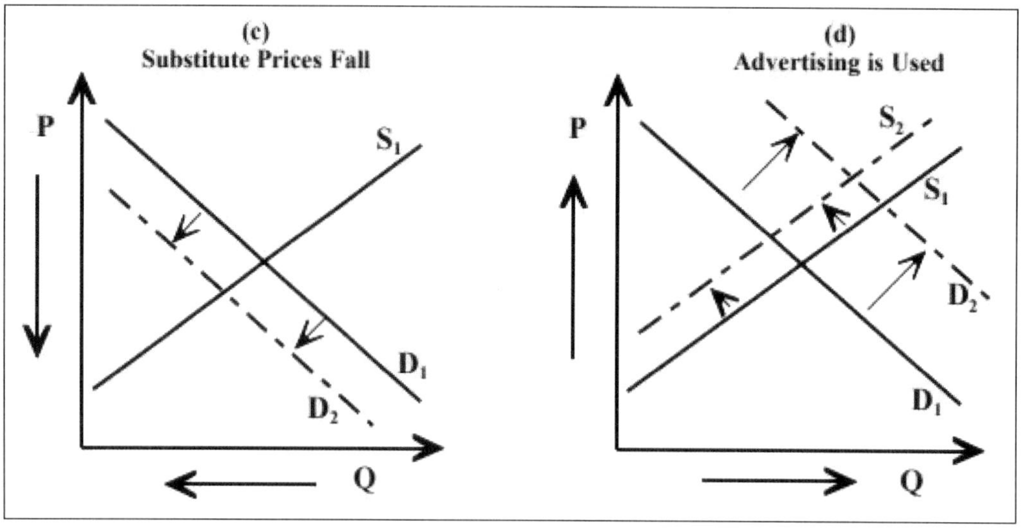

In graph (a) consumer income rises. This causes demand to shift right, raising prices and output.

In graph (b) a fall in the cost of resources used in manufacturing increases supply, causing prices to fall and output to rise.

In graph (c) the price of a substitute good falls, lowering demand for this product, with the obvious result.

In graph (d) advertising influences both demand and supply, the latter because it is a cost.

The **(+)** and **(-)** signs to the right of the variable names indicate the presumed sensitivity of supply or demand to that variable. For example, the **(+)** sign next to **Income** in the list of factors that effect demand indicates that if income rises, demand will rise.

The sensitivity of the price variables are represented by the slopes of the curves. The (-) sign next to the price variable for demand indicates the demand curve will have a negative slope. The equivalent sign on the supply side indicates that the supply curve will have a positive slope. Both were drawn this way in Figure. All other variables cause a shift in their respective curves. The plus **(+)** sign indicates a shift to the right if the variable is rising, and a shift to the left if it is falling. A negative **(-)** sign indicates a shift to the left if the variable is rising and a shift to the right if it is falling.

The (+) sign next to Income in the table, in the figure above, indicates that this should shift the demand curve to the right, as shown. Consequently at the new equilibrium, price and output will be higher. Graph (b) shows the effect of a decline in resource costs. Since the sign associated with costs is negative **(-)**, a decline in costs will cause the supply curve to shift right. (A rise in costs would cause the supply curve to shift left). Prices fall and output grows, a result that confirms intuition.

Suppose in the DVP example, the price of digital VCRs, a close substitute for the DVP, falls. This will cause the demand curve for the DVP to shift left representing a decline in demand, as is shown in graph (c). This makes sense because the price of the competing product, the digital VCR, makes it more attractive, and some consumers are lured away. Hence, the manufacturers of the DVP must lower their prices as well.

The reader should now understand what would happen if the manufacturers of the DVP refused to lower their prices in the face of such competition. Because of the collapse in the demand for their product, they would face an unwanted inventory buildup. Eventually they would have no choice but to cut production and prices.

Finally, graph (d) shows the effect of a variable, advertising, which influences both supply and demand. Demand grows, shifting right (that is the purpose of advertising) but because advertising is a cost, supply also shifts right. Presumably the effect upon demand would be far greater than upon supply, as shown, or the advertising would not be justified.

The Effect of Cost Reductions Upon Quantity Demanded: A Correct and an Incorrect Approach.

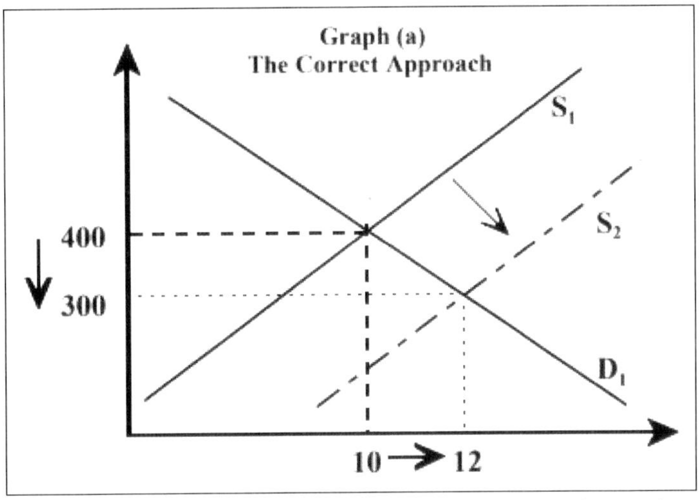

Cost is a factor that effects the Supply Curve only. Therefore only the supply curve shifts.

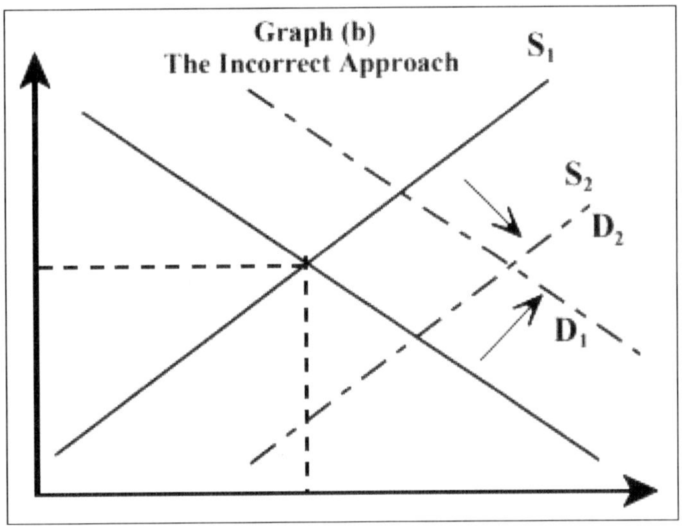

Since none of the factors (except price) effecting the Demand Curve have changed, the Demand Curve should not shift.

Cause and Effect in Comparative Statics Models

Students using comparative statics models sometimes confuse the direction of cause and effect, or the direction of influence of one variable upon another.

For an example, consider the answer to the following question:

"Assume that technology lowers manufacturing costs for this product. How would one show, using the microeconomic supply-and-demand model, that quantity demanded of the product will ultimately rise because of this impact of technology?" Refer to figure. Shown are two answers, one correct and the other incorrect.

Graph (a), where only the supply curve shifts, is the correct answer, and graph (b), which is incorrect, shows an answer often provided by students. In graph (a), the reduction in costs due to new technology causes the supply curve to shift to the right. This causes the equilibrium price to fall, from $400 to $300. The stationary demand curve indicates at this lower price, the quantity demanded will rise. In this example, it rises from 10 million to 12 million units. Quantity demanded has grown by 2 million units because of the decline in price, which in turn is due to cost reduction.

A common mistake among students is to reason ahead of the model, presuming that to show the increase in demand, the demand curve must be shifted. This is a mistake. The slope of the demand curve already represents the response to different prices. Therefore, if the price change is originating on the supply side, the change in equilibrium must be shown as due to a shift in the supply curve, and the change in quantity demanded is shown as a movement along the stable demand curve.

Generally, the following rule must be remembered: A supply or demand curve cannot be shifted unless one of the variables (except price) in the list of factors that effect that curve have changed. In this example, the initial equilibrium was changed because of a change in production costs. This was the initial cause. Costs are included in the list of factors that affect supply but not demand. Therefore, only the supply curve shifts.

The reduction of cost was the initial cause, the decline in price was the intermediate effect, and the resulting decline in quantity demanded was the final effect.

Economic Problem

The economic problem is a theory that scarcity exists in the sense that only finite and insufficient resources are available to satisfy the needs and desires of all human beings. The fundamental economic problem then faced by human society and business operators is how to allocate scarce resources to the provision of various goods and services within the economy.

What to Produce and in What Quantities?

The first central problem of an economy is to decide what goods and services are to be produced and in what quantities. This involves allocation of scarce resources in relation to the composition of total output in the economy. Since resources are scarce, the society has to decide about the goods to be produced: wheat, cloth, roads, television, power, buildings, and so on.

Once the nature of goods to be produced is decided, then their quantities are to be decided. How many tonnes of wheat, how many televisions, how many million kws of power, how many buildings, etc. Since the resources of the economy are scarce, the problem of the nature of goods and their quantities has to be decided on the basis of priorities or preferences of the society.

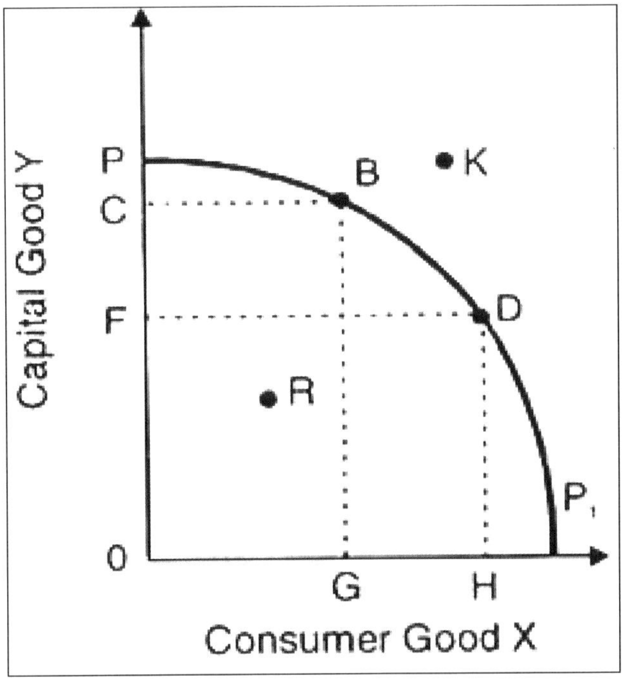

If the society gives priority to the production of more consumer goods now, it will have less in the future. A higher priority on capital goods implies less consumer goods now and more in the future. But since resources are scarce, if some goods are produced in larger quantities, some other goods will have to be produced in smaller quantities. This problem can also be explained with the help of the production possibility curve as shown in figure.

Suppose the economy produces capital goods and consumer goods. In deciding the total output of the economy, the society has to choose that combination of capital goods and consumer goods which is in keeping with its resources.

It cannot choose the combination R which is inside the production possibility curve PP_1 because it reflects economic inefficiency of the system in the form of unemployment of resources. Nor can it choose the combination R which is outside the current production possibilities of the society. The society lacks the resources to produce this combination of capital goods and consumer goods.

It will, therefore, have to choose among the combinations B, E, or D which give the highest level of satisfaction. If the society decides to have more capital goods, it will choose combination B; and if it wants more consumer goods, it will choose combination D.

How to Produce these Goods?

The next basic problem of an economy is to decide about the techniques or methods to be used in order to produce the required goods. This problem is primarily dependent upon the availability of resources within the economy.

If land is available in abundance, it may have extensive cultivation. If land is scarce, intensive methods of cultivation may be used. If labour is in abundance, it may use labour-intensive techniques; while in the case of labour shortage, capital-intensive techniques may be used.

The technique to be used also depends upon the type and quantity of goods to be produced. For producing capital goods and large outputs, complicated and expensive machines and techniques are required. On the other hand, simple consumer goods and small outputs require small and less expensive machines and comparatively simple techniques.

Further, it has to be decided what goods and services are to be produced in the public sector and what goods and services in the private sector. But in choosing between different methods of production, those methods should be adopted which bring about an efficient allocation of resources and increase the overall productivity in the economy.

Suppose the economy is producing certain quantities of consumer and capital goods at point A on PP curve in Figure. y adopting new techniques of production, given the supplies of factors, the productive efficiency of the economy increases. As a result, the PP_0 curve shifts outwards to P_1P_1.

It leads to the production of more quantities of consumer and capital gods from point A on PP_0 curve to point C of PP with be the new production possibility curve and the economy will move from point A to B where more of both the goods are produced.

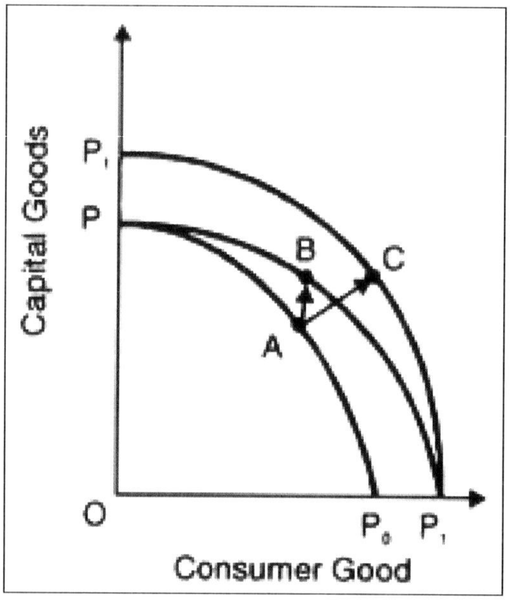

For whom is the Goods Produced?

The third basic problem to be decided is the allocation of goods among the members of the society. The allocation of basic consumer goods or necessities and luxuries comforts and among the household takes place on the basis of among the distribution of national income.

Whosoever possesses the means to buy the goods may have then. A rich person may have a large share of the luxuries goods, and a poor person may have more quantities of the basic consumer goods he needs. This problem is illustrated in figure where the production possibility curve PP shows the combinations of luxuries and necessaries.

At point B on the PP curve, the economy is producing more of luxuries OC for the rich and less of necessaries OC for the at whereas at point D more of necessaries OH are being produced for the poor and less of luxuries OF for the rich.

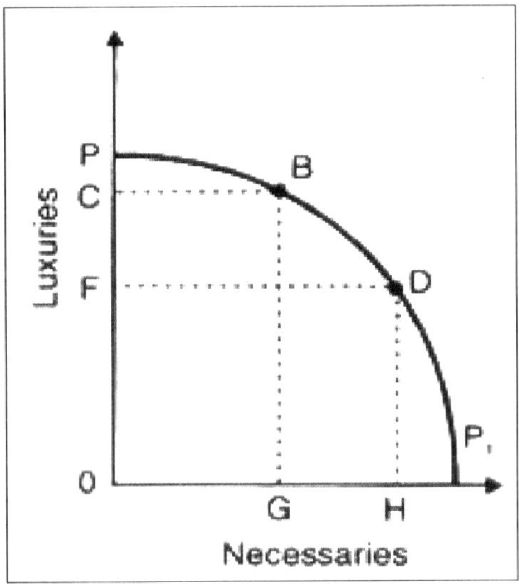

How Efficiently are the Resources being Utilised?

This is one of the important basic problems of an economy because having made the three earlier decisions, the society has to see whether the resources it owns are being utilised fully or not. In case the resources of the economy are lying idle, it has to find out ways and means to utilise them fully.

If the idleness of resources, say manpower, land or capital, is due to their male allocation, the society will have to adopt such monetary, fiscal, or physical measures whereby this is corrected. This is illustrated in figure where the production possibility curve PP reflects idle resources within the economy at point A, while the production possibility curve P_1P_1 reflects the full utilisation of the resources at point B or C.

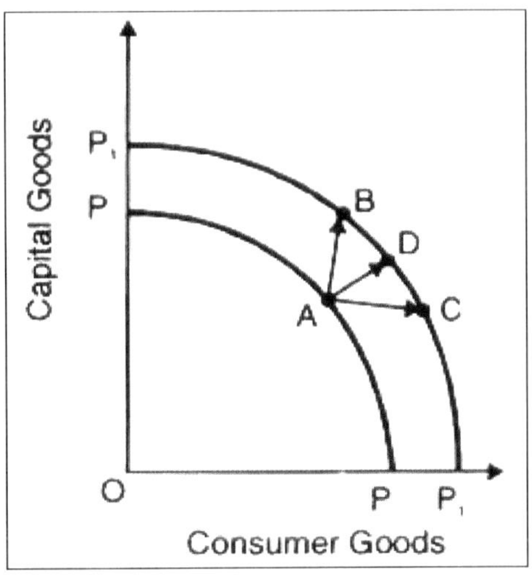

It is for the society to decide whether to produce more capital goods at point B or more consumer goods at point C, or both at point D at the level of full employment represented by the in an economy where the available resources are being fully utilised, it is characterised by technical efficiency or full employment.

To maintain it at this level, the economy must always be increasing the output of some goods and services by giving up something of others.

Is the Economy Growing?

The last and the most important problem is to find out whether the economy is growing through time or is it stagnant. If the economy is stagnant at any point inside the production possibility curve, says in figure, it has to be moved on to the production possibility curve PP whereby the economy now produces larger quantities of consumer goods and capital goods.

Economic growth takes place through a higher rate of capital formation which consists of replacing existing capital goods with new and more productive ones by adopting more efficient production techniques or through innovations.

This leads to the outward shifting of the production possibility curve from PP to P_1P_1. The economy moves, say after 5 years, from point A to B or C or D on the P_1P_1 curve. Point C represents the situation where larger quantities of both consumer and capital goods are produced in the economy. Economic growth enables the economy to have more of both the goods.

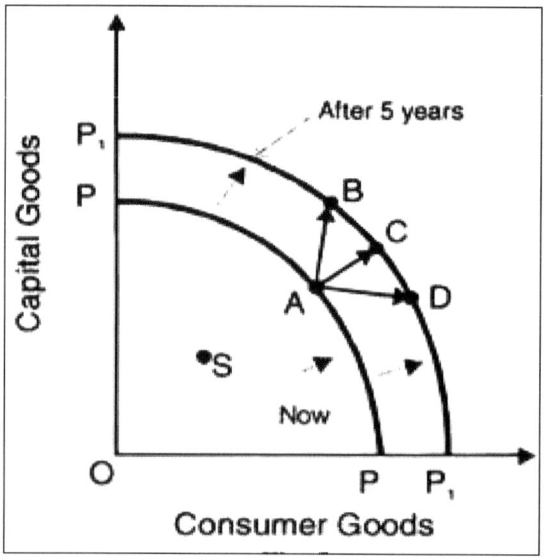

All these central problems of an economy are interrelated and interdependent. They arise from the fundamental economic problems of scarcity of means and multiplicity of ends which lead to the problem of choice or economizing of resources.

Economic Growth

The economic growth of a country is the increase in the market value of the goods and services produced by an economy over time.

Economic growth is measured by the increase in a country's total output or real Gross Domestic Product (GDP) or Gross National Product (GNP). The Gross Domestic Product (GDP) of a country is the total value of all final goods and services produced within a country over a period of time. Therefore an increase in GDP is the increase in a country's production.

Growth doesn't occur in isolation. Events in one country and region can have a significant effect on growth prospects in another.

Most developed economies experience slower economic growth as compared to developing countries. It would be more appropriate to compare their economic growth rates during similar periods in their history.

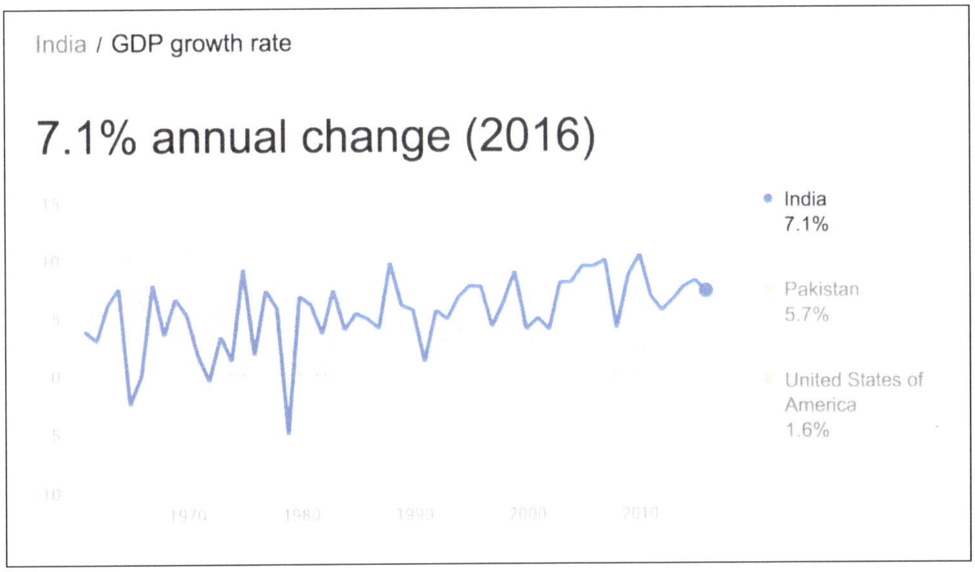

Economic Growth is not the same as Economic Development. Development alleviates people from low standards of living into proper employment with suitable shelter. Economic Growth does not take into account the depletion of natural resources which might lead to pollution, congestion & disease. Development, however, is concerned with sustainability which means meeting the needs of the present without compromising future needs.

Importance of Economic Growth

Economic growth is one of the most important indicators of a healthy economy. One of the biggest impacts of long-term growth of a country is that it has a positive impact on national income and the level of employment, which increases the standard of living. As the country's GDP is increasing, it is more productive which leads to more people being employed. This increases the wealth of the country and its population.

Higher economic growth also leads to extra tax income for government spending, which the government can use to develop the economy. This expansion can also be used to reduce the budget deficit.

Additionally, as the population of a country grows, it requires the growth to keep up its standard of living and wealth.

Economic growth also helps improve the standards of living and reduce poverty, but these improvements cannot occur without economic development. Economic growth alone cannot eliminate poverty on its own.

Six Factors that Affect Economic Growth

The follow six causes of economic growth are key components in an economy. Improving or increasing their quantity can lead to growth in the economy.

Natural Resources

The discovery of more natural resources like oil, or mineral deposits may boost economic growth as this shifts or increases the country's Production Possibility Curve. Other resources include land, water, forests and natural gas.

Realistically, it is difficult, if not impossible, to increase the number of natural resources in a country. Countries must take care to balance the supply and demand for scarce natural resources to avoid depleting them. Improved land management may improve the quality of land and contribute to economic growth. For example, Saudi Arabia's economy has historically been dependent on its oil deposits.

Physical Capital or Infrastructure

Increased investment in physical capital, such as factories, machinery, and roads, will lower the cost of economic activity. Better factories and machinery are more productive than physical labor. This higher productivity can increase output. For example, having a robust highway system can reduce inefficiencies in moving raw materials or goods across the country, which can increase its GDP.

Population or Labor

A growing population means there is an increase in the availability of workers or employees, which means a higher workforce. One downside of having a large population is that it could lead to high unemployment.

Human Capital

An increase in investment in human capital can improve the quality of the labor force. This increase in quality would result in an improvement of skills, abilities, and training. A skilled labor force has a significant effect on growth since skilled workers are more productive. For example, investing in STEM students or subsidizing coding academies would increase the availability of workers for higher-skilled jobs that pay more than investing in blue collar jobs.

Technology

Another influential factor is the improvement of technology. The technology could increase productivity with the same levels of labor, thus accelerating growth and development. This increment means factories can be more productive at lower costs. Technology is most likely to lead to sustained long-run growth.

Law

An institutional framework which regulates economic activity such as rules and laws. There is no specific set of institutions that promote growth.

Six Factors that Limit Economic Growth

Poor Health and Low Levels of Education

People who don't have access to healthcare or education have lower levels of productivity. This lack of access means the labor force is not as productive as it could be. Therefore, the economy does not reach the productivity it could otherwise.

Lack of Necessary Infrastructure

Developing nations often suffer from inadequate infrastructures such as roads, schools, and hospitals. This lack of infrastructure makes transportation more expensive and slows the overall efficiency of the country.

Flight of Capital

If the country is not delivering the returns expected from investors, then investors will pull out their money. Money often flows out of the country to seek higher rates of returns.

Political Instability

Similarly, political instability in the government scares investors and hinders investment. For example, historically, Zimbabwe had been plagued with political uncertainty and laws favoring indigenous ownership. This instability has scared off many investors who prefer smaller but surer returns elsewhere.

Institutional Framework

Often local laws don't adequately protect rights. Lack of an institutional framework can severely impact progress and investment.

The World Trade Organization

Many economists claim that the World Trade Organization (WTO) and other trading systems are biased against developing nations. Many developed nations adopt protectionist strategies which don't help liberalize trade.

Types of Economic Growth

There are primarily four types of economic growth:

Boom and Bust Business Cycles

If economic growth is high-speed and inflationary, then the level of growth will become unsustainable. This could lead to a recession like the Great Recession in 2008. However, this type of growth is typical of a business cycle.

Export-led

The Japanese and Chinese economy have experienced export-led growth thanks to a high current account surplus. This is because they have significantly more exports than imports.

Consumer

The US economy is dependent on consumer spending to stimulate economic growth. As a result, they also have a higher current account deficit.

Commodity Exports

These economies are dependent on their natural resources like oil or iron ore. For example, Saudi Arabia has had a very prosperous economy thanks to its oil exports. However, this can cause a problem when commodity prices fall, and there aren't other industries to balance things out.

Costs of Economic Growth

There are two problems associated with the economic growth:

Environmental Costs

Pollution and other negative externalities often accompany increased production or increased economic growth. Economists usually associate an adverse impact on the environment with rapid growth in developing economies.

Rising Income Inequality

Growth often leads to increased income inequality. Those not involved or related to the growth-generating sector of the economy get left behind. Usually, the rural population suffers the most.

Microeconomics

Microeconomics is the social science that studies the implications of human action, specifically about how those decisions affect the utilization and distribution of scarce resources. Microeconomics shows how and why different goods have different values, how individuals make more efficient or more productive decisions, and how individuals best coordinate and cooperate with one another. Generally speaking, microeconomics is considered a more complete, advanced, and settled science than macroeconomics.

Microeconomics is the study of economic tendencies, or what is likely to happen when individuals make certain choices or when the factors of production change. Individual actors are often grouped into microeconomic subgroups, such as buyers, sellers, and business owners. These groups create the supply and demand for resources, using money and interest rates as a pricing mechanism for coordination.

The uses of Microeconomics

As a purely normative science, microeconomics does not try to explain what should happen in a market. Instead, microeconomics only explains what to expect if certain conditions change. If a manufacturer raises the prices of cars, microeconomics says consumers will tend to buy fewer than before. If a major copper mine collapses in South America, the price of copper will tend to increase, because supply is restricted. Microeconomics could help an investor see why Apple Inc. stock prices might fall if consumers buy fewer iPhones. Microeconomics could also explain why a higher minimum wage might force the Wendy's Company to hire fewer workers. Microeconomics can address questions like these that might have very broad implications for the economy; however, questions about aggregate economic numbers remain the purview of macroeconomics, such as what might happen to the gross domestic product (GDP) of China in 2020.

Method of Microeconomics

Most modern microeconomic study is performed according to general equilibrium theory, developed by Léon Walras in *Elements of Pure Economics* and partial equilibrium theory, introduced by Alfred Marshall in *Principles of Economics*. The Marshallian and Walrasian methods fall under the larger umbrella of neoclassical microeconomics. Neoclassical economics focuses on how consumers and producers make rational choices to maximize their economic well being, subject to the constraints of how much income and resources they have available. Neoclassical economists make simplifying assumptions about markets – such as perfect knowledge, infinite numbers of buyers and sellers, homogeneous goods, or static variable relationships – in order to construct mathematical models of economic behavior.

These methods attempt to represent human behavior in functional mathematical language, which allows economists to develop mathematically testable models of individual markets. As logical positivists, neoclassicals believe in constructing measurable hypotheses about economic events, then using empirical evidence to see which hypotheses work best. Unlike physicists or biologists, economists cannot run repeatable tests, so their empirical research depends on the collection and observation of economic data from real world markets. The economic efficiency of markets is then determined by how well real markets adhere to the rules of the model.

Basic Concepts of Microeconomics

The study of microeconomics involves several key concepts, including (but not limited to):

- Production theory: This is the study of production — or the process of converting inputs into outputs. Producers seek to choose the combination of inputs and method of combining them that will minimize cost in order to maximize their profits.
- Utility theory: Analogous to production theory, consumers will choose to purchase and consume a combination of goods that will maximize their happiness or "utility", subject to the constraint of how much income they have available to spend.
- Price theory: Production theory and utility theory interact to produce the theory of supply and demand, which determine prices in a competitive market. In a perfectly competitive market, it concludes that the price demanded by consumers is the same supplied by producers. That results in economic equilibrium.
- Industrial organization and market structure: Microeconomists study the many ways that markets can be structured, from perfect competition to monopolies, and the ways that production and prices will develop in these different types of markets.

Macroeconomics

Macroeconomics Is the study of the behaviour of a national or regional economy as a whole. It is concerned with understanding economy-wide events such as the total amount of goods and services produced, the level of unemployment, and the general behaviour of prices.

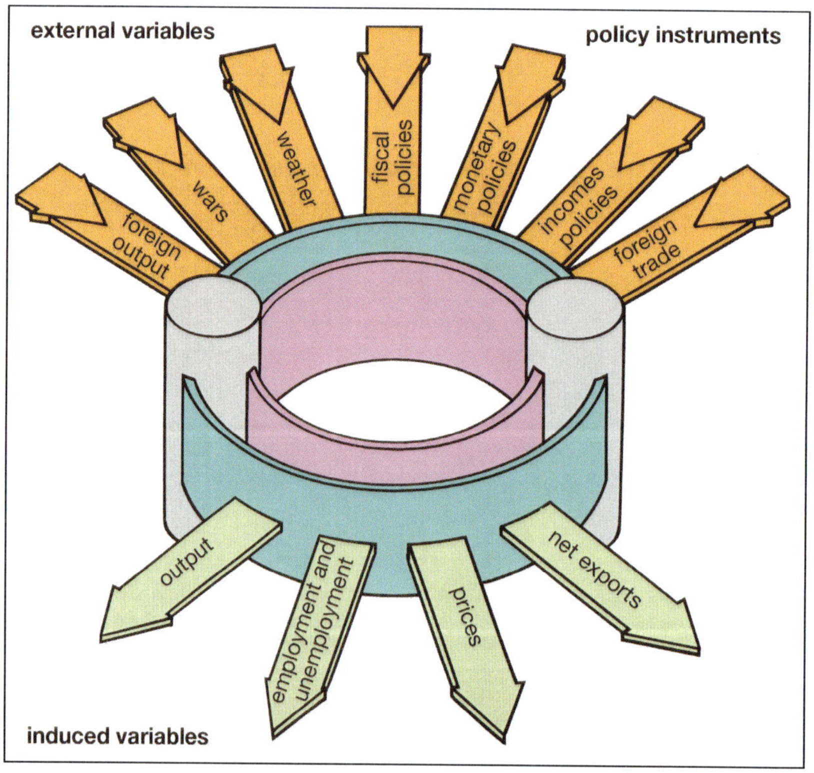

Macroeconomics

Diagram depicting the components of macroeconomic functioning.

Unlike microeconomics—which studies how individual economic actors, such as consumers and firms, make decisions—macroeconomics concerns itself with the aggregate outcomes of those decisions. For that reason, in addition to using the tools of microeconomics, such as supply-and-demand analysis, macroeconomists also utilize aggregate measures such as gross domestic product (GDP), unemployment rates, and the consumer price index (CPI) to study the large-scale repercussions of micro-level decisions.

Classical School

Although complex macroeconomic structures have been characteristic of human societies since ancient times, the discipline of macroeconomics is relatively new. Until the 1930s most economic analysis was focused on microeconomic phenomena and concentrated primarily on the study of individual consumers, firms and industries. The classical school of economic thought, which derived its main principles from Scottish economist Adam Smith's theory of self-regulating markets, was the dominant philosophy. Accordingly, such economists believed that economy-wide events such as rising unemployment and recessions are like natural phenomena and cannot be avoided. If left undisturbed, market forces would eventually correct such problems; moreover, any intervention by the government in the operation of free markets would be ineffective at best and destructive at worst.

Keynesianism

The classical view of macroeconomics, which was popularized in the 19th century as laissez-faire, was shattered by the Great Depression, which began in the United States in 1929 and soon spread to the rest of the industrialized Western world. The sheer scale of the catastrophe, which lasted almost a decade and left a quarter of the U.S. workforce without jobs, threatening the economic and political stability of many countries, was sufficient to cause a paradigm shift in mainstream macroeconomic thinking, including a reevaluation of the belief that markets are self-correcting. The theoretical foundations for that change were laid in 1935–36, when the British economist John Maynard Keynes published his monumental work *The General Theory of Employment, Interest, and Money*. Keynes argued that most of the adverse effects of the Great Depression could have been avoided had governments acted to counter the depression by boosting spending through fiscal policy. Keynes thus ushered in a new era of macroeconomic thought that viewed the economy as something that the government should actively manage. Economists such as Paul Samuelson, Franco Modigliani, James Tobin, Robert Solow, and many others adopted and expanded upon Keynes's ideas, and as a result the Keynesian school of economics was born.

In contrast to the hands-off approach of classical economists, the Keynesians argued that governments have a duty to combat recessions. Although the ups and downs of the business cycle cannot be completely avoided, they can be tamed by timely intervention. At times of economic crisis, the economy is crippled because there is almost no demand for anything. As businesses' sales decline, they begin laying off more workers, which causes a further reduction in income and demand, resulting in a prolonged recessionary cycle. Keynesians argued that, because it controls tax revenues, the government has the means to generate demand simply by increasing spending on goods and services during such times of hardship.

Monetarism

In the 1950s the first challenge to the Keynesian school of thought came from the monetarists, who were led by the influential University of Chicago economist Milton Friedman. Friedman proposed an alternative explanation of the Great Depression: he argued that what had started as a recession was turned into a prolonged depression because of the disastrous monetary policies followed by the Federal Reserve System (the central bank of the United States). If the Federal Reserve had started to increase the money supply early on, instead of doing just the opposite, the recession could have been effectively tamed before it got out of control. Over time, Friedman's ideas were refined and came to be known as monetarism. In contrast to the Keynesian strategy of boosting demand through fiscal policy, monetarists favoured controlled increases in the money supply as a means of fighting off recesssions. Beyond that, the government should avoid intervening in free markets and the rest of the economy, according to monetarists.

Current Developments

A second challenge to the Keynesian school arose in the 1970s, when the American economist Robert E. Lucas, Jr., laid the foundations of what came to be known as the New Classical school of thought in economics. Lucas's key introduced the rational-expectations hypothesis. As opposed to the ideas in earlier Keynesian and monetarist models that viewed the individual decision makers in the economy as shortsighted and backward-looking, Lucas argued that decision makers, insofar as they are rational, do not base their decisions solely on current and past data; they also form expectations about the future on the basis of a vast array of information available to them. That fact implies that a change in monetary policy, if it has been predicted by rational agents, will have no effect on real variables such as output and the unemployment rate, because the agents will have acted upon the implications of such a policy even before it is implemented. As a result, predictable changes in monetary policy will result in changes in nominal variables such as prices and wages but will not have any real effects.

Following Lucas's pioneering work, economists including Finn E. Kydland and Edward C. Prescott developed rigorous macroeconomic models to explain the fluctuations of the business cycle, which came to be known in the macroeconomic literature as real-business-cycle (RBC) models. RBC models were based on strong mathematical foundations and utilized Lucas's idea of rational expectations. An important outcome of the RBC models was that they were able to explain macroeconomic fluctuations as the product of a myriad of external and internal shocks (unpredictable events that hit the economy). Primarily, they argued that shocks that result from changes in technology can account for the majority of the fluctuations in the business cycle.

The tendency of RBC models to overemphasize technology-driven fluctuations as the primary cause of business cycles and to underemphasize the role of monetary and fiscal policy led to the development of a new Keynesian response in the 1980s. New Keynesians, including

John B. Taylor and Stanley Fischer, adopted the rigorous modeling approach introduced by Kydland and Prescott in the RBC literature but expanded it by altering some key underlying assumptions. Previous models had relied on the fact that nominal variables such as prices and wages are flexible and respond very quickly to changes in supply and demand. However, in the real world, most wages and many prices are locked in by contractual agreements. That fact introduces "stickiness," or resistance to change, in those economic variables. Because wages and prices tend to be sticky, economic decision makers may react to macroeconomic events by altering other variables. For example, if wages are sticky, businesses will find themselves laying off more workers than they would in an unrealistic environment in which every employee's salary could be cut in half.

Introducing market imperfections such as wage and price stickiness helped Taylor and Fischer to build macroeconomic models that represented the business cycle more accurately. In particular, they were able to show that in a world of market imperfections such as stickiness, monetary policy will have a direct impact on output and on employment in the short run, until enough time has passed for wages and prices to adjust. Therefore, central banks that control the supply of money can very well influence the business cycle in the short run. In the long run, however, the imperfections become less binding, as contracts can be renegotiated, and monetary policy can influence only prices.

Following the new Keynesian revolution, macroeconomists seemed to reach a consensus that monetary policy is effective in the short run and can be used as a tool to tame business cycles. Many other macroeconomic models were developed to measure the extent to which monetary policy can influence output. More recently, the impact of the financial crisis of 2007–08 and the Great Recession that followed it, coupled with the fact that many governments adopted a very Keynesian response to those events, brought about a revival of interest in the new Keynesian approach to macroeconomics, which seemed likely to lead to improved theories and better macroeconomic models in the future.

Economic Theories

Economic theories try to explain economic phenomena, to interpret why and how the economy behaves and what is the best to solution - how to influence or to solve these economic phenomena.

Nature of Economic Theory:

Economic theory involves generalisations which are statements of general tendencies or uniformities of relationships among various elements of economic phenomena. A generalisation is the establishment of a general truth on the basis of particular experiences.

For example, the generalisation that demand is an inverse function of price expresses a relationship between price and demand, other things remaining the same. If other things remain the same, the law of demand holds valid. If other things do not remain the same, it stands refuted.

Steps of Economic Theory

The various steps required to construct a theory of economics are detailed below:

Selecting the Problem

The first step in the formulation of a theory is the selection of the problem which must be stated clearly and correctly. The problem to be explored may be very wide like poverty, unemployment, inflation, etc., or it may be narrow relating to an industry.

The narrower the problem, the better it would be for a researcher to conduct his enquiry satisfactorily. "It is desirable that investigators should concentrate upon narrow problems—narrow in area or period or aspect of a problem—and the scope for further intensive rather than extensive work should be an important criterion for selecting a problem".

Collection of Data

The second step is to collect data or facts pertaining to the problem to be explored. If the problem is simple the data can be easily collected. However, complicated problems may require many months or even years to collect the necessary data.

This step is called descriptive economics. Sometimes, 'facts' can be known only after careful observation. Many economic principles are based on careful observation, such as the law of diminishing returns, the Malthusian theory of population, the Marshallian price theory, etc.

Classification of Data

After collection, the data are enumerated, classified and analysed. Classification is a way of knowing things. It is the grouping of data or facts according to their resemblances and differences, and to note comparisons and contrasts.

For instance, if the problem is to study the trend in population growth, the census data may be collected and classified by sex, age groups, literacy, marital status, occupational distribution etc. Thus enumeration, classification and analysis of data are crucial to scientific theory.

Formulation of Hypothesis

The next step is to formulate hypothesis about the economic phenomena to be analysed. A hypothesis is a suggested answer to a problem by the aid of which we endeavour to explain facts by discovering their orderliness. The hypothesis arises from the observed facts, experience or previous knowledge of the researcher.

At this stage, simplifying assumptions may be introduced so that a particular hypothesis may be developed fully. It is these special assumptions which become formulated consciously as a hypothesis. For example, the assumption that producers aim at maximising their profits is a plausible hypothesis on which the theory of business behaviour can be constructed.

Testing of Hypothesis

The next step is the testing of the hypothesis formulated. The hypothesis formulated should be such that deductions can be drawn from it and a decision reached as to whether it explains the facts considered or not. The hypothesis should be tested by well-established techniques of logic and statistics which may then be subjected to confirmation.

Further, the hypothesis should provide the answer to the problem which led to the enquiry. This requires prediction. Prediction may refer to past, present or future events as long as it are not known previous to or at the time of prediction. A hypothesis is said to be verified, and not proved, through the successful prediction it makes.

Of the various hypotheses formulated that hypothesis should be preferred "which can predict what will happen, and from which we can infer what has already happened, even if we did not know what has happened when the hypothesis was formulated". A successfully tested hypothesis is a theory.

Verification of Theory

The tested hypothesis or theory should be verified. If it turns out to be true, the theory is said to be confirmed or verified. The process of verification may be carried out by observation or by checking the consistency of the theory with related facts that are believed to be true.

If a theory is proved to be wrong, it stands rejected. But it is a gross error to suppose that a theory which is rejected is useless. Rather, a wrong theory may direct our attention to unsuspected facts or new facts and lead to the amendment of the theory.

Formulation of Solutions

Once the theory is verified and proved true, possible solutions or suggestions to the problem under investigation are to be formulated. This is essential in the case of social sciences like economics "because economists tend to be socially oriented, and do not like spending their energies on trivial and irrelevant issues". This final stage relates to applied economics and involves value judgements.

Uses of Economic Theory

Economic theory provides us with tools of economic analysis, helps in explaining economic phenomena, in predicting economic events, in judging the performance of the economy, and in formulating economic policies.

To Provide Economic Tools

Economic theory provides economic tools to economists. That is why Mrs. Joan Robinson characterised economic theory as a "box of tools". Rightly so. It provides a number of tools with which the economists analyse economic problems.

The methods and techniques used in economics are the "box of tools" of economists. Economic tools are applicable to all economic systems whether they are capitalist, socialist or mixed. They also apply to developed and developing economies.

To Explain Economic Phenomena

Economic theory helps in interpreting and explaining economic phenomena of the real world. By the process of abstraction, it chooses relevant facts, classifies and interprets them in the light of the previous or existing knowledge, establishes a causal relationship among different variables in order to establish the validity of an economic problem.

For instance, to find out the causes of unemployment in the country, data or facts are collected, enumerated, analysed and classified. Then they are interpreted in the light of our knowledge of the nature of unemployment. Ultimately, a causal relationship is established among the probable factors responsible for unemployment in order to arrive at the causes.

To Predict Economic Events

It provides a basis for predicting unobserved economic events. It possesses much predictive accuracy in exploring the economic problems of the real world. For instance, if we find that with the increase in the supply of wheat, its price does not fall, given the demand for wheat, we can predict that there is likely to be shortage of wheat in the coming year.

The reason may be failure of rains or drought conditions, or the expectation of some untoward event like war.

To Judge the Performance of the Economy

Economic theory helps in judging the performance of the various sectors of the economy and of the economy as a whole. For instance, if the prices of vegetable oils are rising, knowledge of the price mechanism is necessary to decide whether the rise in their prices is due to shortage of raw materials, or increase in demand, or due to malfunctioning of the industry or the economy.

To Formulate and Understand Economic Policies

It helps in formulating and understanding economic policies. Suppose the economist is asked to offer advice to reduce unemployment. This problem is complementary to the goals of removal of poverty and reduction of inequitable distribution of income and wealth. But it conflicts with the goal of price stability.

So the economist will have to think out how much unemployment can be sustained with a minimum of inflation. The choice of problem of unemployment is the first step in theoretical economic analysis which is being investigated for policy formulation.

The next step is to collect data, or if they are already available, the economist has to arrange and interpret them in the light of the existing theories of unemployment in order to find out the causes of unemployment.

Then he has to propose alternative means of achieving the given goal of lowering the level of unemployment. "In other words, when faced with evaluating a policy measure for achieving some goal, he must ask whether other measures that are feasible at the time and place would better achieve the desired goal".

To Evaluate Economic Policies

Given the objectives of the society, theoretical economics can be used to evaluate various economic policies. And it is the economist who is called upon to evaluate policy measures. "It is the role of the economist not only to analyse the consequences of a proposed policy (or to compare two or more policies), but also to suggest policies. Given a statement of the objects economic theory can be used to invent or publicize proposed policies that have not previously been under consideration". Thus theoretical economics helps in formulating and understanding economic policies. It also guides consumers, producers, traders, workers, administrators and economists to plan rationally.

Economic Theory and Economic Policy

Economic policy (or practice or applied economics) provides a practical shape to economic theory. In practice, we apply economic principles for analysing the actual conditions of the economy. Economic theory and policy are closely related to each other.

For economic policy to be successful, it has to be formulated on the basis of economic theories. It is the knowledge of economic theories that leads to the laying down of economic policies.

Economic theory is an indispensable tool for understanding the policy measures of the government. And it is the economist who is asked to formulate policy measures. As pointed out by Lipsey, "It is the role of the economist not only to analyse the consequences of a proposed policy (or to compare two or more policies), but also to suggest policies. Given a statement of the objects economic theory can be used to invent or publicize proposed policies that have not previously been under consideration".

First, the economist should know the goals of economic policy. The goals of economic policy may be economic growth, full employment, price stability, removal of poverty and equitable distribution of income and wealth.

Second, suppose he is asked to offer advice about the ways in which unemployment can be reduced. This goal is complementary and overlaps the goals of removal of poverty and equitable distribution of income and wealth. But it conflicts with the goal of price stability. So he will have to think out how much unemployment can be sustained with a minimum of inflation.

Third, he will have to collect data, or if they are already available, arrange and interpret in the light of the existing theories of unemployment in order to find out the causes of unemployment.

Fourth, then he has to propose alternative means of achieving the given goal of lowering the level of unemployment. "In other words, when faced with evaluating a policy measure for achieving some goal, he must ask whether other measures that are feasible at the time and place would better achieve the desired goal".

Lastly, he should point out the probable effects of these measures on the economy. "This entails a clear-cut understanding of the economic impact, costs and political feasibility of alternative programmes".

Limitations of Economic Theory

But too much should not be expected of economic theory. It has its limitations.

Accurate Data not Available

Economic theory being a "kit of tools" presupposes the availability of accurate data or facts which are, however, not easily available. As a matter of fact, a theory is based on facts. If the facts are not true, the theory is also wrong. A theory to be true must be tested against actual economic entities or facts. But the collection and interpretation of data are often arbitrary which make economic theories unrealistic.

Accurate Predictions not Possible

Accurate predictions are not always possible in economic theory. The probability of accurate predictions in economics is much less than in physical sciences. A scientist can conduct his investigations by experimenting under controlled conditions in a laboratory. But an economist is not able to predict accurately because he cannot have controlled experimentation of economic phenomena.

Human Behaviour not Rational

Economic theory deals with the behaviour of human beings who do not always act rationally. Their behaviour is influenced more by the existing social and legal institutions of the society in which they live than by economic principles. "It is impossible to isolate a group of consumers or businessmen in a test-tube to see how they would react to a given change".

Unrealistic Assumptions

All economic theories are based on certain assumptions. But some of the assumptions of economic theory are unrealistic. For instance, we assume that individuals as consumers and producers behave rationally. But we find that consumers and producers Seldom behave rationally. The negation of the assumption of rationality makes wrong the predictions based on this.

As Aptly Put by Boulding

"Economic analysis is not a perfect picture of economic life; it is a map of it. Just as we do not expect a map to show every tree, every house, and every blade of grass in a landscape, so we should not expect economic analysis to take into account every detail and quirk of real economic behaviour".

Not Fully Applicable to Economic Policies

Economic theories are not fully applicable to economic policies. The application of economic theory to economic problems, irrespective of time and place, has led to the failure of many economic policies implemented with good intentions.

Firstly, the applicability and correctness of an economic theory depends upon the fact whether the assumptions of the theory are in keeping with the actual economic condition on which the economist wants to apply it.

If the assumptions are not in agreement with the actual economic situation, the results may be wrong. For instance, if we try to apply the profit-maximisation theory of the firm on a particular industry, our conclusions might turn out to be wrong if the conditions of perfect competition do not prevail in practice in that industry.

Secondly, another reason for the failure of economic theory to be useful in policy is the existence of particular situations in the country which happen to be different from those considered in the theory. Such a situation arises when efforts are made to apply economic theories meant for developed countries on the developing economies.

Thirdly, an economic theory which is the basis of a policy measure at one time in the economy cannot be true for all times because an economy is "a dynamic, changing organism". An economic theory which is correct today may become obsolete tomorrow and the policy based on this might also become useless.

Failure of Economic Theory on Policy

But a blind application of economic theory to policy is not helpful in evolving correct economic policies. The application of economic theory to economic problems, irrespective of time and place, has led to the failure of many economic policies implemented with good intentions. The reasons for such failures have been as under.

Keynesian Economics

Keynesian economics is a theory that says the government should increase demand to boost growth. Keynesians believe consumer demand is the primary driving force in an economy. As a result, the theory supports expansionary fiscal policy. Its main tools are government spending on infrastructure, unemployment benefits, and education. A drawback is that overdoing Keynesian policies increases inflation.

The British economist John Maynard Keynes developed this theory in the 1930s. The Great Depression had defied all prior attempts to end it. President Franklin D. Roosevelt used Keynesian economics to build his famous New Deal program. In his first 100 days in office, FDR increased the debt by $4 billion to create 16 new agencies and laws. For example, the Works Progress Administration put 8.5 million people to work. The Civil Works Administration created 4 million new construction jobs.

Keynes described his premise in "The General Theory of Employment, Interest, and Money". Published in February 1936, it was revolutionary. First, it argued that government spending was a critical factor driving aggregate demand. That meant an increase in spending would increase demand.

Second, Keynes argued that government spending was necessary to maintain full employment.

Keynes advocated deficit spending during the contraction phase of the business cycle. But in recent years, politicians have used it even during the expansionary phase. President Bush's deficit spending in 2006 and 2007 increased the debt. It also helped create a boom that led to the 2007 financial crisis. President Trump is increasing the debt during stable economic growth. That will also lead to a boom-and-bust cycle.

Keynesian Economics	Classical Economics
• Government spending on infrastructure, unemployment benefits, and education will increase consumer demand. • Government spending is necessary to maintain full employment.	• Increasing business growth will boost the economy. • Government should play a limited role and target companies, not consumers.

Keynesian versus Classical Economic Theories

Classical economic theory promotes laissez-faire policy. It says the free market allows the laws of supply and demand to self-regulate the business cycle. It argues that unfettered capitalism will create a productive market on its own. It will enable private entities to own the factors of production. These four factors are entrepreneurship, capital goods, natural resources, and labor. In this theory, business owners use the most efficient practices to maximize profit.

Classical economic theory advocates for a limited government. It should have a balanced budget and incur little debt. Government spending is dangerous because it crowds out private investment. But that only happens when the economy is not in a recession. In that case, government borrowing will compete with corporate bonds. The result is higher interest rates, which make borrowing more expensive. If deficit spending only occurs during a recession, it will not raise interest rates. For that reason, it also won't crowd out private investment.

Criticism

Supply-side economists say that increasing business growth, not consumer demand, will boost the economy. They agree the government has a role to play, but fiscal policy should target companies. They rely on tax cuts and deregulation.

Proponents of trickle-down economics say that all fiscal policy should benefit the wealthy. Since the wealthy are business owners, benefits to them will trickle down to everyone.

Monetarists claim that monetary policy is the real driver of the business cycle. Monetarists like Milton Friedman blame the Depression on high-interest rates. They believe expansion of the money supply will end recessions and boost growth.

Socialists criticize Keynesianism because it doesn't go far enough. They believe the government should take a more active role to protect the common welfare. This means owning some factors of production. Most socialist governments own the nation's energy, health care, and education services.

Even more critical are communists. They believe the people, as represented by the government, should own everything. The government completely controls the economy.

Keynesian Multiplier

The Keynesian multiplier represents how much demand each dollar of government spending generates. For example, a multiplier of two creates $2 of gross domestic product for every $1 of spending. Most economists agree that the Keynesian multiplier is one. Every $1 the government spends adds $1 to economic growth. Since government spending is a component of GDP, it has to have at least this much impact.

The Keynesian multiplier also applies to decreases in spending. The International Monetary Fund estimated that a cut in government spending during a contraction has a multiplier of 1.5 or more. Governments who insist on austerity measures during a recession remove $1.50 from GDP for every $1 cut.

New Keynesian Theory

In the 1970s, rational expectations theorists argued against the Keynesian theory. They said that taxpayers would anticipate the debt caused by deficit spending. Consumers would save today to pay off the future debt. Deficit spending would spur savings, not increase demand or economic growth.

The rational expectations theory inspired the New Keynesians. They said that monetary policy is more potent than fiscal policy. If done right, expansionary monetary policy would negate the need for deficit spending. Central banks don't need politicians' help to manage the economy. They would merely adjust the money supply.

Classical Economics

Classical economics is the English school of economic thought that originated during the late 18th century with Adam Smith and that reached maturity in the works of David Ricardo and John Stuart Mill. The theories of the classical school, which dominated economic thinking in Great Britain until about 1870, focused on economic growth and economic freedom, stressing laissez-faire ideas and free competition.

David Ricardo, in the National Portrait Gallery.

Many of the fundamental concepts and principles of classical economics were set forth in Smith's An Inquiry into the Nature and Causes of the Wealth of Nations. Strongly opposed to the mercantilist theory and policy that had prevailed in Britain since the 16th century, Smith argued that free competition and free trade, neither hampered nor coddled by government, would best promote a nation's economic growth. As he saw it, the entire community benefits most when each of its members follows his or her own self-interest. In a free-enterprise system, individuals make a profit by producing goods that other people are willing to buy. By the same token, individuals spend money for goods that they want or need most. Smith demonstrated how the apparent chaos of competitive buying and selling is transmuted into an orderly system of economic cooperation that can meet individuals' needs and increase their wealth. He also observed that this cooperative system occurs through the process of individual choice as opposed to central direction.

In analyzing the workings of free enterprise, Smith introduced the rudiments of a labour theory of value and a theory of distribution. Ricardo expanded upon both ideas in Principles of Political Economy and Taxation. In his labour theory of value, Ricardo emphasized that the value (i.e., price) of goods produced and sold under competitive conditions tends to be proportionate to the labour costs incurred in producing them. Ricardo fully recognized, however, that over short periods price depends on supply and demand. This notion became central to classical economics, as did Ricardo's theory of distribution, which divided national product between three social classes: wages for labourers, profits for owners of capital, and rents for landlords. Taking the limited growth potential of any national economy as a given, Ricardo concluded that a particular social class could gain a larger share of the total product only at the expense of another.

These and other Ricardian theories were restated by Mill in Principles of Political Economy, a treatise that marked the culmination of classical economics. Mill's work related abstract economic principles to real-world social conditions and thereby lent new authority to economic concepts.

The teachings of the classical economists attracted much attention during the mid-19th century. The labour theory of value, for example, was adopted by Karl Marx, who worked out all of its logical implications and combined it with the theory of surplus value, which was founded on the assumption that human labour alone creates all value and thus constitutes the sole source of profits.

More significant were the effects of classical economic thought on free-trade doctrine. The most influential was Ricardo's principle of comparative advantage, which states that every nation should specialize in the production of those commodities it can produce most efficiently; everything else should be imported. This idea implies that if all nations were to take full advantage of the territorial division of labour, total world output would invariably be larger than it would be if nations tried to be self-sufficient. Ricardo's comparative-advantage principle became the cornerstone of 19th-century international-trade theory.

Development Economics

Development economics is a branch of economics that deals with the improvement of the economies of developing countries. The discipline aims at establishing strategies that apply to different developing countries depending on their unique social, political, and economic factors. Development economics also explores the unique challenges that face developing nations thus helps in the analysis of the opportunities available in these nations and how they can be applied. The

Development economics makes use of economic theory, econometric methods, political science, and demographics in its approaches.

Areas of Relevance

Development economics is often applied to efforts aimed at poverty eradication, achieving millennium development goals (MDGs) set by the United Nations (UN), democratic governance, sustainable environment and energy policies, and crisis prevention and recovery.

Practical Applications

Development economics is applied in the development of strategies that are aimed at improving the economic status of developing nations. Thus, they contribute to bridging the ever-increasing gaps between the poor and the rich in many countries. This economic development is achieved through the application of economic and political theories in the analysis of present and past economic developments as well as the possible opportunities that may be exploited and the methods for using these opportunities to the benefit of the country.

Benefits of using Development Economics

Development economics offers a more comprehensive view and understanding of economic, political, and social impacts, as well as of influences on the economic state of a country. Besides, it examines areas that can be improved such as infrastructure, education, health and technology that is critical to positive economic growth through empowerment of the population. Besides, Economic Development examines the macroeconomic and micro-economic factors that relates to the structure of the developing country and how the country can create both domestic and international growth.

Criticisms of Development Economics

The measures used in quantifying the progress of economic development have been criticized for their failure to include smaller, yet significantly important economic activities, such as housekeeping and home building, that are not listed in financial transactions. Therefore, this shortcoming is likely to misrepresent the economic position of a country as the economic progress is measured in financial terms. Fraud and lack of data on funding also compromise the effectiveness of calculating the Gross Domestic Product (GDP) of a country.

Development Economics in Practice

The United Nations Development Program (UNDP) has applied development economics in an attempt to help developing countries to improve their economic positions by assisting them in developing strategies and analyzing growth trends. The UNDP program works through women empowerment and gender equality, poverty reduction, sustainable environmental management, disease eradication, and treatment, as well as strengthening partnerships for cooperation between rich and developing nations in a view to achieving the Millennium Development Goals.

Strengths of Development Economics

The most important and significant aspect of development economic is the realization that economic development strategies to be applied are not to be found in predefined formulas, but differ according to the political, economic, and social factors affecting any given economy. This realization is important in the development of tailored growth strategies that will best serve the economy in question.

Business Economics

Business economics is a field of applied economics that studies the financial, organizational, market-related, and environmental issues faced by corporations. Economic theory and quantitative methods form the basis of assessments on factors affecting corporations such as business organization, management, expansion, and strategy. Studies might include how and why corporations expand, the impact of entrepreneurs, the interactions among corporations, and the role of governments in regulation.

Economics, broadly, refers to the study of the components and functions of a particular marketplace or economy, such as supply and demand, and the effect of the concept of scarcity. Within an economy, production factors, distribution methods, and consumption are important subjects of study. Business economics focuses on the elements and factors within business operations and how they relate to the economy as a whole.

The field of business economics addresses economic principles, strategies, standard business practices, the acquisition of necessary capital, profit generation, the efficiency of production, and overall management strategy. Business economics also includes the study of external economic factors and their influence on business decisions such as a change in industry regulation or a sudden price shift in raw materials.

Managerial Economics

Managerial economics is a sub-focus of business economics that focuses on the microeconomic factors pertinent to the decision-making process with an organization. Corporations make strategic decisions that result in a profit or loss. Managerial economic principles influence and guide corporate strategy and decisions.

Managerial economics apply to the public and private sectors and for-profit and not-for-profit organizations. All organizations must assess the internal and external economic climate to remain solvent because all organizations require a source of funding to continue operations. The goal of managerial economics is to use available resources and maximize production while minimizing waste.

Business Economics of Non-profits

While non-profits may focus on raising donations, for-profits instead focus on the sale of goods or services. Each organization strives to limit waste to maximize the overall usefulness of the available resources. Each type of organization uses the same principles to meet the associated goals of maintaining the necessary capital to continue working within the economy.

Both for-profit and non-profit organizations perform similar business functions and require similar expertise. For example, all types of organizations engage in advertising, community, or customer support and need leadership to make appropriate strategic decisions.

Real-world Example of Business Economics

There are various organizations associated with the field of business economics. In the United States, the National Association for Business Economics (NABE) is the professional association for business economists. The organization's mission is "to provide leadership in the use and understanding of economics". In the United Kingdom, the equivalent organization is the Society of Business Economists.

Behavioral Economics

Behavioural economics is a recent field of mainstream economics; it predominantly deals with human behaviour's deviations from the model of the *homo economicus* or rational man. These deviations from rational calculation are introduced as "non-standard" (the standard being neoclassical economics) or reflections of "bias". Behavioural research explains human behaviour through the lens of social preferences, heuristics and norms, from which new behavioural models are constructed. Scientific findings are mainly taken from field or laboratory experiments. Furthermore, findings from neighbouring disciplines (psychology, social sciences, neuroscience, cognitive science etc.) are used and transferred to the economic discipline in order to improve the reliability and precision of explaining human behaviour in the economic realm.

Analysis and Conception of the Economy

In general, behavioural economics does not have strong theoretical or normative assumptions about how an economic system works or should work. Instead, prominent (neoclassical) economic theories are analysed and reviewed with respect to human behaviour, flagging deviations from the neoclassical model in concrete economic contexts, e.g. markets or public goods (Weber and Dawes 2010, 91). Hence, behavioural economics focuses on the observable behaviour of humans. Central concepts particularly refer to humans and their decisions. Thereby, humans are described as behaving in accordance with 'bounded rationality'.

There are different explanations for the causes. A prominent idea is the dual process theory: According to Daniel Kahneman, there are two different ways of thinking based on the systems involved in decision making, depending on the situation: One, the intuitive system, is described as being fast, effortless and volatile with respect to its performance, while the other, the reasoning system is more elaborate, reliable and slow. Since the intuitive system deviates from predictions of the rational behavioural model, humans are considered as behaving with bounded rationality.

Based on neoclassical decision theory, the behavioural economist Matthew Rabin developed three deviations from neoclassical economics' 'expected utility theory'; these have become vital differentiations in behavioural economics research. Rabin developed 'non-standard preferences', 'non-standard beliefs' and 'non-standard decision making' (the three respectively refer to one part of the mathematical function in the neoclassical expected utility theory). These are described in the following, with two examples presented for each case:

- Non-standard preferences refer to elements that form part of the utility function:
  - Social preferences: These include evidence for altruism and reciprocity. Example: Humans do not only care for their own share, but also care for the distribution.
  - Time preferences: Humans do not consistently discount over time, but do often have a preference for the present. As a result decisions concerning future investments and savings deviate from neoclassical predictions.
- Non-standard beliefs concerns the part of the decision making process in which probabilities need to be taken into account:
  - Overconfidence: Humans tend to overestimate their own capabilities. For instance, 93% of all drivers in the U.S.A. assume they drive better than the average driver. Similarly, managers of big companies overestimate their capabilities.
  - The law of small numbers: Humans tend to extrapolate from a small sample to the whole statistical population. For example, even if a fund manager works better than the market average for three years, this does not imply that high performance will necessarily continue for years to come.
- Non-standard decision-making concerns the guideline of decisions, maximization being the normal case:
  - Framing: Decisions do not only depend on the expected results but also on the way the result is presented. Doctors rather tend to use a risky medication if it is promoted using the phrase 'saves 90 out of 100' rather than 'kills 10 out of 100'.
  - Heuristics: Humans use a variety of rules of thumb in order to reach a decision more quickly. The Availability Heuristic describes the overestimation of probabilities if an event is cognitively available. For example, after a plane crash that has been covered by the media worldwide, humans overestimate the probability of a plane crash in comparison to periods of time in which no accidents occur.

The use of the term 'non-standard' in Rabin's classification clearly illustrates the orientation towards mainstream economics. While doing so, this version of behavioural economics claims to, first, generate better theories, second, make better predictions and, third, present better policy recommendations.

There is disagreement on how the mentioned findings should influence decision theory. Some researchers just extend neoclassical expected utility theory by adding findings from behavioural economics. For instance, Daniel Kahneman and Amos Tversky's 'prospect theory' mostly maintains the concept of utility maximisation although in their model losses are weighted twice as much as gains. Alternatively, there are concepts that reject a vast part of the homo economicus concept, or which use other behavioural models as their basis. This includes research on social norms, where other people's expectations directly influence an individual's behaviour. Regarding theoretical approaches, apart from employing the neoclassical rational choice approach, behavioural economics also brings concepts into play from an array of fields including sociology and social psychology, which have different scientific assumptions. In some studies, the impact of social norms is used to induce a behavioural change, for instance in order to save energy.

Ontology

Behavioural economics' focus on human behaviour makes the individual the central unit of analysis. Nevertheless, in contrast to mainstream economics, human behaviour is conceptualised in a more complex manner at the ontological level. Neoclassical economics assumes a reductionist ideal type of homo economicus, characterised by a stable set of preferences with regards to a bundle of goods. Meanwhile in behavioural economics, for modelling purposes, individual behaviour is determined by rules, heuristics, desires, moods, emotions, and other things (Anger 2014). As neoclassical theory does not correspond to real behaviour, behavioural economics has historically and continues to develop new behavioural models that are more accurate.

In the first instance it is not clear what causes deviations from the model of *homo economicus* at the ontological level. In the scientific discourse there are competing and complementary theoretical explanations which see the root cause arising from a reductionist focus on the individual in isolation rather than the individual in a group or decision making context. An example of the reductionist approach is the analysis of cognitive capacities. The authors Sendhil Mullainathan and Eldar Sharif (2013) describe that each individual has what they call a cognitive scarcity. Hence, decisions are boundedly rational due to the limitation of human thought. Examples of theories in line with the contextual approach include publications on social norms, which emphasise the influence of context on individual decisions.

Behavioural economic research does not present a universal answer to the question of whether reductionist or contextual approaches are more adequate for yielding trustworthy results. Another still contested question that figures as an issue of ongoing debate is whether preferences are rooted inside human beings (methodological individualism with stable preferences and reactions to results) or whether they are influenced by external factors and thus considered endogenous.

Moreover, scarcity of resources is often understood as the central economic problem in behavioural economics. Derived from this understanding, the question arises as to which external conditions must be present in order for people to behave in line with the assumptions of homo economicus, since this would result in an efficient outcome. The central economic problem of scarcity can be derived from applied behavioural research in the discipline "market design". Market design deals with the architecture of markets while accounting for certain aims. In the economic encyclopedia Gabler Wirtschaftslexikon "the maximization of returns, efficiency or liquidity, the minimization of costs, the revelation of information" are named as market design's principal aims.

Additionally, uncertainty is a factor in behavioural economics. People in an uncertain environment are assumed not to calculate the optimal choice rationally in order to arrive at a decision. Instead, they make use of decision making heuristics. As opposed to neoclassical economics, behavioural economics sets out to analyse decisions taken under fundamental uncertainty, where the level of risk remains unknown. But heuristics are not limited to decisions under uncertainty and can be applied in manifold situations in which decisions are made. In comparison to other schools of thought, such as Austrian economics or Post-Keynesian economics, uncertainty is only a subordinate role and is only relevant to a subfield of behavioural economics.

How does behavioural economics deal with temporal successions on an ontological level? In most theories and models they are treated as being static. This means that models aim at predicting future events in grouped time periods. Time inconsistent preferences display a certain degree of dynamics, yet the results of such dynamics are not open or undetermined. Also, other approaches such as the prospect theory commit themselves to an understanding in which past points of reference dynamically influence future behaviour, but not in an open and undetermined way.

Epistemology

Behavioural economics assumes that the behaviour that is assigned to the *homo economicus* is not adequate for describing human (decision) behaviour. This is the central topic of behavioural economics. Instead, behavioural economics' point of departure is the real world in which theories and hypotheses are tested by means of experiments. This descriptive orientation corresponds to an epistemological realism by assuming that scientists can observe and describe human behaviour relatively easily. Questions concerning knowledge production and the self-referential dynamics of science and scientific concepts, which are addressed by constructivist approaches, do not play an important role in behavioural economics, even if the application of behavioural findings is promoted by scientists of this field.

Concerning the classification of empirical findings, the assumed behaviour of the *homo economicus* is taken as a benchmark for measuring observable behaviour. This becomes, for instance, apparent in the speech of Kahneman, winner of the Nobel memorial prize, where he explains that in his research he intends to explore 'the systematic biases that separate the beliefs that people have and the choices they make from the optimal beliefs and choices assumed in rational-agent models'. By this kind of proceeding, it can be determined whether a person behaves in line with the assumptions of *homo economicus* and to what extent behaviour deviates from the concept. For some researchers, the neoclassical benchmark is at the same time a normative ideal. Thus, Richard Thaler writes: "Expected utility theory remains the gold standard for how decisions should be made in the face of risk". This position is formulated even more drastically by Colin Camerer: "The challenge is figuring out what sorts of 'idiotic' behaviours are likely to arise routinely and how to prevent them, while imposing minimal restrictions on those who behave rationally". The aspiration to reduce the difference between observable behaviour and the benchmark by means of prescriptive theories, includes constructivist elements.

Concerning epistemology, behavioural economics focuses on human behaviour in economic (decision-making) situations (object-driven, i.e. a specific issue or phenomena is considered to be very important), and at the same time hypotheses are derived from a generalized theoretical framework and applied to many aspects of the economy (perspective-driven). This distinguishes behavioural economics from other theory schools, which are usually clearly object-oriented or perspective-driven. Thus, the focus lies in the analysis of human behaviour in economic (decision) situations on the one hand, and the theoretical affiliation to (neoclassical) economic theories on the other hand. Behavioural economics faces this tension as a perspective that follows certain interests and at the same time follows theoretical considerations.

Methodology

The methodological focus of behavioural economics is on experiments. A distinction is made between laboratory and field experiments. In the experimental research design, only the measured behaviour is used as a basis for the analysis.

Vernon Smith laid the foundation of standardised economic experiments. His goal was to set up an experimental situation similar to a theoretical agent-principal situation, with a fixed set of choices in order to reveal the preferences of the participants. All other influencing factors are eliminated in order to compare model predictions with observed behaviour. He developed this approach to the Induced-Value Theory. For this, he received the Sveriges Riksbank Prize in Economic Sciences in Memory of Alfred Nobel. Smith describes certain methodological conditions that have to hold to deliver unbiased results. For instance, different choices must have different rewards. This requires a rewarding medium with certain properties. For example, the participant must always prefer having more of it (monotonicity) and other factors must be rather irrelevant compared to the medium (dominance).

While laboratory experiments were dominant in the early days of behavioural economics, field experiments have become increasingly important. In addition to this, the application of neuro-scientific measurements has proliferated. Often, the goal of the methodology is to determine causal effects. The frequently used experimental design, with a randomized treatment and control group, is intended to simulate a counterfactual situation as closely as possible, in order to isolate the effect of a single measure or situation change. The methodological orientation focuses on the ideal of the natural sciences.

Qualitative research is a rare exception and its methodology is clearly different from standardised experiments. For instance, Truman F. Bewley conducted 300 interviews with business people asking why wages don't fall during a recession. Instead of measuring observed behaviour, Bewley investigated individual motives.

Hypothesis generation does not follow a uniform pattern in the branch of behavioural economics. The empirical orientation towards observable behaviour implies an inductive approach (which is also postulated in some cases as evidenced by statements such as: "Let the data tell you what is going on, both in empirical work and in theory development"). But, usually, hypotheses are derived from the deductive construct of homo economicus and its altered forms. Moreover, experiments are conducted if theory does not suggest distinct predictions, or any predictions whatsoever.

Ideology and Political Goals

The aim of behavioural economic research is to gain more knowledge about human decision making behaviour and also to better inform and politically shape social phenomena (such as investment in private pensions, health care, decisions on finance and education), mostly in accordance with the normative ideal of rational choice. This means that behavior which is considered not to be economically rational should be incrementally reduced. Nudges (such as default settings in pension systems, the arrangement of vegetables in a cafeteria or the presentation of information) are seen as an appropriate instruments to lead humans to decide as if there was no bounded rationality, e.g. due to lack of self-control. It is assumed that humans themselves prefer these devices and these decisions in comparison to those driven by bounded rationality. Richard Thaler and Cass Sunstein understand such approaches as liberal paternalism. Liberal paternalism differs from a pure paternalism insofar that the opportunities are not restricted. Instead, the choice architecture is changed in favor of the prefered outcome.

Furthermore, the findings of behavioural economics are used to test the effectiveness of an envisaged policy toward a certain goal. For behavioural economists, experiments are an adequate method in order to compare different options in politics. The *Behavioural Insights Team* in the UK, which works for the government, developed instructions for public authorities in order to carry out experiments locally. This implies a shift towards concrete situations as a point of departure for policies. This approach is also applied in development economics by Abhijit Banerjee and Esther Duflo, who also take up the idea of a liberal paternalism.

Current Debates and Analyses

A recurring debate in behavioural economics literature discusses the question of whether preferences are endogenous or exogenous. A well-known study by Joseph Henrich draws the following conclusion: 'preferences over economic choices are not exogenous as the canonical model would have it, but rather are shaped by the economic and social interactions of everyday life'. A large survey by Armin Falk, elivered similar results. This is connected to a debate in welfare economics, a field of mainstream economics which permits normative statements. However, if preferences are considered endogenous, normative statements are no longer possible because welfare economics assumes stable and exogenous preferences. Therefore, a debate in the field of the Philosophy of Economics on 'preference purification' discusses if assumptions on true statements are still possible in welfare economics.

Further current research deals with the reconception of ideas about the individual. This seems necessary since behavioural economics rejects *homo economicus* as the agent of economic models. In this context, George Akerlof and Rachel Kronton established identity, mainly understood as a preference to conform to norms, as part of economic research. (Another identity concept can be found in the work of. The current state of the debate is summarised by Rachel Kranton, and for a critical analysis compare John Davis.

Test persons in laboratory experiments are also an object of debate (for an overview cf. Levitt and List 2007 and for a. In an article that received much attention, Henrich characterised test persons as the 'weirdest people in the world'. In this context, 'weird' stands for 'Western, Educated, Industrialised, Rich, and Democratic'. According to the authors of the studies, even if the results of economic laboratory experiments do not show average or usual behaviour, general conclusions are still drawn from those experiments. Hence, the external validity of those experiments is questioned. In contrast, Armin Falk and James Heckman consider those problems less severe and point to the high internal validity, the possibility to identify causal effects as well as the possibility of combining experimental proceedings with survey data in order to improve the external validity.

Concerning the political implications of behavioural economics, the works of Thaler and Sunstein on nudging and liberal paternalism are often debated, especially in other social sciences than economics. The basic theses of the authors are that boundedly rational behaviour leads to 'behavioural market failures' and that persons often unconsciously act to his/her detriment. In those cases, institutions or the state have to 'nudge' persons in the right direction, since otherwise he/she will be nudged in a direction by other persons, firms or institutions which entirely lack democratic accountability. In Germany, the psychologist Gerd Gigerenzer rejects nudging since it mainly relies on rational choice as the normative ideal and does not operate through better educational offers concerning, for example, financial decisions.

Delineation: Subschools, other Economic Theories and other Disciplines

It is not possible to consistently differentiate between different currents of behavioural economics, behavioural economics research areas are often delineated by the following subjects:

- Analysis of heuristics e.g. representativeness heuristic, availability heuristic,
- Discounting and time preferences,
- Altruism, fairness, reciprocity,
- Emotions,
- Happiness research.

Further distinctions, in particular with respect to the practical application of theoretical findings, can be made between different areas such as behavioural finance, behavioural macroeconomics, social policy and liberal paternalism.

Moreover, there have been attempts to classify particular aspects of research in relation to who it was that undertook the substantial body of that research: one example is the Satisficing Theory of Herbert Simon, according to which individuals do not maximize their utility but are satisfied as soon as their expectations are met. A further example is George Akerlof's work to integrate the findings of behavioural economics into neoclassical macroeconomics. Another is Vernon Smith's significant influence on experimental economics, derived from his analysis of the functioning and design of markets.

While the mainstream of behavioural economics tries to improve, not to revolutionise, neoclassical concepts, there are some authors who distance themselves from neoclassical concepts. Hermann Brandstätter and Werner Güth referred to much of the aforementioned brand of research programs as 'neoclassical repair shop[s], since standard models are extended by behavioural economic findings but the assumptions on rational maximisation are maintained. Yet theories exist that reject the concept of utility maximisation. Examples of this rejection are the Satisficing Theory, Aspiration Adaptation Theory, Case-based Decision Making, as well as Fast and Frugal Heuristics.

Finally, the area of neuro-economics, with its strong focus on medical research, is worth mentioning, the point of departure of these analyses being neuro-scientific findings. Often, behaviour is analysed here by means of functional magnetic resonance imaging (fMRI).

Delineation from the Mainstream

One main difference between behavioural economics and the core theories of the mainstream is the way in which human behaviour is classified. While the neoclassical mainstream considers the conception of behaviour in terms of *homo economicus* as descriptively and normatively adequate, in behavioural economics, behaviour in terms of *homo economicus* is a normative guideline. The descriptive foundation is observable human behaviour.

Apart from this difference, behavioural economics is an acknowledged field of mainstream economics. Acknowledgement and compatibility are due to the experimental methods that are also the standard in other empirical areas of mainstream economic research.

References

- What-is-economics, Competitive-markets: economicsonline.co.uk, Retrieved 18 April, 2019
- Economic-system, economics: corporatefinanceinstitute.com, Retrieved 10 May, 2019
- Basic-problems-of-an-economy-with-diagram, economic-problems-18173: economicsdiscussion.net, Retrieved 02 August, 2019
- Economic-growth: intelligenteconomist.com, Retrieved 05 January, 2019
- Microeconomics: investopedia.com, Retrieved 25 June, 2019
- Macroeconomics: britannica.com, Retrieved 28 March, 2019
- Essay-on-economic-theory-17668: economicsdiscussion.net, Retrieved 03 July, 2019
- Keynesian-economics-theory-definition-4159776: thebalance.com, Retrieved 14 July, 2019
- What-is-development-economics: worldatlas.com, Retrieved 18 August, 2019

2

Fundamentals of Market and Firm

Market is any structure that facilitates trade and allows the exchange of goods and services for buyers and sellers. A few fundamentals of market and firm are theory of production, market forms, market equilibrium, market failure, etc. This chapter has been carefully written to provide an easy understanding of these fundamentals of market and firm.

Market

Market is a means by which the exchange of goods and services takes place as a result of buyers and sellers being in contact with one another, either directly or through mediating agents or institutions.

Markets in the most literal and immediate sense are places in which things are bought and sold. In the modern industrial system, however, the market is not a place; it has expanded to include the whole geographical area in which sellers compete with each other for customers. Alfred Marshall, whose Principles of Economics (first published in 1890) was for long an authority for English-speaking economists, based his definition of the market on that of the French economist A. Cournot:

> *Economists understand by the term Market, not any particular market place in which things are bought and sold, but the whole of any region in which buyers and sellers are in such free intercourse with one another that the prices of the same goods tend to equality easily and quickly.*

To this Marshall added:

> *The* more *nearly perfect a market is, the stronger is the tendency for the same price to be paid for the same thing at the same time in all parts of the market.*

The concept of the market as defined above has to do primarily with more or less standardized commodities, for example, wool or automobiles. The word market is also used in contexts such as the market for real estate or for old masters; and there is the "labour market," although a contract to work for a certain wage differs from a sale of goods. There is a connecting idea in all of these various usages—namely, the interplay of supply and demand.

Most markets consist of groups of intermediaries between the first seller of a commodity and the final buyer. There are all kinds of intermediaries, from the brokers in the great produce exchanges down to the village grocer. They may be mere dealers with no equipment but a telephone, or they may provide storage and perform important services of grading, packaging, and so on. In general, the function of a market is to collect products from scattered sources and channel them to scattered outlets. From the point of view of the seller, dealers channel the demand for his product; from the point of view of the buyer, they bring supplies within his reach.

There are two main types of markets for products, in which the forces of supply and demand operate quite differently, with some overlapping and borderline cases. In the first, the producer offers his goods and takes whatever price they will command; in the second, the producer sets his price and sells as much as the market will take. In addition, along with the growth of trade in goods, there has been a proliferation of financial markets, including securities exchanges and money markets.

Market Theory

The Abstract Nature of Traditional Market Theory

The key to the modern concept of the market may be found in the famous observation of the 18th-century British economist Adam Smith that "The division of labour depends upon the extent of the market". He foresaw that modern industry depended for its development upon an extensive market for its products. The factory system developed out of trade in cotton textiles, when merchants, discovering an apparently insatiable worldwide market, became interested in increasing production in order to have more to sell. The factory system led to the use of power to supplement human muscle, followed in turn by the application of science to technology, which in an ever-accelerating spiral has produced the scope and complexity of modern industry.

The economic theory of the late 19th century, which is still influential in academic teaching, was, however, concerned with the allocation of existing resources between different uses rather than with technical progress. This theory was highly abstract. The concept of the market was most systematically worked out in a general equilibrium system developed by the French economist Léon Walras, who was strongly influenced by the theoretical physics of his time. His system of mathematical equations was ingenious, but there are two serious limitations to the mechanical analogy upon which they were based: it omitted the factor of time—the effect upon peoples' present behaviour of their expectations about the future; and it ignored the consequences for the human beings concerned of the distribution of purchasing power among them. Though economists have always admitted the abstract nature of the theory, they generally have accepted the doctrine that the free play of market forces tended to bring about full employment and an optimum allocation of resources. On this view, unemployment could only be caused by wages being too high. This doctrine was still influential in the Great Depression of the 1930s.

Modifications of the Theory

The change in view that was to become known as the Keynesian Revolution was largely an escape to common sense, as opposed to abstract theory. In a private-enterprise economy, investment in industrial installations and housing construction is aimed at profitability in the future. Because investment therefore depends upon expectations, unfavourable expectations tend to fulfill themselves—when investment outlay falls off, workers become unemployed; incomes fall, purchases fall, unemployment spreads to the consumer goods industries, and receipts are reduced all the more. The operation of the market thus generates instability. The market may also generate instability in an upward direction. A high level of effective demand leads to a scarcity of labour; rising wages raise both costs of production and incomes so that there is a general tendency to inflation.

While the English economist John Maynard Keynes was attacking the concept of equilibrium in the market as a whole, the notion of equilibrium in the market for particular commodities was also being undermined. Traditional theory had conceived of a group of producers as operating in a perfect market for a single commodity; each produced only a small part of the whole supply; for each, the price was determined by the market; and each maximized its profits by selling only as much as would make marginal cost equal to price—that is to say, only so much that to produce a little more would add more to costs than it would to proceeds. Each firm worked its plant up to capacity—*i.e.*, to the point where profitability was limited by rising costs. This state of affairs, known as "perfect competition," is quite contrary to the general run of business experience, particularly in bad times when under-capacity working is prevalent. A theory of imperfect competition was invented to reconcile the traditional theory with under-capacity working but was attacked as unrealistic. The upshot was a general recognition that strict profit maximizing is impossible in conditions of uncertainty; that prices of manufactures are generally formed by adding a margin to direct costs, large enough to yield a profit at less than capacity sales; and that an increase in capacity generally has to be accompanied by a selling campaign to ensure that it will be used at a remunerative level.

Once it is recognized that competition is never perfect in reality, it becomes obvious that there is great scope for individual variations in the price policy of firms. No precise generalization is possible. The field is open for study of what actually happens, and exploration is going on.

The Origin of Markets

Markets as centres of commerce seem to have had three separate points of origin. The first was in rural fairs. A typical cultivator fed his family and paid the landlord and the moneylender from his chief crop. He had sidelines that provided salable products, and he had needs that he could not satisfy at home. It was then convenient for him to go to a market where many could meet to sell and buy.

The second point was in service to the landlords. Rent, essentially, was paid in grain; even when it was translated into money, sales of grain were necessary to supply the cultivator with funds to meet his dues. Payment of rent was a one-way transaction, imposed by the landlord. In turn, the landlord used the rents to maintain his warriors, clients, and artisans, and this led to the growth of towns as centres of trade and production. An urban class developed with a standard of life enabling its members to cater to each other as well as to the landlords and officials.

The third, and most influential, origin of markets was in international trade. From early times, merchant adventurers (the Phoenicians, the Arabs) risked their lives and their capital in carrying the products of one region to another. The importance of international trade for the development of the market system was precisely that it was carried on by third parties. Within a settled country, commercial dealings were restrained by considerations of rights, obligations, and proper behaviour. In medieval Europe, for example, dealings were regulated in the main by the concept of the "just price," that is, a system of valuations that assured the producers and merchants an income sufficient to maintain life at a level suited to their respective positions in society. But in trade in which the dealer is not subject to any obligation at either end, no holds are barred; purely commercial principles have free play. It was in trade (for instance, the export of English wool to the weavers of Italy) that the commercial principle undermined feudal conceptions of rights and duties. As Adam Smith observed, a great leap occurred when trade released the forces of industrial production.

Throughout history the relations between the trader and the producer have changed with the development of technique and with changes in the economic power of the parties. The 19th century was the heyday of the import–export merchant. Traders from a metropolitan country could establish themselves in a foreign centre, become experts on its needs and possibilities, and deal with a great variety of producers and customers, on a relatively small scale with each. With the growth of giant corporations, the scope of the merchant narrowed; his functions were largely taken over by the sales departments of the industrial concerns. Nowadays it is common to hold international fairs at which industrial products are displayed for inspection by customers, a grand and glorified version of the village market; the business, however, consists in placing orders rather than buying on the spot and carrying merchandise home. The function of the independent wholesaler, like that of the merchant, has declined as great retail businesses have grown to a scale whereby they can deal directly with manufacturers; but specialized exchanges for primary commodities are still important.

Markets under Socialism

Markets are essential to the free enterprise system; they grew and spread along with it. The propensity "to truck, barter, and exchange one thing for another" (in Adam Smith's words) was exalted into a principle of civilization by the doctrine of laissez-faire, which taught that the pursuit of self-interests by the individual would be to the benefit of society as a whole. In the Soviet Union and other Socialist countries, a different kind of economy existed and a different ideology was dominant. There were two interlocking systems in the economy of the Soviet Union: one for industry and one for agriculture; and the same pattern was followed, with variations, in the other Socialist countries. Industrially, all equipment and materials were owned by the state, and production was directed according to a central plan. In theory, payments to workers were thought of as their share of the total production of the economy; in practice, however, the system of wages was very much like that in capitalist industry except that rates as a rule were set by decree and the managers of enterprises had little scope for bargaining. Workers might move around looking for jobs, but there was no "labour market" in the capitalist sense. Materials and equipment were distributed among enterprises by the state planning offices. (Faulty planning gave rise to intermediaries who operated between enterprises, but this is not at all the same thing as the highly developed markets in materials, components, and equipment that exist under capitalism).

Consumption goods, on the other hand, were distributed to Soviet households through a retail market. Though some Socialist idealists, regarding buying and selling as the essence of capitalism, have advocated that money should be abolished altogether, in a large community it has proved to be most convenient to provide incomes in the form of generalized purchasing power and to allow each to choose what he pleases from whatever goods are available. Classical economists usually assert that the advantage of the retail market system is that it runs itself without excessive regulation; consumers who go shopping are in charge of their own money and need account to no one for what they do with it. Retail markets in the Soviet economy differed from those in capitalist economies in that, while in both systems the buyer is in this sense a principal, the seller in the Soviet model was an agent. Retailers and manufacturers all served as agents of the same authority—the central plan. Rather than making it their business to woo and cajole the customer, sellers threw supplies into the shops in a somewhat arbitrary way and customers would search for what they wanted.

Soviet agriculture was organized on principles quite different from those operative for manufacturing. Collective farms, though managed in an authoritarian way, were like cooperatives in which members shared in the income of their farm in respect to the "work points" each could earn. The value of a work point was affected by the prices set for the products of the farm, and these were politically, rather than only economically, determined. In the Western industrial economies, there is also a political element involved in the setting of agricultural prices; generally the problem here is to prevent excess production from driving prices too low. For the Soviets, the problem was the opposite. There, agricultural output failed to expand rapidly enough to keep pace with the requirements of the growing industrial labour force, and prices were therefore kept down so that they would not be unfavourable to the industrial sector. At the same time, individual members of the collective farms were permitted to sell the produce of their household plots on a free market. In this specific market, the peasant was as much a principal as the buyer.

In China, cooperative farms established after 1949 were much more genuinely cooperatives than were those in the Soviet Union, and trade with the cities in China is organized through a kind of Socialist wholesaling. City authorities place contracts with neighbouring farms, specifying prices, varieties, quantities, and delivery dates, and then direct the supplies to retail outlets, which are part of the Socialist economy. A similar system controls trade in manufactured consumer goods. Through the retail shops, the authorities monitor demand and guide supply as far as possible to meet it by the contracts that they place with the Socialist manufacturers. By adapting the wholesale trade to its own requirements, the Chinese economy seems to have avoided some of the difficulties that the Soviets encountered.

An example of socialism without a formal market was seen in the early days of the cooperative settlements known as kibbutzim in Israel, where cultivators shared the proceeds of their work without any distinction of individual incomes. (Because a kibbutz could trade with the surrounding market economy, its members were not confined to consuming only the produce of their own soil). At the outset some of the kibbutzim carried the objection to private property so far that a man who gave a shirt to the laundry received back just some other shirt. But to dispense altogether with market relationships is apparently possible only in a small community in which all share a common ideal, and the austere standards of the original kibbutzim have softened somewhat with growing prosperity; but they still maintain a small-scale example of economic efficiency without commercial incentives.

Commodity Markets

The general run of agricultural commodities is produced under competitive conditions by relatively small-scale cultivators scattered over a large area. The final purchasers are also scattered, and centres of consumption are distant from regions of production. The dealer, therefore, since he is indispensable, is in a stronger economic position than the seller. This situation is markedly true when the producer is a peasant who lacks both commercial knowledge and finance so that he is obliged to sell as soon as his harvest comes in; it is true also, though to a lesser extent, of the capitalist plantation for which the only source of earnings is a particular specialized product. In this kind of business, both demand and supply are said to be inelastic in the short run—that is, a fall in price does not have much effect in increasing purchases and a rise in price cannot quickly increase supplies. Supplies are subject to natural variations, weather conditions, pests, and so forth; and demand varies with the level of activity in the centres of industry and with changes in tastes and technical requirements. Under a regime of unregulated competition such markets are, therefore, tormented with continual fluctuations in prices and volume of business. Though dealers may mitigate this to some extent by building up stocks when prices are low and releasing them when demand is high, such buying and selling often turns into speculation, which tends to exacerbate the fluctuations.

The behaviour of primary commodity markets is a serious matter when whole communities depend upon a single commodity for income or for employment and wages. The agricultural communities that form part of an industrial economy are therefore generally sheltered from the operation of supply and demand by government regulations of various types, price supports, or tariff protection. Though some attempts have been made to control world commodity markets, these are generally more talk than performance. Some nations, Australia for example, have been able to make enough profit from primary commodity exports to attract capital into the development of industry; but most of the so-called developing countries find their export earnings insecure and insufficient. Their spokesmen complain that the world market system operates in favour of the industrialized nations.

Firm

A firm is a commercial enterprise, a company that buys and sells products and services to consumers with the aim of making a profit. In the world of commerce, the term is usually synonymous with 'company', or 'business'.

A business entity such as a corporation, limited liability company, public limited company, sole proprietorship, or partnership that has products or services for sale is a firm.

Law, accountancy and management consultancy partnerships are known as firms, and are rarely referred to as companies.

In 1744, the term first emerged in the English language with the meaning of 'business house.

Theory of the Firm

The Theory of the Firm comprises several economic theories that explain and predict the nature of the firm (company), including its structure, relationship to the market, behavior, and its very existence.

The theory aims to answer the following questions:

- Existence: Why do firms emerge. Why aren't all transactions in the economy mediated over the market?

- Boundaries: Why is the boundary between the market and firms located exactly there, in relation to output variety and size. Which transactions are negotiated on the market and which are performed internally?
- Organization: Why are firms structured the way they are, with hierarchy, a central point, etc.?
- Heterogeneity of Firm Actions/Performances: Why do firms do things, what drives them?
- Evidence: What tests currently exist for respective theories?

Adam Smith, a Scottish moral philosopher and pioneer of political economy, known by many today as the 'father of modern economics', discussed firms in his work – *The Wealth of Nations*. He established that in the world of manufacturing, they were more efficient in producing than laborers or craftsmen were when working individually.

Mr. Smith explained that a manufacturing firm used a more intense form of division of labor than can be coordinated through market exchange. His view of firms in terms of their different kind of division of labor was widely accepted by classical economists.

Karl Marx, a Prussian (German) philosopher, economist and revolutionary socialist, wrote in his work – *Das Kapital* – about the Smithian type of manufactures and how they exploited the more intense division of labor.

Mr. Marx found the division of labor in firms highly problematic, because the individual worker, he believed, was separated from the end product and therefore was 'alienated' through work performed within the manufacturing process.

Regarding Mr. Marx' attitude to the economic aspects of efficient firms, Per Bylund writes:

"Marx was obviously not very interested in the economic analysis — division of labor increases productivity and increases prosperity for all individuals involved as well as society as a whole — and so focuses solely on the problem he identifies".

Over the following century, sociologists and economists have contributed extensively to the Theories of the Firm.

Put simply, firms exist as an alternative system to the market-price mechanism, when producing in a non-market environment is more efficient.

For example, in a labor market, it may be costly and difficult for commercial entities to engage in production when they have to take on and lay off workers, depending on levels of demand and supply.

For employees, it is costly and inconvenient to shift companies on a daily basis looking for better alternatives.

Companies, similarly, will find it costly to seek out new suppliers every day. That is why firms engage in long-term contracts with their workers and suppliers to minimize the cost or optimize the value of property rights.

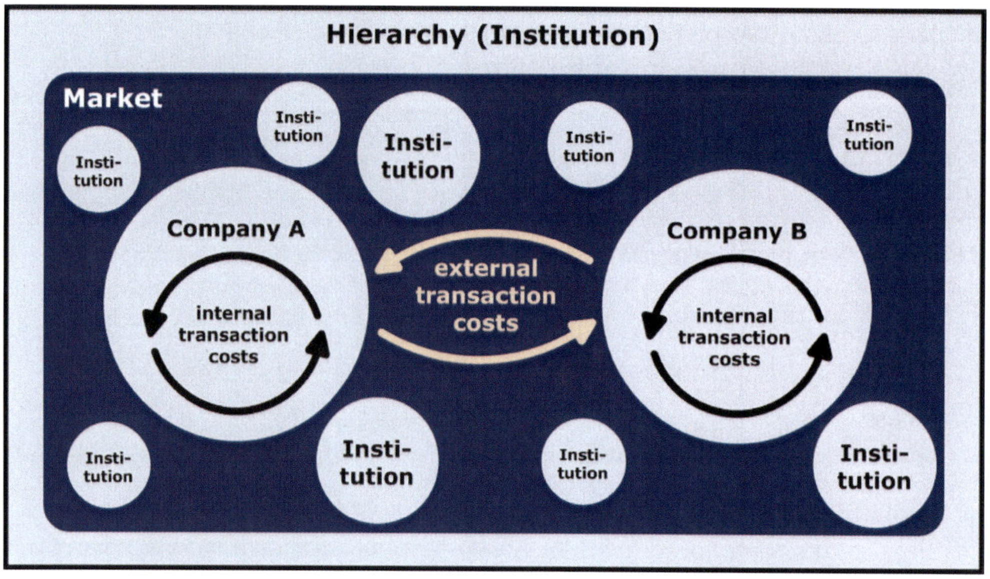

The model above shows institutions and market as a possible form of organization to coordinate economic transactions. When the external transaction costs are greater than the internal ones, the firm will grow.

Economic Objectives of Firms

The main objectives of firms are:

- Profit maximisation,
- Sales maximisation,
- Increased market share/market dominance,
- Social/environmental concerns,
- Profit satisficing,
- Co-operatives.

Sometimes there is an overlap of objectives. For example, seeking to increase market share, may lead to lower profits in the short-term, but enable profit maximisation in the long run.

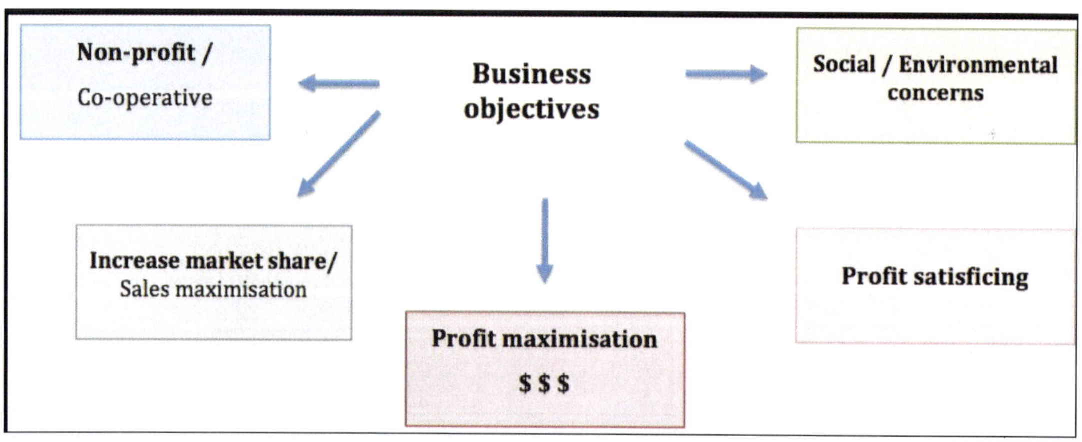

Profit Maximisation

Usually, in economics, we assume firms are concerned with maximising profit. Higher profit means:

- Higher dividends for shareholders.
- More profit can be used to finance research and development.
- Higher profit makes the firm less vulnerable to takeover.
- Higher profit enables higher salaries for workers.

Alternative Aims of Firms

However, in the real world, firms may pursue other objectives apart from profit maximisation.

Profit Satisficing

- In many firms, there is a separation of ownership and control. Those who own the company (shareholders) often do not get involved in the day to day running of the company.
- This is a problem because although the owners may want to maximise profits, the managers have much less incentive to maximise profits because they do not get the same rewards, (share dividends).
- Therefore managers may create a minimum level of profit to keep the shareholders happy, but then maximise other objectives, such as enjoying work, getting on with other workers. (e.g. not sacking them) This is the problem of separation between owners and managers.
- This 'principal-agent' problem can be overcome, to some extent, by giving managers share options and performance related pay although in some industries it is difficult to measure performance.

Sales Maximisation

Firms often seek to increase their market share – even if it means less profit. This could occur for various reasons:

- Increased market share increases monopoly power and may enable the firm to put up prices and make more profit in the long run.
- Managers prefer to work for bigger companies as it leads to greater prestige and higher salaries.
- Increasing market share may force rivals out of business. E.g. the growth of supermarkets have lead to the demise of many local shops. Some firms may actually engage in predatory pricing which involves making a loss to force a rival out of business.

Growth Maximisation

This is similar to sales maximisation and may involve mergers and takeovers. With this objective, the firm may be willing to make lower levels of profit in order to increase in size and gain more market share. More market share increases its monopoly power and ability to be a price setter.

Long Run Profit Maximisation

In some cases, firms may sacrifice profits in the short term to increase profits in the long run. For example, by investing heavily in new capacity, firms may make a loss in the short run but enable higher profits in the future.

Social/Environmental Concerns

A firm may incur extra expense to choose products which don't harm the environment or products not tested on animals. Alternatively, firms may be concerned about local community/charitable concerns.

- Some firms may adopt social/environmental concerns as part of their branding. This can ultimately help profitability as the brand becomes more attractive to consumers.
- Some firms may adopt social/environmental concerns on principal alone – even if it does little to improve sales/brand image.

Co-operatives

Co-operatives may have completely different objectives to a typical PLC. A co-operative is run to maximise the welfare of all stakeholders – especially workers. Any profit the co-operative makes will be shared amongst all members.

Diagram showing different objectives of firms.

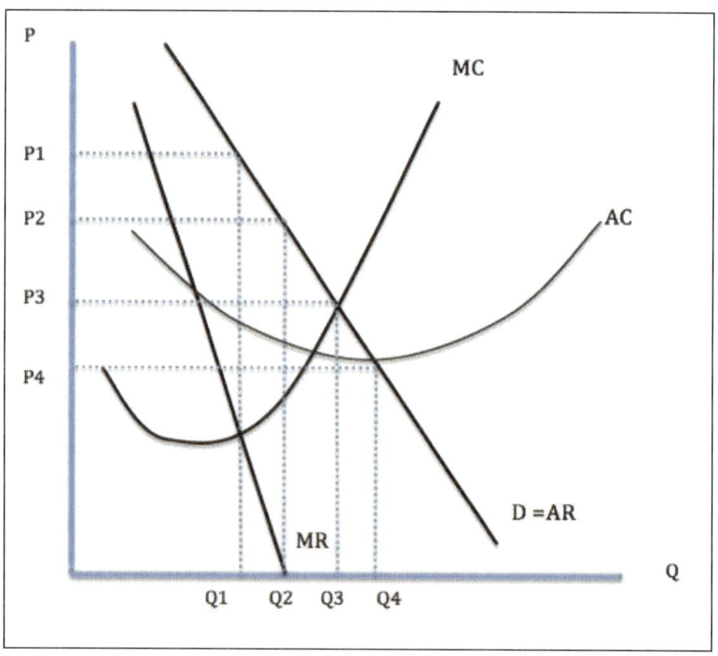

- Q1 = Profit maximisation (MR=MC).

- Q2 = Revenue Maximisation (MR=0).
- Q3 = Marginal cost pricing (P=MC) – allocative efficiency.
- Q4 = Sales maximisation – maximum sales while still making normal profit (AR=ATC).

Consumer

Consumers are the basic economic entities of an economy. All the consumers consume goods and services directly and indirectly to maximise satisfaction and utility.

Consumers have limited income and by which they want to satisfy their maximum utility (utility is the want satisfying capacity of a commodity).

Generally, consumer means an individual only; however, consumers will consist of a particular individual, a group of individuals, institutions etc.

Types (Kinds) of Consumers

According to the nature of consumption, consumers are of following types:

Direct Consumers

History tells us that at the very early stage of civilisation producers produced all the basic needs of life for themselves and their families. All the basic needs like food, clothing and shelter they produced for their own and their family's consumption. Hence, the producers were producing goods for their self- consumption. Thus, they were called as direct consumers or direct producers also.

Consumers by Exchanging Products

With passage of time and civilisation people understood the benefits of exchange. Hence, they tried to specialise on a particular or few products and then tried to exchange the product with the other product(s). The exchange started with barter system and now continuing with monetary system.

This will create the concept of marketable surplus, i.e., the producers are not only producing goods for self-consumption, but some excess or surplus product(s) they are keeping to get other product(s) in exchange. For example, a farmer producing pulse not only for self-consumption but the extra or surplus pulse he will exchange with the producer of other product, say paddy.

Modern Consumers

These consumers only go to the market to buy the goods and services available in the market through money only. Here, the producers are also producing goods or services directly sent to the market for the consumers. These consumers buy all the goods and services in lieu of money. The modern consumers are the outcome of monetary system.

Importance (Significance) of Consumers

The importance of consumers in different avenues is discussed below.

Encourage Demand

Consumers are the main source of demand for all the goods. The producers of industrial goods or the producers of agricultural products are all producing the various items according to the demand in the market. According to Prof. Marshall, it is the demand which controls the production or market. Hence, the consumers create demand in the market and producers produce goods or services accordingly.

Create Demand for Various Products

The different consumers have different types of demand or a single consumer can also demand different types of products. These will encourage the producers to produce various types of products in the market. For example, some consumers want to consume paddy, whereas some consumers want to consume wheat.

However, there are some consumers; who want different qualities of paddy and wheat also. Thus, there are some consumers who prefer red colour soap whereas other' consumers prefer green colour soap. Therefore, to satisfy all the types of consumers, producers must increase the production of various products.

Increase Demand for Consumer Goods

Consumers create more demand for all the types of consumer goods, like durable, semi- durable and perishable goods. Durable consumer goods include furniture, utensils, televisions, etc. and for semi-durable goods like clothes, books, shoes etc. On the other hand, perishable goods like bread, butter, vegetables, fruits etc. are all demanded by the consumers for their consumption purposes. Naturally, all these create an atmosphere to increase demand for consumer goods.

Enhance Service Diversification

Consumers not only consume different varieties of goods, but also consume large varieties of services to maintain the standard of living. These include health service, educational service, banking and insurance service, transport and communication service, etc. Day by day the consumption of these services is rising. This will lead to expansion or enhancement of service sector within the economy.

Producer

In economics, a producer is an economic unit that manufactures or commercializes goods or services. Simply put, these are entities that supply the economic system.

A producer might have different shapes. Since this is an economic term this definition is very wide and includes any economic activity that supplies a good or service to society. By using and combining the factors of production (land, labor, capital and technology) these organizations or individuals produce an output. This output constitutes the supply side of the market. To some economic schools and theories, producers are defined even more widely to include federal governments, municipalities, government agencies and even households. Producers are essential for an economic system to function properly.

Having a low number of producers can increase the chances of getting high inflation rates, unemployment, monopolies and scarcity. By widening the range and number of producers within a given economy the supply increases and these producers start competing with each other, which in turn increases productivity and a better economic environment.

Example:

Mr. Donahue is a farmer that owns a small family ranch in Dallas, Texas. His family has been working their ranch for many years and most of what they produce they use it to sustain themselves, but they also sell a portion of the production to the open market. One of their main products is butter. The family has a small company called Donahue Butters Co. and they sell butter in different presentations to the local stores. According to our definition, can they be considered producers?

Producers, as we previously defined them, are those who manufacture or commercialize goods or services. The Donahue family does this with many of the things they produce in their ranch and also trough the butter company. This means both the family and the company should be considered producers from an economic standpoint.

Cost is the monetary value of goods and services that producers and consumers purchase. In a basic economic sense, cost is the measure of the alternative opportunities foregone in the choice of one good or activity over others. This fundamental cost is usually referred to as opportunity cost. For a consumer with a fixed income, the opportunity cost of purchasing a new domestic appliance may be, for example, the value of a vacation trip not taken.

More conventionally, cost has to do with the relationship between the value of production inputs and the level of output. Total cost refers to the total expense incurred in reaching a particular level of output; if such total cost is divided by the quantity produced, average or unit cost is obtained. A portion of the total cost known as fixed cost—e.g., the costs of a building lease or of heavy machinery—does not vary with the quantity produced and, in the short run, does not alter with changes in the amount produced. Variable costs, like the costs of labour or raw materials, change with the level of output.

An aspect of cost important in economic analysis is marginal cost, or the addition to the total cost resulting from the production of an additional unit of output. A firm desiring to maximize its profits will, in theory, determine its level of output by continuing production until the cost of the last additional unit produced (marginal cost) just equals the addition to revenue (marginal revenue) obtained from it.

Another consideration involves the cost of externalities—that is, the costs that are imposed either intentionally or unintentionally on others. Thus the cost of generating electricity by burning high-sulfur bituminous coal can be measured not only by the cost of the coal and its transport to the power plant (among other economic considerations) but also by its cost in terms of air pollution.

Concept of Optimum Firm in Economics

It is important to explain the concept of optimum firm. The optimum firm refers to the best or ideal size of the firm. More specifically optimum or best firm is considered as one that has set up a plant with lowest possible cost and is also operating it at its lowest average cost point. E.A.G. Robinson who has done a good deal of research on the issue of optimum firm writes, "an optimum firm is the one which operates at the scale at which, in the existing conditions of technique and organising ability, has the lowest average cost of production when all those costs which must be covered in the long run are included".

This means that optimum firm is one which operates at the lowest point of long-run average cost curve of production. Production at the minimum point of the long-run average cost curve is called optimum because at it resources of the society are most efficiently used.

When a firm expands its size to the lowest point of the long-run average cost (LAC), it sets up a plant which, given the state of technology, has the lowest unit cost of production when operated at its full capacity. As has been explained above that long-run average cost of a firm is influenced by the various economies and diseconomies of scale. These economies and diseconomies are determined by various technical, managerial, financial and marketing factors.

The optimum size is achieved when all the internal economies of scalc such as division of labour, use of specialised machinery, managerial advantage of large scale production etc. are being fully enjoyed by the firm and the internal diseconomies of scale have not yet started accruing to it.

It is worth noting that in the determination of optimum size, the state of technology and methods of organising business remain unchanged. In figure. optimum firm is one that has set up a plant represented by short-run average cost curve SAC_4 and operating at the minimum point P on it and producing output OQ.

It is clear from figure. that in the continuous long-run average cost curve both for outputs less than OQ and more than OQ no plant is used at its point of minimum average cost. It is only the plant, the minimum point of whose short-run average cost curve coincides with the minimum point of the long-run average cost curve, which is operated at the point of minimum point of its short-run average cost curve. In figure for producing output OQ, the plant of SAC_4 is being utilized to produce its optimum output OQ, that is to say, it is being used at its full capacity.

It should be noted that in figure the plant of SAC_4 is optimum plant, since its minimum cost of production is the lowest of the minimum costs of all other plants. If the size of the plant is increased beyond SAC_4, it results in higher average cost of production.

Similarly, if the size of the plant is smaller than SAC_4, average cost of production is higher. Further, the least-cost output, or in other words, the optimum output of the plant SAC_4 is OQ. Now, if the firm produces output OQ with the optimum plant SAC_4, it is said to have achieved the optimum size.

Thus, an optimum firm is that firm which is producing optimum output (i.e., least-cost output) with the optimum plant. In figure the firm is of optimum size if it employs plant SAC_4 and uses it to produce OQ. Since the point of minimum cost of the optimum plant SAC_4 coincides with the minimum point of the long-run average cost curve, the optimum firm can also be defined as one which produces at the minimum point of the long-run average cost curve (LAC).

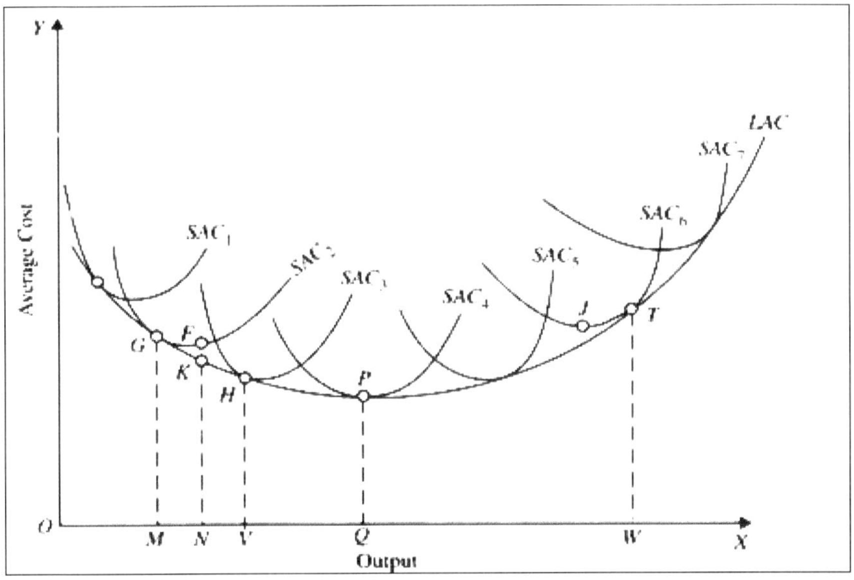

Deriving long run cost curve from short run average cost curves.

The optimum size of the firm varies a great deal in different industries. In agriculture, extractive industries, wholesale and retail trade, optimum size is relatively small, that is, the minimum point of the long-run average cost curve is reached at a comparatively small output.

Figure shows a firm whose optimum size is relatively small. On the other hand, the optimum size of the firm in steel industry, automobile industry, other heavy industries and public utilities is relatively very large, that is, the minimum point of their long-run average cost curve is reached at a relatively very large output. Figure depicts a firm whose optimum size is very large. In the industry in which the optimum size of the firm is very large, there are generally a few numbers of firms, each with a large size

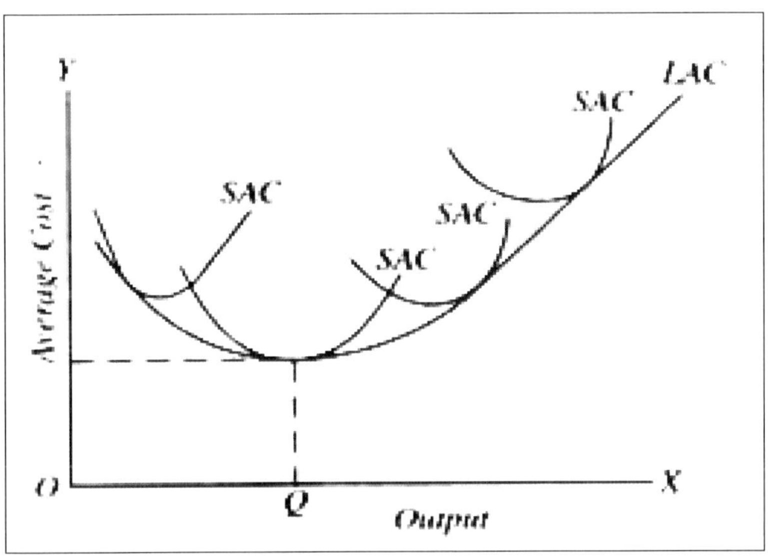

Small optimum size.

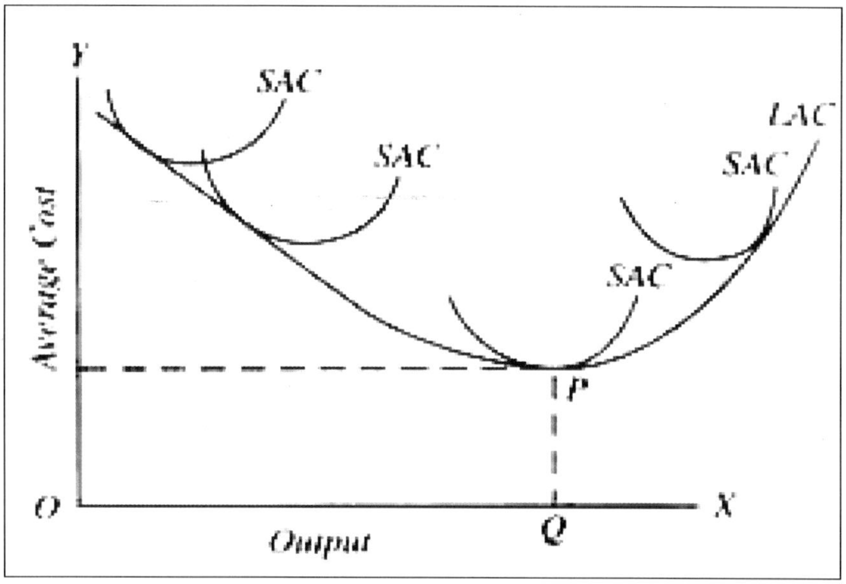

Large optimum size.

Theory of Production

Theory of production, in economics, is an effort to explain the principles by which a business firm decides how much of each commodity that it sells (its "outputs" or "products") it will produce, and how much of each kind of labour, raw material, fixed capital good, etc., that it employs (its "inputs" or "factors of production") it will use. The theory involves some of the most fundamental principles of economics. These include the relationship between the prices of commodities and the prices (or wages or rents) of the productive factors used to produce them and also the relationships between the prices of commodities and productive factors, on the one hand, and the quantities of these commodities and productive factors that are produced or used, on the other.

The various decisions a business enterprise makes about its productive activities can be classified into three layers of increasing complexity. The first layer includes decisions about methods of producing a given quantity of the output in a plant of given size and equipment. It involves the problem of what is called short-run cost minimization. The second layer, including the determination of the most profitable quantities of products to produce in any given plant, deals with what is called short-run profit maximization. The third layer, concerning the determination of the most profitable size and equipment of plant, relates to what is called long-run profit maximization.

Minimization of Short-run Costs

The Production Function

However much of a commodity a business firm produces, it endeavours to produce it as cheaply as possible. Taking the quality of the product and the prices of the productive factors as given, which is the usual situation, the firm's task is to determine the cheapest combination of factors of production that can produce the desired output. This task is best understood in terms of what is called the production function, *i.e.*, an equation that expresses the relationship between the quantities of factors employed and the amount of product obtained. It states the amount of product that can be obtained from each and every combination of factors. This relationship can be written mathematically as $y = f(x_1, x_2, \ldots, x_n; k_1, k_2, \ldots, k_m)$. Here, y denotes the quantity of output. The firm is presumed to use n variable factors of production; that is, factors like hourly paid production workers and raw materials, the quantities of which can be increased or decreased. In the formula the quantity of the first variable factor is denoted by x_1 and so on. The firm is also presumed to use m fixed factors, or factors like fixed machinery, salaried staff, etc., the quantities of which cannot be varied readily or habitually. The available quantity of the first fixed factor is indicated in the formal by k_1 and so on. The entire formula expresses the amount of output that results when specified quantities of factors are employed. It must be noted that though the quantities of the factors determine the quantity of output, the reverse is not true, and as a general rule there will be many combinations of productive factors that could be used to produce the same output. Finding the cheapest of these is the problem of cost minimization.

The cost of production is simply the sum of the costs of all of the various factors. It can be written:

$$C = p[x] + \ldots + p_n x_n + r_1 k_1 + \ldots + r_n k_n$$

in which p_1 denotes the price of a unit of the first variable factor, r_1 denotes the annual cost of owning and maintaining the first fixed factor, and so on. Here again one group of terms, the first, covers variable cost (roughly"direct costs" in accounting terminology), which can be changed readily; another group, the second, covers fixed cost (accountants' "overhead costs"), which includes items not easily varied.

The principles involved in selecting the cheapest combination of variable factors can be seen in terms of a simple example. If a firm manufactures gold necklace chains in such a way that there are only two variable factors, labour (specifically, goldsmith-hours) and gold wire, the production function for such a firm will be $y = f(x_1, x_2; k)$, in which the symbol k is included simply as a reminder that the number of chains producible by x_1 feet of gold wire and x_2 goldsmith-hours depends on the amount of machinery and other fixed capital available. Since there are only two variable factors, this production function can be portrayed graphically in a figure known as an isoquant diagram. In the graph, goldsmith-hours per month are plotted horizontally and the number of feet of gold wire used per month vertically. Each of the curved lines, called an isoquant, will then represent a certain number of necklace chains produced. The data displayed show that 100 goldsmith-hours plus 900 feet of gold wire can produce 200 necklace chains. But there are other combinations of variable inputs that could also produce 200 necklace chains per month. If the goldsmiths work more carefully and slowly, they can produce 200 chains from 850 feet of wire; but to produce so many chains more goldsmith-hours will be required, perhaps 130. The isoquant labelled "200" shows all the combinations of the variable inputs that will just suffice to produce 200 chains. The other two isoquants shown are interpreted similarly. It is obvious that many more isoquants, in principle an infinite number, could also be drawn. This diagram is a graphic display of the relationships expressed in the production function.

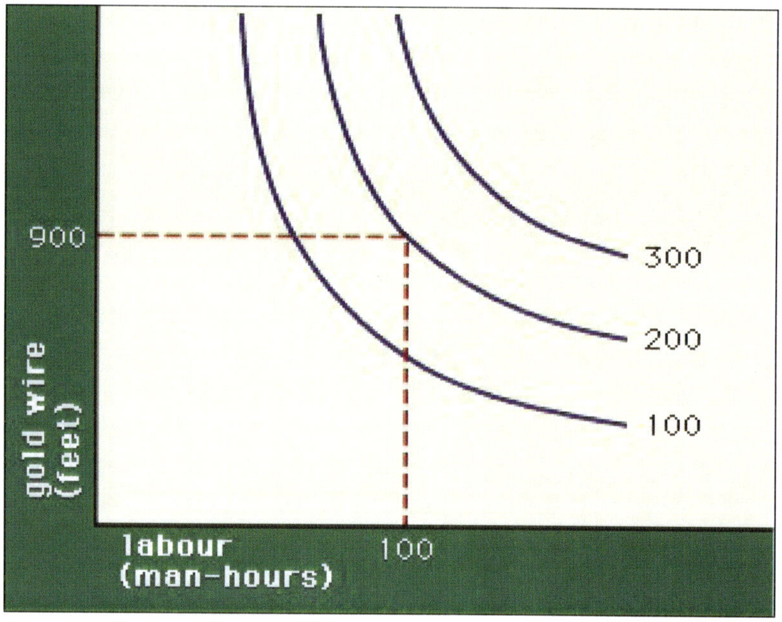

Isoquant diagram of hours of labour and feet of gold wire used per month.

Substitution of Factors

The isoquants also illustrate an important economic phenomenon: that of factor substitution. This means that one variable factor can be substituted for others; as a general rule a more lavish use of one variable factor will permit an unchanged amount of output to be produced with fewer units of some or all of the others. In the example above, labour was literally as good as gold and could be substituted for it. If it were not for factor substitution there would be no room for further decision after y, the number of chains to be produced, had been established.

The shape of the isoquants shown, for which there is a good deal of empirical support, is very important. In moving along any one isoquant, the more of one factor that is employed, the less of the other will be needed to maintain the stated output; this is the graphic representation of factor substitutability. But there is a corollary: the more of one factor that is employed, the less it will be possible to reduce the use of the other by using more of the first. This is the property known as "diminishing marginal rates of substitution". The marginal rate of substitution of factor 1 for factor 2 is the number of units by which x_1 can be reduced per unit increase in x, output remaining unchanged. In the diagram, if feet of gold wire are indicated by x_1 and goldsmith-hours by x_2, then the marginal rate of substitution is shown by the steepness (the negative of the slope) of the isoquant; and it will be seen that it diminishes steadily as x_2 increases because it becomes harder and harder to economize on the use of gold simply by taking more care. The remainder of the analysis rests heavily on the assumption that diminishing marginal rates of substitution are characteristic of the production process generally.

The cost data and the technological data can now be brought together. The variable cost of using x_1, x_2 units of the factors of production is written $p_1x_1 + p_2x_2$, and this information can be added to the isoquant diagram. The straight line labelled v_2, called the v_2-isocost line, shows all the combinations of input that can be purchased for a specified variable cost, v_2. The other two isocost lines shown are interpreted similarly. The general formula for an isocost line is $p_1x_1 + p_2x_2 = v$, in which

v is some particular variable cost. The slope of an isocost line is found by dividing p_2 by p_1 and depends only on the ratio of the prices of the two factors.

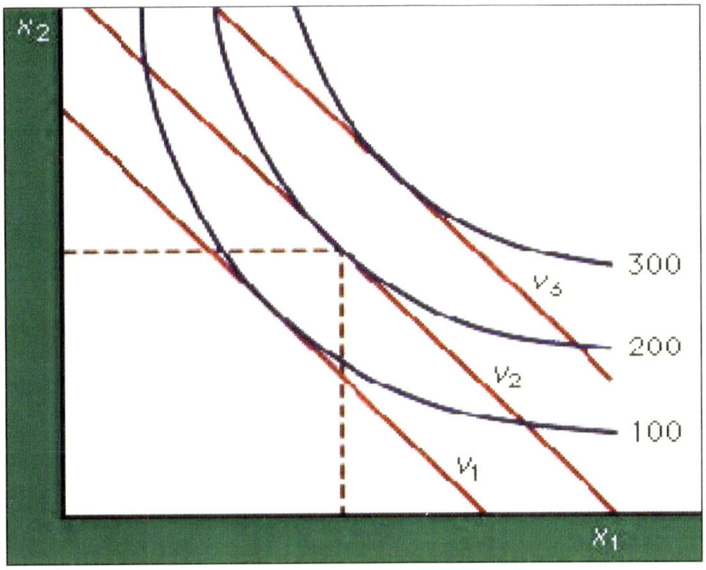

Isoquant diagram for two factors of production, x_1 and x_2.

Three isocost lines are shown, corresponding to variable costs amounting to v_1, v_2, and v_3. If 200 units are to be produced, expenditure of v_1 on variable factors will not suffice since the v_1-isocost line never reaches the isoquant for 200 units. An expenditure of v_3 is more than sufficient; and v_2 is the lowest variable cost for which 200 units can be produced. Thus v_2 is found to be the minimum variable cost of producing 200 units (as v_3 is of 300 units) and the coordinates of the point where the v_2 isocost line touches the 200-unit isoquant are the quantities of the two factors that will be used when 200 units are to be produced and the prices of the two factors are in the ratio p_2/p_1. It may be noted that the cheapest combination for the production of any quantity will be found at the point at which the relevant isoquant is tangent to an isocost line. Thus, since the slope of an isoquant is given by the marginal rate of substitution, any firm trying to produce as cheaply as possible will always purchase or hire factors in quantities such that the marginal rate of substitution will equal the ratio of their prices.

The isoquant–isocost diagram (or the corresponding solution by the alternative means of the calculus) solves the short-run cost minimization problem by determining the least-cost combination of variable factors that can produce a given output in a given plant. The variable cost incurred when the least-cost combination of inputs is used in conjunction with a given outfit of fixed equipment is called the variable cost of that quantity of output and denoted VC(y). The total cost incurred, variable plus fixed, is the short-run cost of that output, denoted SRC(y). Clearly SRC(y) = VC(y) + R(K), in which the second term symbolizes the sum of the annual costs of the fixed factors available.

Marginal Cost

Two other concepts now become important. The average variable cost, written AVC(y), is the variable cost per unit of output. Algebraically, AVC(y) = VC(y)/y. The marginal variable cost, or simply marginal cost [MC(y)] is, roughly, the increase in variable cost incurred when output is increased by one unit; *i.e.*, MC(y) = VC(y + 1) - VC(y). Though for theoretical purposes a more precise definition can be obtained by regarding VC(y) as a continuous function of output, this is not necessary in the present case.

The usual behaviour of average and marginal variable costs in response to changes in the level of output from a given fixed plant is shown in Figure. In this figure costs (in dollars per unit) are measured vertically and output (in units per year) is shown horizontally. The figure is drawn for some particular fixed plant, and it can be seen that average costs are fairly high for very low levels of output relative to the size of the plant, largely because there is not enough work to keep a well-balanced work force fully occupied. People are either idle much of the time or shifting, expensively, from job to job. As output increases from a low level, average costs decline to a low plateau. But as the capacity of the plant is approached, the inefficiencies incident on plant congestion force average costs up quite rapidly. Overtime may be incurred, outmoded equipment and inexperienced hands may be called into use, there may not be time to take machinery off the line for routine maintenance; or minor breakdowns and delays may disrupt schedules seriously because of inadequate slack and reserves. Thus the AVC curve has the flat-bottomed U-shape shown. The MC curve, as might be expected, falls faster and rises more rapidly than the AVC curve.

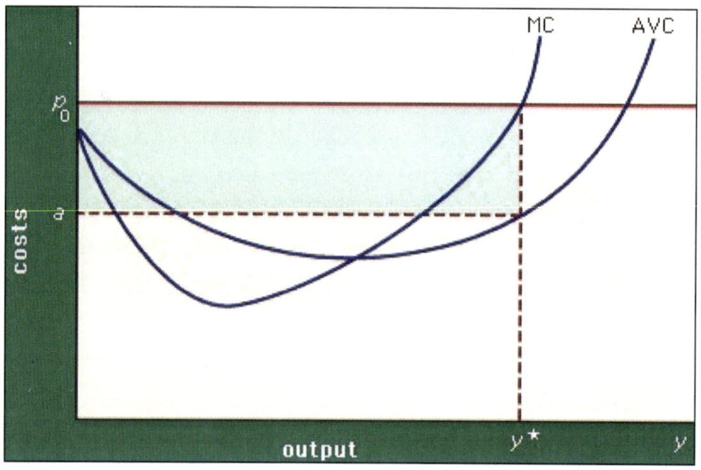

Average variable costs (AVC) and marginal variable costs (MC) in relation to output.

Maximization Of Short-run Profits

The average and marginal cost curves just deduced are the keys to the solution of the second-level problem, the determination of the most profitable level of output to produce in a given plant. The only additional datum needed is the price of the product, say p_0.

The most profitable amount of output may be found by using these data. If the marginal cost of any given output (y) is less than the price, sales revenues will increase more than costs if output is increased by one unit (or even a few more); and profits will rise. Contrariwise, if the marginal cost is greater than the price, profits will be increased by cutting back output by at least one unit. It then follows that the output that maximizes profits is the one for which MC(y) = p_0. This is the second basic finding: in response to any price the profit-maximizing firm will produce and offer the quantity for which the marginal cost equals that price.

Such a conclusion is shown in Figure. In response to the price, p_0, shown, the firm will offer the quantity y^* given by the value of y for which the ordinate of the MC curve equals the price. If a denotes the corresponding average variable cost, net revenue per unit will be equal to $p_0 - a$, and the total excess of revenues over variable costs will be $y^*(p_0 - a)$, which is represented graphically by the shaded rectangle in the figure.

Marginal Cost and Price

The conclusion that marginal cost tends to equal price is important in that it shows how the quantity of output produced by a firm is influenced by the market price. If the market price is lower than the lowest point on the average variable cost curve, the firm will "cut its losses" by not producing anything. At any higher market price, the firm will produce the quantity for which marginal cost equals that price. Thus the quantity that the firm will produce in response to any price can be found in figure by reading the marginal cost curve, and for this reason the marginal cost curve is said to be the short-run supply curve for the firm.

The short-run supply curve for a product—that is, the total amount that all the firms producing it will produce in response to any market price—follows immediately, and is seen to be the sum of the short-run supply curves (or marginal cost curves, except when the price is below the bottoms of the average variable cost curves for some firms) of all the firms in the industry. This curve is of fundamental importance for economic analysis, for together with the demand curve for the product it determines the market price of the commodity and the amount that will be produced and purchased.

One pitfall must, however, be noted. In the demonstration of the supply curves for the firms, and hence of the industry, it was assumed that factor prices were fixed. Though this is fair enough for a single firm, the fact is that if all firms together attempt to increase their outputs in response to an increase in the price of the product, they are likely to bid up the prices of some or all of the factors of production that they use. In that event the product supply curve as calculated will overstate the increase in output that will be elicited by an increase in price. A more sophisticated type of supply curve, incorporating induced changes in factor prices, is therefore necessary.

Marginal Product

It is now possible to derive the relationship between product prices and factor prices, which is the basis of the theory of income distribution. To this end, the marginal product of a factor is defined as the amount that output would be increased if one more unit of the factor were employed, all other circumstances remaining the same. Algebraically, it may be expressed as the difference between the product of a given amount of the factor and the product when that factor is increased by an additional unit. Thus if $MP_1(x_1)$ denotes the marginal product of factor 1 when x_1 units are employed, then $MP_1(x_1) = f(x_1 + 1, x_2, \ldots, x_n; k) - f(x_1, x_2 \ldots, x_n; k)$. The marginal products are closely related to the marginal rates of substitution previously defined. If an additional unit of factor 1 will increase output by f_1 units, for example, then one more unit of output can be obtained by employing $1/f_1$ more units of factor 1. Similarly, if the marginal product of factor 2 is f_2, then output will fall by one unit if the use of factor 2 is reduced by $1/f_2$ units. Thus output will remain unchanged, to a good approximation, if $1/f_1$ units of factor 1 are used to replace $1/f_2$ units of factor 2. The marginal rate of substitution is therefore f_2/f_1, or the ratio of the marginal products of the two factors. It has already been shown that the marginal rate of substitution also equals the ratio of the prices of the factors, and it therefore follows that the prices (or wages) of the factors are proportional to their marginal products.

This is one of the most significant theoretical findings in economics. To restate it briefly: factors of production are paid in proportion to their marginal products. This is not a question of social equity but merely a consequence of the efforts of businessmen to produce as cheaply as possible.

Further, the marginal products of the factors are closely related to marginal costs and, therefore, to product prices. For if one more unit of factor 1 is employed, output will be increased by $MP_1(x_1)$ units and variable cost by p_1; so the marginal cost of additional units produced will be $p_1/MP_1(x_1)$. Similarly, if additional output is obtained by employing an additional unit of factor 2, the marginal cost will be $p_2/MP_2(x_2)$. But, as shown above, these two numbers are the same; whichever factor i is used to increase output, the marginal cost will be $p_i/MP_i(x_i)$ and, furthermore, the firm will choose its output level so that the marginal cost will be equal to the price, p_0.

Therefore it has been established that $p_1 = p_0MP_1(x_1)$, $p_2 = p_0MP_2(x_2)$, . . ., or the price of each factor is the price of the product multiplied by its marginal product, which is the value of its marginal product. This, also, is a fundamental theorem of income distribution and one of the most significant theorems in economics. Its logic can be perceived directly. If the equality is violated for any factor, the businessman can increase his profits either by hiring units of the factor or by laying them off until the equality is satisfied, and presumably the businessman will do so.

The theory of production decisions in the short run, as just outlined, leads to two conclusions (of fundamental importance throughout the field of economics) about the responses of business firms to the market prices of the commodities they produce and the factors of production they buy or hire: (1) the firm will produce the quantity of its product for which the marginal cost is equal to the market price and (2) it will purchase or hire factors of production in such quantities that the price of the commodity produced multiplied by the marginal product of the factor will be equal to the cost of a unit of the factor. The first explains the supply curves of the commodities produced in an economy. Though the conclusions were deduced within the context of a firm that uses two factors of production, they are clearly applicable in general.

Maximization of Long-run Profits

Relationship between the Short Run and the Long Run

The theory of long-run profit-maximizing behaviour rests on the short-run theory that has just been presented but is considerably more complex because of two features: (1) long-run cost curves, to be defined below, are more varied in shape than the corresponding short-run cost curves, and (2) the long-run behaviour of an industry cannot be deduced simply from the long-run behaviour of the firms in it because the roster of firms is subject to change. It is of the essence of long-run adjustments that they take place by the addition or dismantling of fixed productive capacity by both established firms and new or recently created firms.

At any one time an established firm with an existing plant will make its short-run decisions by comparing the ruling price of its commodity with cost curves corresponding to that plant. If the price is so high that the firm is operating on the rising leg of its short-run cost curve, its marginal costs will be high—higher than its average costs—and it will be enjoying operating profits, as shown in Figure. The firm will then consider whether it could increase its profits by enlarging its plant. The effect of plant enlargement is to reduce the variable cost of producing high levels of output by reducing the strain on limited production facilities, at the expense of increasing the level of fixed costs.

In response to any level of output that it expects to continue for some time, the firm will desire and eventually acquire the fixed plant for which the short-run costs of that level of output are as low as possible. This leads to the concept of the long-run cost curve: the long-run costs of any level of output are the short-run costs of producing that output in the plant that makes those short-run costs as low as possible. These result from balancing the fixed costs entailed by any plant against the short-run costs of producing in that plant. The long-run costs of producing y are denoted by LRC(y). The average long-run cost of y is the long-run cost per unit of y [algebraically LAC(y) = LRC(y)/y]. The marginal long-run cost is the increase in long-run cost resulting from an increase of one unit in the level of output. It represents a combination of short-run and long-run adjustments to a slight increase in the rate of output. It can be shown that the long-run marginal cost equals the marginal cost as previously defined when the cost-minimizing fixed plant is used.

Long-run Cost Curves

Cost curves appropriate for long-run analysis are more varied in shape than short-run cost curves and fall into three broad classes. In constant-cost industries, average cost is about the same at all levels of output except the very lowest. Constant costs prevail in manufacturing industries in which capacity is expanded by replicating facilities without changing the technique of production, as a cotton mill expands by increasing the number of spindles. In decreasing-cost industries, average cost declines as the rate of output grows, at least until the plant is large enough to supply an appreciable fraction of its market. Decreasing costs are characteristic of manufacturing in which heavy, automated machinery is economical for large volumes of output. Automobile and steel manufacturing are leading examples. Decreasing costs are inconsistent with competitive conditions, since they permit a few large firms to drive all smaller competitors out of business. Finally, in increasing-cost industries average costs rise with the volume of output generally because the firm cannot obtain additional fixed capacity that is as efficient as the plant it already has. The most important examples are agriculture and extractive industries.

Criticisms of the Theory

The theory of production has been subject to much criticism. One objection is that the concept of the production function is not derived from observation or practice. Even the most sophisticated firms do not know the direct functional relationship between their basic raw inputs and their ultimate outputs. This objection can be got around by applying the recently developed techniques of linear programming, which employ observable data without recourse to the production function and lead to practically the same conclusions.

On another level the theory has been charged with excessive simplification. It assumes that there are no changes in the rest of the economy while individual firms and industries are making the adjustments described in the theory; it neglects changes in the technique of production; and it pays no attention to the risks and uncertainties that becloud all business decisions. These criticisms are especially damaging to the theory of long-run profit maximization. On still another level, critics of the theory maintain that businessmen are not always concerned with maximizing profits or minimizing costs.

Though all of the criticisms have merit, the simplified theory of production does nevertheless indicate some basic forces and tendencies operating in the economy. The theorems should be understood as conditions that the economy tends toward, rather than conditions that are always and instantaneously achieved. It is rare for them to be attained exactly, but it is just as rare for substantial violations of the theorems to endure.

Only the simplest aspects of the theory were described above. Without much difficulty it could be extended to cover firms that produce more than one product, as almost all firms do. With more difficulty it could be applied to firms whose decisions affect the prices at which they sell and buy (monopoly, monopolistic competition, monopsony). The behaviour of other firms that recognize the possibility that their competitors may retaliate (oligopoly) is still a theory of production subject to controversy and research.

Market Forms

The different market forms depend on the degree of competition prevailing in the market.

Pure Competition

Pure Competition is said to exist when the following two conditions are fulfilled.

Large Number of Buyers and Sellers

The first condition is that there should be operating in the market a large number of buyers and sellers. If that is so, no single producer or purchaser will be able to influence the market price by varying respectively his supply or demand. The output of any single firm is only a small portion of the total output and the demand of any single purchaser is only a small portion of the total demand. Hence, the market price has to be taken as given and unalterable by every purchaser and seller. This happens when the number of buyers and sellers is very large.

Homogeneous Product

The second condition is that the articles produced by all firms should be standardised or identical. In case of farm produce, e.g., Kalyan wheat, it is immaterial for the purchaser as to who has produced it. He can buy it as well from the one as from the other. This condition ensures that the same price rules in the market for the same commodity. In case the output is not standardised (i.e., it is differentiated), each individual firm will be in a position to influence the market price.

Whether the products are identical or not has to be looked at from the purchaser's angle. Even if the products are identical, the purchaser may have a prejudice against the output of a particular firm and may consider it different. That is, if the consumers regard the commodities as different, they should be considered different for purposes of classification in spite of the fact that they are actually identical.

The consumers generally believe that the products are different. They generally believe that the commodities that they purchase from a particular shop are superior, even though they may actually be of the same quality. When the quality is the same, the commodities are perfect substitutes of one another and their cross-elasticity is infinity.

In these circumstances, if a firm raises its prices, it will lose all customers. It can sell as much as it likes at the prevailing price. Why should it then think of lowering its price? Hence it cannot raise its price and it need not lower it. That is why the prevailing market price is accepted and acted upon by all dealers. Thus, if the above two conditions, viz., homogeneous products and a large number of buyers and sellers are found in a market, it is said to be under pure competition.

Diagrammatic Representation

Under pure competition, the average revenue curve (also called demand curve) of a firm will be a horizontal straight line, which means that any firm can sell any quantity at the prevailing price. Since the number of firms is very large, no individual firm has the power to vary the market price. Also, since the products are identical from the consumers' point of view, the price paid by them cannot be different. This is represented by the following diagram.

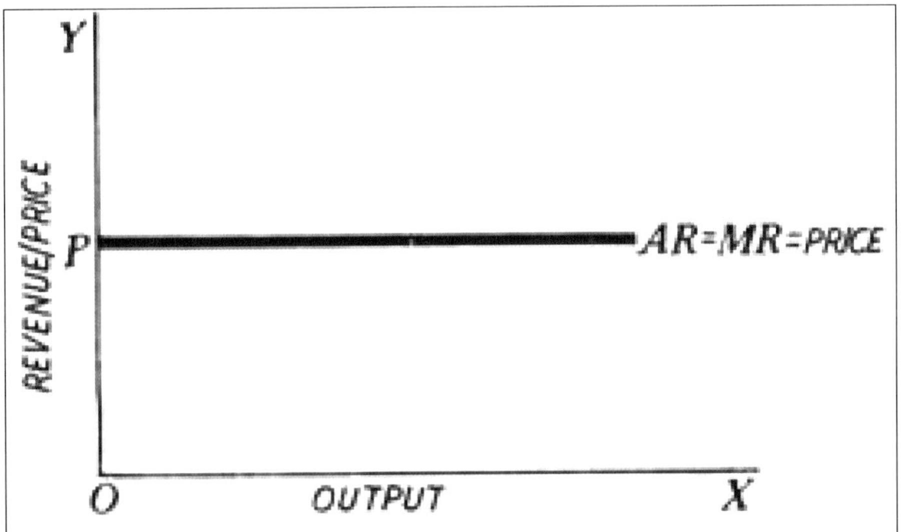

AR Curve Under Perfect Competition

OX and OY are the two axes. Along OX is represented the output and along OY the price/Revenue. At OP price, the sellers can sell as much as they like. They cannot charge more and they will not charge less. If they raise the price, they will lose their customers, and if they charge less, they will be unnecessarily losing.

Examples of pure competition are to be found in the case of farm products, e.g., wheat, cotton, rice. There are a large number of producers, each producing an insignificant proportion of the total market supply. Their product is similar and none of them is in a position to influence the market price by his own individual action. In other fields, we seldom come across pure competition.

Perfect Competition

Perfect competition, on the other hand, is a wider term. It includes the two conditions of pure competition mentioned above as well as some more conditions mentioned below.

The existence of the following conditions in a market will make it a perfect competition market:

- Large number of buyers and sellers.
- Homogeneous product.
- Free Entry or Exit.

Under perfect competition, all firms in the industry will be earning normal profit. This will happen only if there are no restrictions on the firms' entry into, or exit from, that industry. If the profit is more, new firms will enter and the extra profit will be competed away; and if, on the other hand, profit is less, some firms will quit raising the profits for the remaining firms.

But if there are restrictions on the entry of new firms, the existing firms may enjoy super-normal profit and the competition will be imperfect. Only when there are no restrictions on entry or exit, the competition is said to be perfect.

- Perfect Knowledge.

Another assumption of perfect competition is that the purchasers and sellers should be fully aware of the prices that are being offered and accepted. In case there is ignorance among the dealers, the same price cannot rule in the market for the same commodity. When the producers and the customers have full knowledge of the prevailing price, nobody will offer more and none will accept less, and the same price will rule throughout the market. The producers can sell at that price as much as they like, and the buyers also can buy as much as they like.

- Absence of Transport Costs.

If the same price is to rule, it is necessary that no cost of transport has to be incurred. If the cost of transport is there, prices must differ in different sectors of the market.

- Perfect Mobility of the Factors of Production.

This mobility is essential in order to enable the firms to adjust their supply to demand. If the demand exceeds supply, additional factors will move into the industry, and, in the opposite case, move out. Mobility of the factors of production is essential to enable the firms and the industry to achieve an equilibrium position.

Imperfect Competition

In real life, perfect competition or even pure competition are seldom met with. On the other hand, it is imperfect competition which is the rule, and perfect competition is the exception. However, there are different degrees of imperfect competition, ranging from what is called-'monopolistic competition' to 'simple monopoly'. In between these two forms of imperfect competition are 'oligopoly' and 'duopoly".

Monopolistic Competition

The main features of monopolistic competition are:

- In monopolistic competition, the number of dealers is quite large but not as large as under perfect competition.
- The products are not homogeneous; they are, on -the other hand, differentiated by means of different labels attached to them, such as different brands of toilet requisites.
- Either in ignorance or on account of transport costs or lack of mobility of the factors of production, the same price does not rule in the market throughout. Rather different prices are charged by different producers for products which are really similar but are made to appear different through advertisements, high pressure salesmanship and labelling and branding. The result is that each producer comes to have a hold on a clientele from whom he can charge higher prices.
- Under monopolistic competition, the demand curve or sales curve, or what is also called average revenue curve, is not a horizontal straight line. II is, on the other hand, a downward sloping curve, i.e., the seller can sell more by reducing price. Under perfect competition, he need not reduce the price, for he can sell any amount at the prevailing price.

  Under monopolistic competition, the seller can also charge higher prices because his customers are attached to him. He can thus have a price policy of his own, whereas a seller under perfect competition has no price policy; he has merely to accept the market price as given.
- Under imperfect competition, the demand for the product is not perfectly elastic; it is responsive to changes in price.

This form of market is a blend of monopoly and competition and has been called monopolistic competition by Chamberlin, an American economist. In the real world, we have neither monopoly (i.e., absence of competition) nor perfect competition but imperfect competition, i.e. partly monopoly and partly competition. In this market form, the products are not perfect substitutes for one another but they are close substitutes.

Duopoly

In duopoly, there are two sellers, selling either a homogeneous product or a differentiated product. These two sellers between them enjoy a monopoly in the sale of the product produced by them.

Oligopoly

Thus, a market form, in which there are only a few sellers, is called oligopoly. They may be producing and selling either a homogeneous or a differentiated product, the former is called perfect oligopoly and the latter imperfect or differentiated oligopoly.

Monopoly

In monopoly, a single producer or seller controls the market. There are no close substitutes for his product. He controls the supply and he can fix the price. He is the firm and he also constitutes the industry. Thus, under monopoly the distinction between the firm and industry disappears. The average revenue curve or the demand curve always slopes downwards to the right as in monopolistic competition, but it is less elastic in monopoly than in monopolistic competition.

In monopoly, there is one seller and in monopolistic competition many sellers. In monopoly, there is no need to differentiate products because no close substitutes are available. It is one homogeneous product and completely under the control of the monopolist.

Classification of Market Forms

The following chart shows at a glance different types of market forms on the basis of the nature of competition.

Type of the market	No. of firms	Nature of the commodity
Perfect or pure competition	A. Perfect competition Infinite	Homogeneous

Imperfect Competition

- Monopolistic Competition – Many – Differentiated,
- Perfect Oligopoly – A few – Homogeneous,
- Imperfect Oligopoly – A few – Differentiated.

Pure or Absolute Monopoly

Pure or Absolute Monopoly – One – Homogeneous.

Market Equilibrium

Market equilibrium occurs where supply = demand. When the market is in equilibrium, there is no tendency for prices to change. We say the market clearing price has been achieved. A market occurs where buyers and sellers meet to exchange money for goods.

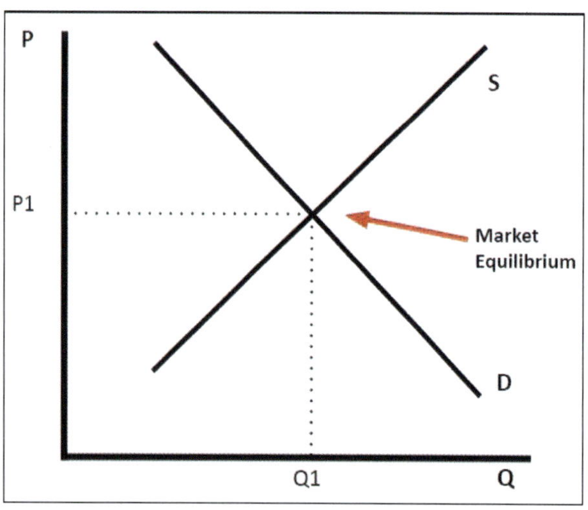

The price mechanism refers to how supply and demand interact to set the market price and amount of goods sold. At most prices planned demand does not equal planned supply. This is a state of disequilibrium because there is either a shortage or surplus and firms have an incentive to change the price. Market equilibrium can be shown using supply and demand diagrams.

In the diagram, the equilibrium price is P1. The equilibrium quantity is Q1.

If price is below the equilibrium.

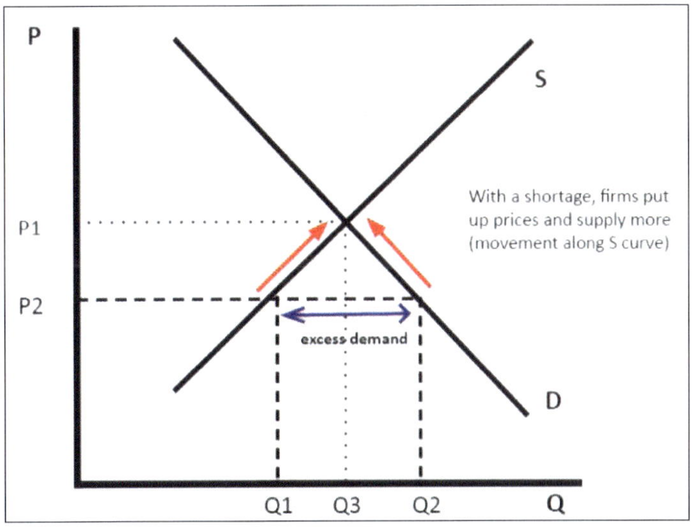

In the above diagram, price (P2) is below the equilibrium. At this price, demand would be greater than the supply. Therefore there is a shortage of (Q2 – Q1).

If there is a shortage, firms will put up prices and supply more. As price rises, there will be a movement along the demand curve and less will be demanded.

Therefore the price will rise to P1 until there is no shortage and supply = demand.

If price is above the equilibrium.

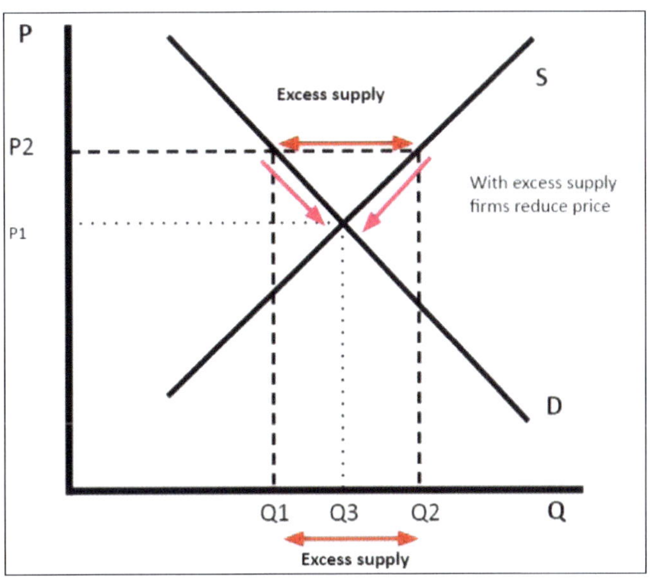

If price was at P2. This is above the equilibrium of P1. At the price of P2, then supply (Q2) would be greater than demand (Q1) and therefore there is too much supply. There is a surplus. (Q2-Q1).

Therefore firms would reduce price and supply less. This would encourage more demand and therefore the surplus will be eliminated. The new market equilibrium will be at Q3 and P1.

Movements to a New Equilibrium

- Increase in demand.

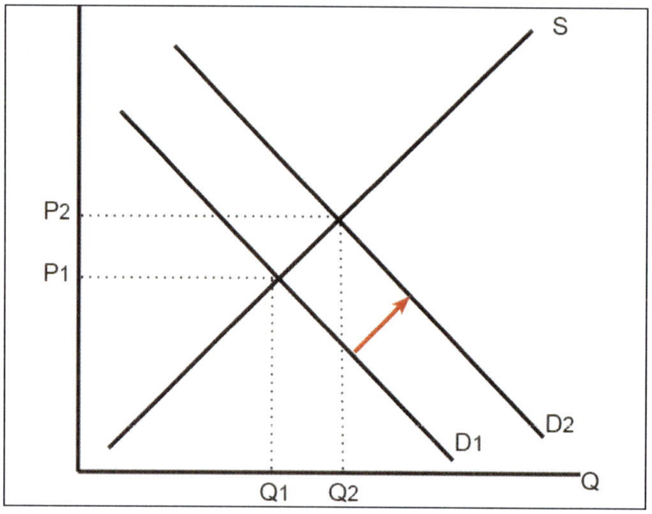

If there was an increase in income the demand curve would shift to the right (D1 to D2). Initially, there would be a shortage of the good. Therefore the price and quantity supplied will increase leading to a new equilibrium at Q2, P2.

- Increase in supply.

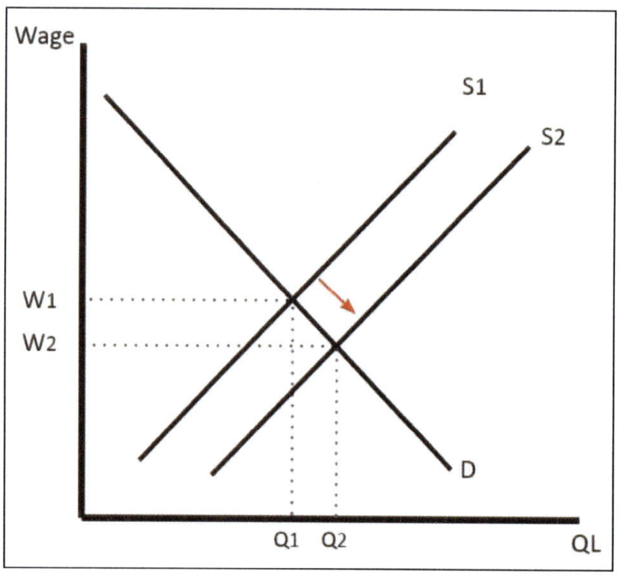

An increase in supply would lead to a lower price and more quantity sold.

Market Failure

Market failure occurs when the price mechanism fails to account for all of the costs and benefits necessary to provide and consume a good.

Market failure occurs when the price mechanism fails to account for all of the costs and benefits necessary to provide and consume a good. The market will fail by not supplying the socially optimal amount of the good.

Prior to market failure, the supply and demand within the market do not produce quantities of the goods where the price reflects the marginal benefit of consumption. The imbalance causes allocative inefficiency, which is the over- or under-consumption of the good.

The structure of market systems contributes to market failure. In the real world, it is not possible for markets to be perfect due to inefficient producers, externalities, environmental concerns, and lack of public goods. An externality is an effect on a third party which is caused by the production or consumption of a good or service.

Air pollution is an example of a negative externality. Governments may enact tradable permits to try and reduce industrial pollution.

During market failures the government usually responds to varying degrees. Possible government responses include:

- Legislation: Enacting specific laws. For example, banning smoking in restaurants, or making high school attendance mandatory.
- Direct provision of merit and public goods: Governments control the supply of goods that have positive externalities. For example, by supplying high amounts of education, parks, or libraries.
- Taxation: Placing taxes on certain goods to discourage use and internalize external costs. For example, placing a 'sin-tax' on tobacco products, and subsequently increasing the cost of tobacco consumption.

- Subsidies: Reducing the price of a good based on the public benefit that is gained. For example, lowering college tuition because society benefits from more educated workers. Subsidies are most appropriate to encourage behavior that has positive externalities.
- Tradable permits: Permits that allow firms to produce a certain amount of something, commonly pollution. Firms can trade permits with other firms to increase or decrease what they can produce. This is the basis behind cap-and-trade, an attempt to reduce of pollution.
- Extension of property rights: Creates privatization for certain non-private goods like lakes, rivers, and beaches to create a market for pollution. Then, individuals get fined for polluting certain areas.
- Advertising: Encourages or discourages consumption.
- International cooperation among governments: Governments work together on issues that affect the future of the environment.

Causes of Market Failure

Market failure occurs due to inefficiency in the allocation of goods and services.

Market failure occurs due to inefficiency in the allocation of goods and services. A price mechanism fails to account for all of the costs and benefits involved when providing or consuming a specific good. When this happens, the market will not produce the supply of the good that is socially optimal – it will be over or under produced.

In order to fully understand market failure, it is important to recognize the reasons why a market can fail. Due to the structure of markets, it is impossible for them to be perfect. As a result, most markets are not successful and require forms of intervention.

Reasons for market failure include:

- Positive and negative externalities: An externality is an effect on a third party that is caused by the consumption or production of a good or service. A positive externality is a positive spillover that results from the consumption or production of a good or service. For example, although public education may only directly affect students and schools, an educated population may provide positive effects on society as a whole. A negative externality is a negative spillover effect on third parties. For example, secondhand smoke may negatively impact the health of people, even if they do not directly engage in smoking.
- Environmental concerns: Effects on the environment as important considerations as well as sustainable development.
- Lack of public goods: Public goods are goods where the total cost of production does not increase with the number of consumers. As an example of a public good, a lighthouse has a fixed cost of production that is the same, whether one ship or one hundred ships use its light. Public goods can be underproduced; there is little incentive, from a private standpoint, to provide a lighthouse because one can wait for someone else to provide it, and then use its light without incurring a cost. This problem – someone benefiting from resources or goods and services without paying for the cost of the benefit – is known as the free rider problem.

- Underproduction of merit goods: A merit good is a private good that society believes is under consumed, often with positive externalities. For example, education, healthcare, and sports centers are considered merit goods.
- Overprovision of demerit goods: A demerit good is a private good that society believes is over consumed, often with negative externalities. For example, cigarettes, alcohol, and prostitution are considered demerit goods.
- Abuse of monopoly power: Imperfect markets restrict output in an attempt to maximize profit.

When a market fails, the government usually intervenes depending on the reason for the failure.

Introducing Externalities

An externality is a cost or benefit that affects an otherwise uninvolved party who did not choose to be subject to the cost or benefit.

In economics, an externality is a cost or benefit resulting from an activity or transaction, that affects an otherwise uninvolved party who did not choose to be subject to the cost or benefit. An example of an externality is pollution. Health and clean-up costs from pollution impact all of society, not just individuals within the manufacturing industries. In regards to externalities, the cost and benefit to society is the sum of the value of the benefits and costs for all parties involved.

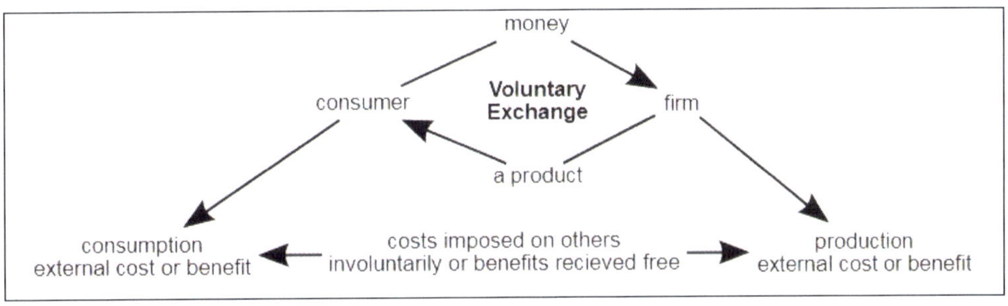

Externality: An externality is a cost or benefit that results from an activity or transaction and that affects an otherwise uninvolved party who did not choose to incur that cost or benefit.

Negative vs. Positive

Negative Externality: Air pollution caused by motor vehicles is an example of a negative externality.

A negative externality is an result of a product that inflicts a negative effect on a third party. In contrast, positive externality is an action of a product that provides a positive effect on a third party.

Externalities originate within voluntary exchanges. Although the parties directly involved benefit from the exchange, third parties can experience additional effects. For those involuntarily impacted, the effects can be negative (pollution from a factory) or positive (domestic bees kept for honey production, pollinate the neighboring crops).

Economic Strain

Neoclassical welfare economics explains that under plausible conditions, externalities cause economic results that are not ideal for society. The third parties who experience external costs from a negative externality do so without consent, while the individuals who receive external benefits do not pay a cost. The existence of externalities can cause ethical and political problems within society.

In regards to externalities, one way to correct the issue is to internalize the third party costs and benefits. However, in many cases, internalizing the costs is not financially possible. Governments may step in to correct such market failures.

Externality Impacts on Efficiency

Economic efficiency is the use resources to maximize the production of goods; externalities are imperfections that limit efficiency.

Economic Efficiency

In economics, the term "economic efficiency" is defined as the use of resources in order to maximize the production of goods and services. An economically efficient society can produce more goods or services than another society without using more resources.

A market is said to be economically efficient if:

- No one can be made better off without making someone else worse off.
- No additional output can be obtained without increasing the amounts of inputs.
- Production proceeds at the lowest possible cost per unit.

Externalities

An externality is a cost or benefit that results from an activity or transaction and affects a third party who did not choose to incur the cost or benefit. Externalities are either positive or negative depending on the nature of the impact on the third party. An example of a negative externality is pollution. Manufacturing plants emit pollution which impacts individuals living in the surrounding areas. Third parties who are not involved in any aspect of the manufacturing plant are impacted negatively by the pollution. An example of a positive externality would be an individual who lives by a bee farm. The third parties' flowers are pollinated by the neighbor's bees. They have no cost or investment in the business, but they benefit from the bees.

Externalities and Efficiency

Positive and negative externalities both impact economic efficiency. Neoclassical welfare economics states that the existence of externalities results in outcomes that are not ideal for society as a whole. In the case of negative externalities, third parties experience negative effects from an activity or transaction in which they did not choose to be involved. In order to compensate for negative externalities, the market as a whole is reducing its profits in order to repair the damage that was caused which decreases efficiency. Positive externalities are beneficial to the third party at no cost to them. The collective social welfare is improved, but the providers of the benefit do not make any money from the shared benefit. As a result, less of the good is produced or profited from which is less optimal society and decreases economic efficiency.

In order to deal with externalities, markets usually internalize the costs or benefits. For costs, the market has to spend additional funds in order to make up for damages incurred. Benefits are also internalized because they are viewed as goods produced and used by third parties with no monetary gain for the market. Internalizing costs and benefits is not always feasible, especially when the monetary value or a good or service cannot be determined.

Externalities directly impact efficiency because the production of goods is not efficient when costs are incurred due to damages. Efficiency also decreases when potential money earned is lost on non-paying third parties.

In order to maximize economic efficiency, regulations are needed to reduce market failures and imperfections, like internalizing externalities. When market imperfections exist, the efficiency of the market declines.

References

- Firm-definition-meaning, financial-glossary: marketbusinessnews.com, Retrieved 17 August, 2019
- Objectives-firms, microessays: economicshelp.org, Retrieved 18 April, 2019
- Top-3-theories-of-firm-with-diagram- 19519: economicsdiscussion.net, Retrieved 16 May, 2019
- The-concept-of-optimum-firm-in-economics, economics- 36973: yourarticlelibrary.com, Retrieved 29 July, 2019
- Theory-of-production: britannica.com, Retrieved 14 June, 2019
- Market-forms-pure-competition-perfect-competition-and-imperfect-competition- 1685: economicsdiscussion.net, Retrieved 05 August, 2019
- Market-equilibrium, microessays-equilibrium: economicshelp.org, Retrieved 18 January, 2019
- Introducing-market-failure, boundless-economics: courses.lumenlearning.com, Retrieved 05 February, 2019

3

Consumer's Equilibrium, Elasticity, Demand and Supply

Consumer equilibrium refers to the balance between the expenditure of income on goods and services and maximum satisfaction achieved from the spending on consumption. Supply and demand refers to the amount of goods and services that are available for people to buy compared to the amount of goods and services that people want to buy. All the aspects of consumer equilibrium, demand and supply have been carefully analyzed in this chapter.

General Equilibrium

General equilibrium analysis is an extensive study of a number of economic variables, their interrelations and interdependences for understanding the working of the economic system as a whole. It brings together the cause and effect sequences of changes in prices and quantities of commodities and services in relation to the entire economy.

An economy can be in general equilibrium only if all consumers, all firms, all industries and all factor-services are in equilibrium simultaneously and they are interlinked through commodity and factor prices. As Stigler has said: "The theory of General Equilibrium is the theory of interrelationship among all parts of the economy".

General equilibrium exists when all prices are in equilibrium; each consumer spends his given income in a manner that yields him the maximum satisfaction; all firms in each industry are in equilibrium at all prices and output; and the supply and demand for productive resources (factors of production) are equal at equilibrium prices.

Assumptions

The general equilibrium analysis is based on the following assumptions:

- There is perfect competition both in the commodity and factor markets.
- Tastes and habits of consumers are given and constant.
- Incomes of consumers are given and constant.
- Factors of production are perfectly mobile between different occupations and places.
- There are constant returns to scale.
- All firms operate under identical cost conditions.
- All units of a productive service are homogeneous.

- There are no changes in the techniques of production.
- There is full employment of labour and other resources.

Working of the General Equilibrium System

Given these assumptions, the economy is in a state of general equilibrium when the demand for every commodity and service is equal to the supply for it. It implies perfect harmony of the decisions made by all the market participants. The decisions of consumers for the purchase of each commodity must be in perfect accord with the decisions of producers for the production and sale of each commodity.

Similarly, the decisions of owners for selling each factor service must be in perfect harmony with the decisions of their employers. It is only when the decisions of buyers of goods and services fit in perfectly with the decisions of sellers that the market is in general equilibrium.

Product Market

Given the tastes, preferences and aims of the consumers in the economy, the quantity of each commodity demanded depends not only on its own price but also on the price of each other commodity available in the market. Thus, each consumer maximizes his satisfaction relative to the prices ruling the market. For him, the marginal utility of each commodity equals its price.

Each consumer is assumed to spend his entire income on consumption, so his expenditure equals his income. His income, in turn, depends on the prices at which he is selling his productive services. In other words, a consumer earns by selling the productive services he owns. Thus, the demand of consumers for the various commodities depends upon their prices and the prices of services.

Let us take the supply side. Given the market structure, the state of technology and the aims of firms, the price at which a commodity sells depends on its costs of production. The costs of production, in turn, depend on the quantities of the various productive services employed and the prices paid for them.

Assuming constant returns to scale and identical cost conditions for all firms, each producer will produce and sell that quantity of output at which the demand price for the commodity equals both the minimum average cost and the marginal cost. The equilibrium of the commodity market is illustrated in Figure.

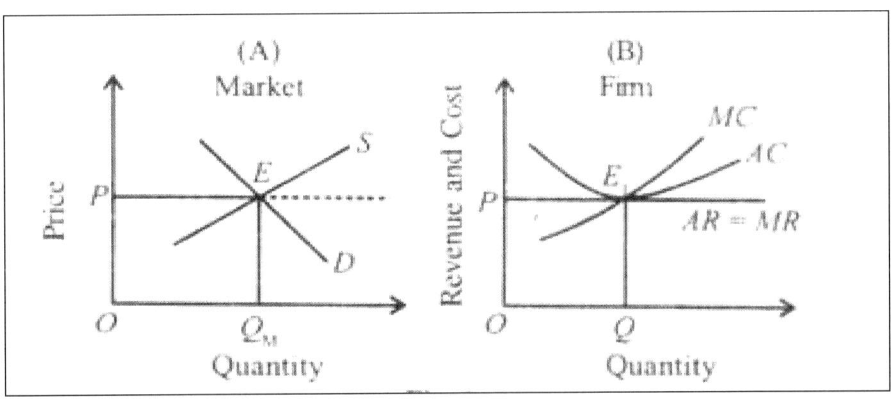

The market is in equilibrium at point E where the market demand and supply curves D and S intersect. It determines OP price at which OQ_M quantity of the product is bought and sold in the market. There being identical cost conditions, each firm in the market produces and sells the commodity at the given price OP.

It is in equilibrium when MC=MR and AC=AR at point E_1producing OQ units of the commodity, as shown in Panel B. If, say, there are 100 firms in the market each producing 60 units of the commodity, the total production will be 6000 (=100 x 60) units. This analysis inter alia can be extended to all commodities being produced in the economy.

Factor Market

Like the equality of demand and supply of commodities, the equality of demand and supply of factor services is also essential for the general equilibrium system. The demand for productive services comes from the producers and supply from the consumers. Given the state of technology and the profit maximisation objective of the producers, the quantity of a factor used in producing a commodity depends on the relationship between the prices of that factor and of all other factors and on the prices of commodities.

Each producer maximises his profits relative to the ruling factor prices by employing the various factors in such proportions and quantities that their marginal revenue productivities are equal to their prices. Since there is full employment in the economy, the markets for factors are in equilibrium when the total quantities of factors offered and the total quantities employed are equal.

The equilibrium of the factor market is illustrated in Figure, where in Panel (A), the price of a factor OP and its quantity ON are determined in the market by the interaction of its demand and supply curves D and 5 respectively at point E. Panel (B) shows that the supply curve of this factor to an individual firm is perfectly elastic and is the same as the marginal cost of that factor, MFC.

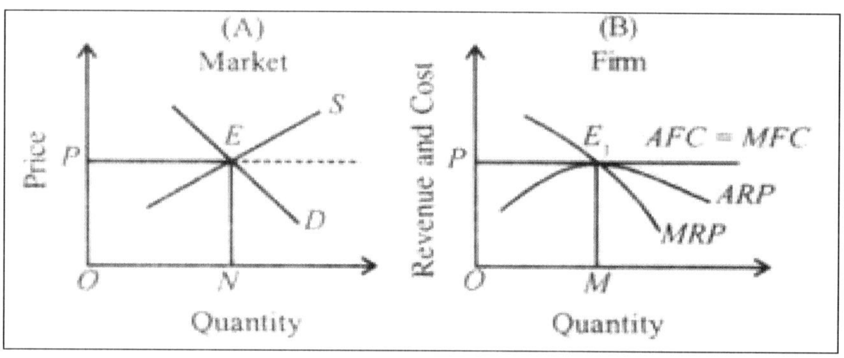

The firm will employ units of the factor at the given factor price OP where MFC=MRP and average factor cost, AFC=ARP (average revenue product) to the firm. Such an equilibrium point is E_1 at which it employs OM units of the factor. If there are 10 identical cost firms and each employs 100 units of the factor, the total market demand and supply of this factor will be 1000 units in the market. This analysis can be extended to the economy as a whole.

Thus the economy is in general equilibrium when commodity prices make each demand equal to its supply and factor prices make the demand for each factor equal to its supply so that all product markets and factor markets are simultaneously in equilibrium.

Such a general equilibrium is characterised by two conditions in which the set of prices in all product and factor markets is such that:

- All consumers maximise their satisfactions and all producers maximise their profits; and
- All markets are cleared which means that the total amount demanded equals the total amount supplied at a positive price in both the product and factor markets.

To explain it, we begin with a simple hypothetical economy where there are only two sectors, the household and the business. The economic activity takes the form of flow of goods and services between these two sectors and monetary flow between them.

These two flows which are called real and monetary are shown in figure where the product market is shown in the lower portion and the factor market in the upper portion. In the product market, consumers purchase goods and services from producers while in the factor market, consumers receive income from the former for providing services.

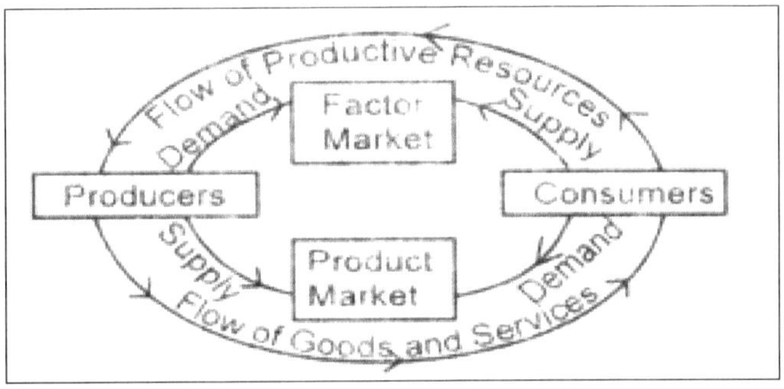

Thus consumers purchase all goods and services provided by producers and make payments to the latter in lieu of these. The producers, in turn, make payments to consumers for the services rendered by the latter to the business, wage payments for labour services, interest for capital supplied, etc. Thus payments go around in a circular manner from producers to consumers and from consumers to producers, as shown by arrows in the outer portion of the figure.

There are also flows of goods and services in the opposite direction to the money payments flows. Goods flow from the business sector to the household sector in the product market, and services flow from the household sector to the business sector in the factor market, as shown in dies inner portion of the figure.

These two flows are linked by product prices and factor prices. The economy is in general equilibrium when a set of prices is allowed at which the magnitude of income flow from producers to consumers is equal to the magnitude of the money expenditure from consumers to producers.

Limitations

The general equilibrium analysis of the economy has several limitations:

- It is based on a number of unrealistic assumptions which are contrary to the actual conditions prevailing in the world. Perfect competition, the very basis of this analysis, is a myth.
- It is a static analysis. All consumers and producers in this analysis consume and produce

the same products day in and day out without any time-lag. Their tastes, preferences, and aims are the same, and their economic decisions are in perfect harmony with each other.

In reality, nothing of this sort happens. Producers and consumers never act and think alike. Changes are taking place continuously in tastes and preferences. There are no constant returns to scale and no two factor services are homogeneous. Thus cost conditions differ from producer to producer. Since the given conditions are continuously changing, the movement towards general equilibrium is ever thwarted and its attainment has ever remained a wishful ideal.

Stigler regards general equilibrium as a misnomer. According to him, "No economic analysis has ever been general in the sense that it considered equilibrium studies as more inclusive than partial equilibrium studies, never that they are complete. Moreover, the more general the analysis, the less specific its content must necessarily be".

Consumer's Equilibrium

A consumer is said to be in equilibrium when he feels that he "cannot change his condition either by earning more or by spending more or by changing the quantities of thing he buys". A rational consumer will purchase a commodity up to the point where price of the commodity is equal to the marginal utility obtained from the thing.

If this condition is not fulfilled the consumer will either purchase more or less. If he purchases more, MU will go on falling and a situation will develop where price paid will exceed MU. In order to avoid negative utility, i.e., dissatisfaction, he will reduce consumption and MU will go on increasing till P = MU.

On the other hand, if MU is greater than the price paid, the consumer will enjoy surplus satisfaction from the units he has already consumed. This will induce him to buy more and more units of the commodity leading to successive fall in MU till it is equated to its price. Thus, by a process of trial and error — by buying more or less units, a consumer will ultimately settle at the point where P = MU. Here, his is total utility is maximum.

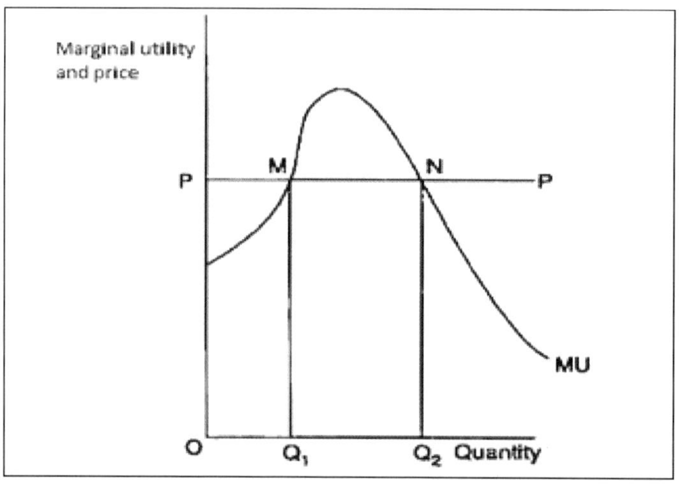

Necessary and sufficient conditions of consumer's equilibrium.

However, P = MU is a necessary but not a sufficient condition for a consumer's equilibrium. In figure we find that the MU curve is intersecting the price curve PP at two different points M and N. So far M is concerned, although by having OA quantity the consumer is reaching the point where P – MU but it is not equilibrium.

For by purchasing extra units above OA he can enjoy surplus satisfaction. Why then will he stop at OA? He will continue using the thing till he reaches OB. If he goes beyond this point, for every extra unit P is greater than MU and he shall have to suffer dissatisfaction. Thus, the sufficient condition of consumer equilibrium is that the MU curve must cut the price curve at its downward segment and not at its rising segment.

The objective of a rational consumer is to maximise utility (welfare) subject to:

- A fixed level of money income.
- A fixed set of commodity prices.

Now, what is fundamental equilibrium condition that has to be satisfied if a consumer is spending his income on different goods so as to make himself truly best off in terms of utility or satisfaction?

Certainly he would not expect that the last egg he is buying brings him exactly the same marginal utility as the last cake he is buying. One cake costs much more than an egg. One may guess that he should go on buying a good which costs twice as much per unit as another until he ends up in his equilibrium bringing him just twice as much in marginal utility.

Thus, if the consumer has arranged his consumption so that every single good brings him marginal utility just exactly proportional to its price, then he could not gain extra utility and thus improve his position by departing from such an equilibrium.

This Fundamental Condition can now be Stated

A consumer with a fixed money income and facing a fixed set of market prices of goods can reach equilibrium or the level of maximum satisfaction or utility only when he acts thus;

Law of Equal Marginal Utilities per Rupee

Each good — such as egg — is demanded up to the point where the marginal utility per rupee spent on it is exactly the same as the marginal utility of a rupee spend on any other good—such as cake.

Why does this law hold? If any one good gave more marginal utility per rupee the consumer would gain by taking money away from other goods and spending more on that good — up to the point where the law of diminishing marginal utility brought its marginal utility per rupee down to equality. If any good gave less marginal utility per rupee than the common level, the consumer would buy less of it's until the marginal utility of the last rupee spent on it had risen back to the common level.

The Law of Equi-marginal Utility (or the Principle of Substitution) follows from the Law of Diminishing Marginal Utility. According to the latter, a person goes on buying the units of a commodity one after another till its marginal utility becomes equal to its price. In the case of more than one commodity, he examines the marginal utility of the last unit of money spent on the different commodities.

More precisely, for the maximization of satisfaction, income must be allocated in such a way that the marginal utility of an unit of money's worth (for example, one rupee's worth) is the same for every commodity. If it is found that the marginal utility of the last unit of money spent on say, X commodity is greater than that derived from another commodity, say, Y commodity, he substitutes X for Y. Such a process of substitution goes on till the marginal utility of the last unit of money spent on X and on Y becomes equal to each other.

Beyond this point, further substitution will not be beneficial to him, for that would involve a decrease in his total utility. This is known as the Law of Equi-marginal Utility. Marshall puts the Law in the following words: "If a person has a thing which he can put to several uses, he will distribute it between these uses in such a way that it has the same marginal utility in all". If he has a greater utility in one use than in another, he would gain by taking away some of it from the second use and applying it to the first.

Proof of the Law

The Law of Equi-marginal Utility can be proved as follows- Let us suppose that a person has Rs. 5 to spend on X and Y commodities during a particular period of time, say a day, and he gets marginal utility from each of these two commodities as shown in the following table:

Table: Rational Allocation of a Consumer's Income (Expenditure).

Amount of money spent	X commodity and its marginal utility	Y commodity and its marginal utility
1st Re.	25 units	21 units
2nd Re.	20 units	16 units
3rd Re.	16 units	12 units
4th Re.	13 units	9 units
5th Re	10 units	6 units

The table shows that a person can either spend all the five rupees on X or Y or divide these between the two. If he spends all the five rupees on X, the last rupee spent on X would give 10 units utility, but if that rupee is spent on Y (i.e., four rupees for X and one rupee for Y) he will get a greater amount of utility. So, he will substitute Y for X.

This process continues till the marginal utility of the last rupee spent on X and on Y will give him the same marginal utility, and he will attain this stage when he spends Rs. 3 on X and Rs. 2 on Y. At this stage, his total utility from his spending will become (25 + 20 + 16 = 61 units from X and 21 + 16 = 37 units from Y) 98 units and this will be the maximum amount of total utility that he can get from his spending. Thus, if a person equalises the marginal utility from each of his purchases, he gets the maximum amount of satisfaction. So, the doctrine of maximum satisfaction can be deduced from this law.

This law can also be explained in another way to show the optimum purchase of the consumer or the consumer's equilibrium. A consumer buys a commodity up to that amount at which its price is equal to its marginal utility. In the case of purchase of many commodities, maximum satisfaction requires the allocation of income in such a way that the marginal utilities of units of various goods bought are proportional to their prices.

In other words, if apples cost twice as much per kg. as potatoes, the consumer must adjust his purchases of these two goods until the marginal utility of a kg. of apple is twice as great as the marginal utility of a kg. of potatoes. So, in equilibrium, the marginal utilities of the different commodities purchased are proportional to their prices and these ratios of marginal utility to price must be equal to the common marginal utility of money.

If he distributes his expenditure rationally among commodities, X, Y, Z, etc., the following relationship will hold good in equilibrium:
MU of X/Price of X = MU of Y/Price of Y = MU of Z/Price of Z = MU_M
where, MU_M is the common marginal utility of money (i.e., marginal utility of a rupee).
The equi-marginal principle can be illustrated in figure to show the maximum satisfaction.

Figure illustrates quantity consumed of two commodities, X shown on the right side and Y on the left side. The marginal utility curves for each use are also shown. The curve X is farther from the vertical axis (OM) than the Y curve to indicate the relatively stronger desire for X.

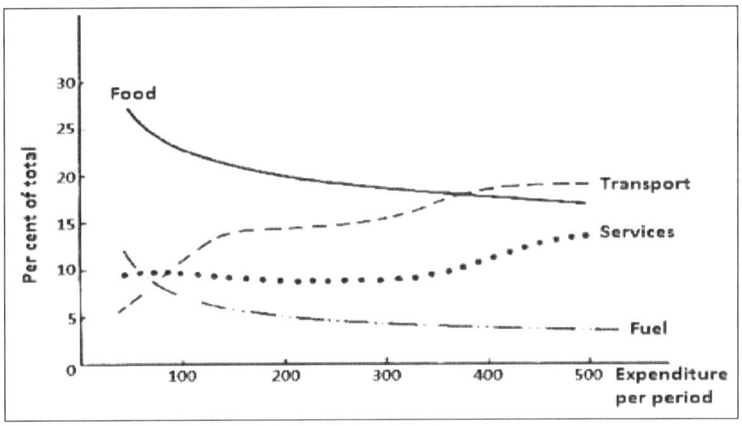

Engel Curves

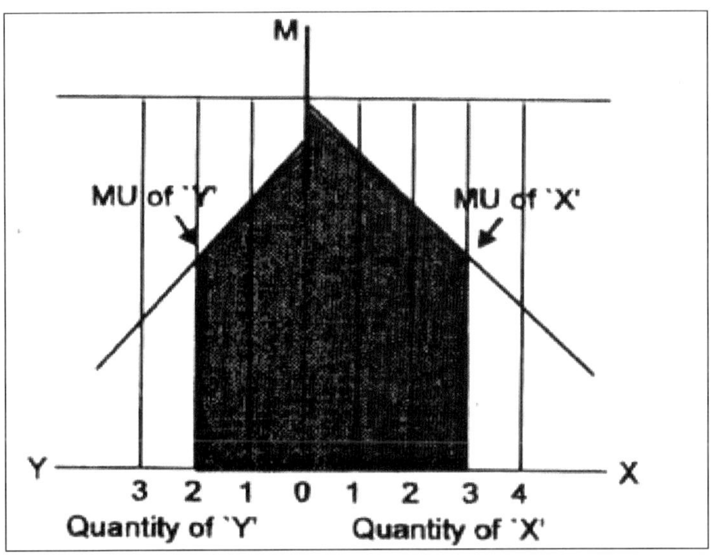

Let us suppose that a consumer has Rs. 5 to spend and $P_X = P_Y$ = Re.1. Given the MU curves for X and Y the best allocation of his income is 3 units of X and 2 units of Y, because with these quantities the marginal utilities are equal. Any other allocations will lower the total satisfaction (the entire shaded area in the diagram).

Let us show it by devoting 4 units in X and 1 unit in Y. In such a case, the area between 3 and 4 under M U curve of X would be a gain, but there would be a loss of the area between 2 and 1 under the MU curve of Y. Clearly the loss is greater than the gain. Any other allocations excepting 3 units in X and 2 units in Y would give the consumer a lower total utility.

Application of the Principle

The principle of substitution applies to production also. A producer varies the quantities of the different factors of production in such a way that he gets equal marginal returns from all the lines of expenditure. For this purpose, he will employ each factor up to that quantity at which the earning or price of each factor is equal to the value of marginal product of each factor. By doing so, he can produce at the lowest possible cost of per unit. As applied in production, this principle is known as the Law of Equi-marginal Returns.

Limitations

The principle of substitution and the law of equi-marginal utility have the following limitations:

Too Much Rationality

The law of equi-marginal utility assumes too much rationality in the behaviour of a consumer. In real life, consumers do not always make their purchases considering minutely the relative marginal utilities of the different commodities; they make their purchases very often out of fancy or emotion or social needs without judging carefully their marginal utilities. In such cases the law does not hold.

Indivisible Units

The law does not operate in the cases of the goods which cannot be divided into small parts or are not available in small units (e.g., motor cars, refrigerators, TV sets, etc). In such cases the perfect adjustment of marginal utilities is not possible and for this reason the law cannot be applied.

Mistake in Calculation

The law may fail to operate in the cases where consumers or producers commit mistakes in calculating marginal utility of the commodity or marginal product of the factor of production.

Difference between Utility and Satisfaction

The law of equi-marginal utility states that the equalisation of marginal utility in all the cases of purchases maximises total utility and thus total satisfaction of a consumer. But, it is pointed out that 'utility' and 'satisfaction' are not the same thing; so the maximisation of utility may not cause the maximisation of satisfaction. In answer to this criticism it is, however, pointed out that, although 'utility' and 'satisfaction' are not identical they are closely related; that an increase of utility would cause an increase in satisfaction cannot be denied.

Difficulty in Measuring Utility

The law assumes, as in the utility analysis of the neo-classical writers, that utility can be measured. But, it is pointed out that utility, being a subjective concept, cannot be measured.

Changing Marginal Utility of Money

Finally, the law assumes that the marginal utility of money remains constant at different levels of income. But as income increases marginal utility of money falls. So, the law cannot be applied in practice.

Elasticity

Elasticity is a measure of a variable's sensitivity to a change in another variable. In business and economics, elasticity refers the degree to which individuals, consumers or producers change their demand or the amount supplied in response to price or income changes. It is predominantly used to assess the change in consumer demand as a result of a change in a good or service's price.

How Elasticity Works

When the value of elasticity is greater than 1, it suggests that the demand for the good or service is affected by the price. A value that is less than 1 suggests that the demand is insensitive to price.

Elasticity is an economic concept used to measure the change in the aggregate quantity demanded for a good or service in relation to price movements of that good or service. A product is considered to be elastic if the quantity demand of the product changes drastically when its price increases or decreases. Conversely, a product is considered to be inelastic if the quantity demand of the product changes very little when its price fluctuates.

For example, insulin is a product that is highly inelastic. For diabetics who need insulin, the demand is so great that price increases have very little effect on the quantity demanded. Price decreases also do not affect the quantity demanded; most of those who need insulin aren't holding out for a lower price and are already making purchases.

On the other side of the equation are highly elastic products. Bouncy balls, for example, are highly elastic in that they aren't a necessary good, and consumers will only decide to make a purchase if the price is low. Therefore, if the price of bouncy balls increases, the quantity demanded will greatly decrease, and if the price decreases, the quantity demanded will increase.

Elasticity can be calculated using the following formula:

$$\text{Elasticity} = \frac{\%\,\text{change in quantity}}{\%\,\text{change in price}}$$

Factors Affecting Demand Elasticity

There are three main factors that influence a good's price elasticity of demand:

- Availability of Substitutes: In general, the more good substitutes there are, the more elastic the demand will be. For example, if the price of a cup of coffee went up by $0.25, consumers might replace their morning caffeine fix with a cup of strong tea. This means that coffee is an elastic good because a small increase in price will cause a large decrease in demand as consumers start buying more tea instead of coffee. However, if the price of caffeine itself were to go up, we would probably see little change in the consumption of coffee or tea because there may be few good substitutes for caffeine. Most people in this case might not willing to give up their morning cup of caffeine no matter what the price. We would say, therefore, that caffeine is an inelastic product. While a specific product within an industry can be elastic due to the availability of substitutes, an entire industry itself tends to be inelastic. Usually, unique goods such as diamonds are inelastic because they have few if any substitutes.
- Necessity: If something is needed for survival or comfort, people will continue to pay higher prices for it. For example, people need to get to work or drive for any number of reasons. Therefore, even if the price of gas doubles or even triples, people will still need to fill up their tanks.
- Time: The third influential factor is time. If the price of cigarettes goes up $2 per pack, a smoker with very few available substitutes will most likely continue buying his or her daily cigarettes. This means that tobacco is inelastic because the change in price will not have a significant influence on the quantity demanded. However, if that smoker finds that he or she cannot afford to spend the extra $2 per day and begins to kick the habit over a period of time, the price elasticity of cigarettes for that consumer becomes elastic in the long run.

The Importance of Price Elasticity in Business

Understanding whether or not a business's good or service is elastic is integral to the success of the company. Companies with high elasticity ultimately compete with other businesses on price and are required to have a high volume of sales transactions to remain solvent. Firms that are inelastic, on the other hand, have goods and services that are must-haves and enjoy the luxury of setting higher prices.

Beyond prices, the elasticity of a good or service directly affects the customer retention rates of a company. Businesses often strive to sell goods or services that have inelastic demand; doing so means that customers will remain loyal and continue to purchase the good or service even in the face of a price increase.

Theory of Consumer Behaviour

Rationality

The consumer is assumed to be rational he aims at the maximization of his utility, given his income and market prices. It is assumed he has full knowledge (certainty) of all relevant information.

Utility is Ordinal

It is taken as axiomatically true that the consumer can rank his preferences (order the various 'baskets of goods') according to the satisfaction of each basket. He need not know precisely the amount of satisfaction. It suffices that he expresses his preference for the various bundles of commodities. It is not necessary to assume that utility is cardinally measurable. Only ordinal measurement is required.

Diminishing Marginal Rate of Substitution

Preferences are ranked in terms of indifference curves, which are assumed to be convex to the origin. This implies that the slope of the indifference curves increases. The slope of the indifference curve is called the marginal rate of substitution of the commodities. The indifference-curve theory is based, thus, on the axiom of diminishing marginal rate of substitution.

The total utility of the consumer depends on the quantities of the commodities consumed.

$$U = f(q_1, q_2, \ldots, q_x, q_y, \ldots.. q_n)$$

Consistency and Transitivity of Choice

It is assumed that the consumer is consistent in his choice, that is, if in one period he chooses bundle A over B, he will not choose B over A in another period if both bundles are available to him.

The Consistency Assumption may be Symbolically Written as Follows:

If A > B, then B !> A

Similarly, it is assumed that consumer's choices are characterised by transitivity: if bundle A is preferred to B, and B is preferred to C, then bundle A, is preferred to C.

Symbolically we may write the transitivity assumption as follows:

If A > B, and B > C, then A > C

Equilibrium of the Consumer

To define the equilibrium of the consumer (that is, his choice of the bundle that maximizes his utility) we must introduce the concept of indifference curves and of their slope (the marginal rate of substitution), and the concept of the budget line. These are the basic tools of the indifference curves approach.

Indifference Curves

An indifference curve is the locus of points – particular combinations or bundles of goods-which yield the same utility (level of satisfaction) to the consumer, so that he is indifferent as to the particular combination he consumes.

An indifference map shows all the indifference curves which rank the preferences of the consumer. Combinations of goods situated on an indifference curve yield the same utility. Combinations of goods lying on a higher indifference curve yield higher level of satisfaction and are preferred. Combinations of goods on a lower indifference curve yield a lower utility.

An indifference curve is shown in figure and a partial indifference map is depicted in figure It is assumed that the commodities y and x can substitute one another to a certain extent but are not perfect substitutes.

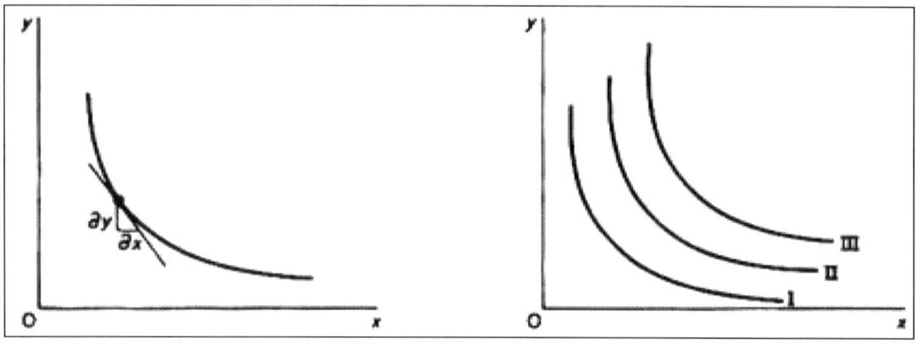

The negative of the slope of an indifference curve at any one point is called the marginal rate of substitution of the two commodities, x and y, and is given by the slope of the tangent at that point.

$$[\text{Slope of indifference curve}] = -\,dy/dx = MRS_{x,y}$$

The marginal rate of substitution of x for y is defined as the number of units of commodity y that must be given up in exchange for an extra unit of commodity x so that the consumer maintains the same level of satisfaction. With this definition the proponents of the indifference-curves approach thought that they could avoid the non-operational concept of marginal utility.

In fact, what they avoid is the assumption of diminishing individual marginal utilities and the need for their measurement. The concept of marginal utility is implicit in the definition of the MRS, since it can be proved that the marginal rate of substitution (the slope of the indifference curve) is equal to the ratio of the marginal utilities of the commodities involved in the utility function.

$$MRS_{x,y} = MU_x/MU_y \text{ or } MRS_{y,x} = MU_y/Mu_x$$

Furthermore, the indifference-curves theorists substitute the assumption of diminishing marginal utility with another which may also be questioned, namely the assumption that the indifference curves are convex to the origin, which implies diminishing MRS of the commodities.

Properties of the Indifference Curves

- An indifference curve has a negative slope, which denotes that if the quantity of one commodity (y) decreases, the quantity of the other (x) must increase, if the consumer is to stay on the same level of satisfaction.
- The further away from the origin an indifference curve lies, the higher the level of utility it denotes bundles of goods on a higher indifference curve are preferred by the rational consumer.
- Indifference curves do not intersect. If they did, the point of their intersection would imply two different levels of satisfaction, which is impossible.

Proof:

The slope of a curve at any one point is measured by the slope of the tangent at that point. The equation-of a tangent is given by the total derivative or total differential, which shows the total change of the function as all its determinants change.

The total utility function in the case of two commodities x and y is:

$$U = f(x,y)$$

The equation of an indifference curve is:

$$U = f(x,y) = k$$

Where k is a constant. The total differential of the utility function is:

$$dU = \frac{\partial U}{\partial y} dy + \frac{\partial U}{\partial x} dx = (MU_y)dy + (MU_x)dx$$

It shows the total change in utility as the quantities of both commodities change. The total change in U caused by changes in y and x is (approximately) equal to the change in y multiplied by its marginal utility, plus the change in x multiplied by its marginal utility.

Along any particular indifference curve the total differential is by definition equal to zero. Thus for any indifference curve:

$$dU = (MU_y)dy + (MU_x)dx = 0$$

Rearranging we obtain:

$$\text{either} = \frac{dy}{dx} = \frac{MU_x}{MU_y} = MRS_{x,y} \text{ or } -\frac{dx}{dy} = \frac{MU_y}{MU_x} = MRS_{y,x}$$

The indifference curves are convex to the origin. This implies that the slope of an indifference curve decreases (in absolute terms) as we move along the curve from the left downwards to the right: the marginal rate of substitution of the commodities is diminishing. This axiom is derived from introspection, like the 'law of diminishing marginal utility' of the cardinalist school.

The axiom of decreasing marginal rate of substitution expresses the observed behavioural rule that the number of units of x the consumer is willing to sacrifice in order to obtain an additional unit of y increases as the quantity of y decreases. It becomes increasingly difficult to substitute x for y as we move along the indifference curve. In figure the fifth unit of y can be substituted for x by the consumer giving up $x_1 x_2$ of x; but to substitute the second unit of y and still retain the same satisfaction the consumer must give up a much greater quantity of x, namely $x_3 x_4$.

The Budget Constraint of the Consumer

The consumer has a given income which sets limits to his maximizing behaviour. Income acts as a constraint in the attempt for maximizing utility. The income constraint, in the case of two commodities, may be written:

$$Y = P_x q_x + P_y q_y$$

We may present the income constraint graphically by the budget line, whose equation is derived from expression 2.1, by solving for q_y:

$$q_y = 1/P_y \; Y - p_x/p_y \; q_x$$

Assigning successive values to q_x (given the income, Y and the commodity prices, P_x, P_y), we may find the corresponding values of q_y. Thus, if $q_x = 0$ (that is, if the consumer spends all his income on y) the consumer can buy Y/P_y units of y. Similarly, if $q_y = 0$ (that is, if the consumer spends all his income on x) the consumer can buy Y/P_x units of x. In figure these results are shown by points A and B. If we join these points.

This assumption implies that the commodities can substitute one another, but are not perfect substitutes. If the commodities are perfect substitutes the indifference curve becomes a straight line with negative slope. If the commodities are complements the indifference curve takes the shape of a right angle.

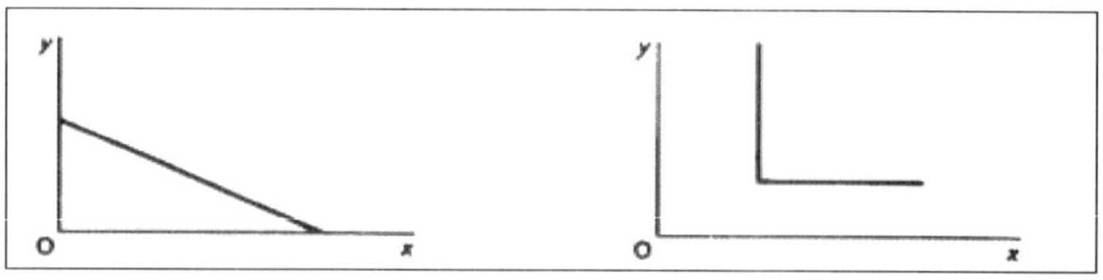

In the first case the equilibrium of the consumer may be a corner solution, that is, a situation in which the consumer spends all his income on one commodity. This is sometimes called 'monomania'. Situations of 'monomania' are not observed in the real world and are usually ruled out from the analysis of the behaviour of the consumer. In the case of complementary goods, indifference-curves analysis breaks down, since there is no possibility of substitution between the commodities.

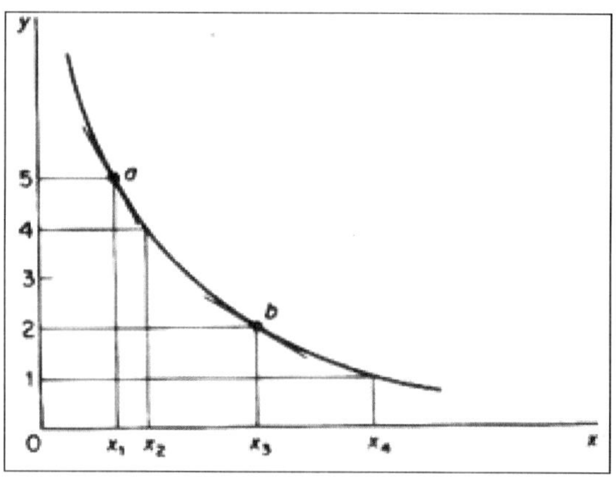

with a line we obtain the budget line, whose slope is the ratio of the prices of the two commodities. Geometrically the slope of the budget line is:

$$OA/OB = Y/P_y/Y/P_x = P_x/P_y$$

Mathematically the slope of the budget line is the derivative.

$$\frac{\partial q_y}{\partial q_x} = \frac{P_x}{P_y}$$

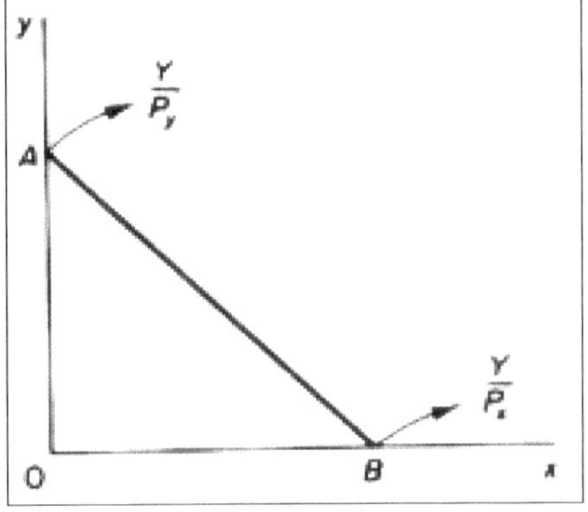

Derivation of the Equilibrium of the Consumer

The consumer is in equilibrium when he maximizes his utility, given his income and the market prices. Two conditions must be fulfilled for the consumer to be in equilibrium.

The first condition is that the marginal rate of substitution be equal to the ratio of commodity prices.

$$MRS_{x,y} = MU_x/MU_y = P_x/P_y$$

This is a necessary but not sufficient condition for equilibrium. The second condition is that the indifference curves be convex to the origin. This condition is fulfilled by the axiom of diminishing $MRS_{x,y}$, which states that the slope of the indifference curve decreases (in absolute terms) as we move along the curve from the left downwards to the right.

Graphical Presentation of the Equilibrium of the Consumer

Given the indifference map of the consumer and his budget line, the equilibrium is defined by the point of tangency of the budget line with the highest possible indifference curve (point e in figure).

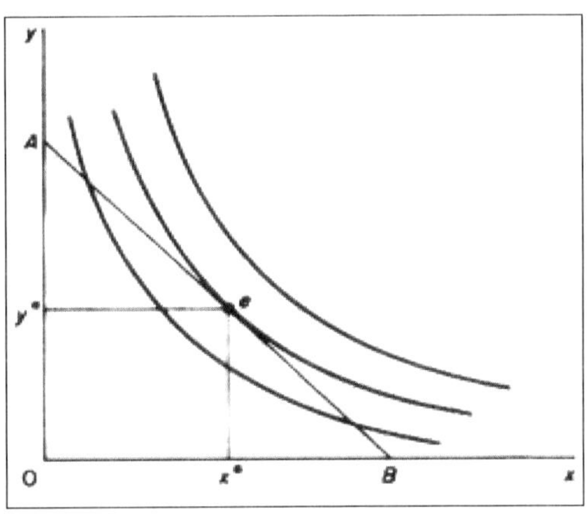

At the point of tangency the slopes of the budget line (P_x/P_y) and of the indifference curve ($MRS_{x,y} = MU_x/MU_y$) are equal:

$$MU_x = MU_y = P_{x/}P_y$$

Thus, the first-order condition is denoted graphically by the point of tangency of the two relevant curves. The second-order condition is implied by the convex shape of the indifference curves. The consumer maximizes his utility by buying x and y of the two commodities.

Mathematical Derivation of the Equilibrium

Given the market prices and his income, the consumer aims at the maximization of his utility. Assume that there are n commodities available to the consumer, with given market prices $P_1, P_2, .., P_n$. The consumer has a money income (V), which he spends on the available commodities.

Formally the problem may be stated as follows:

$$\text{Maximise} \qquad U = f(q_1, q_2 \ldots, q_n)$$

$$\text{subject to} \quad \sum_{i=1}^{n} q_i P_i = q_1 P_1 + q_2 p_2 + \cdots + q_n P_n = Y$$

We usc thc 'Lagrangian multipliers' method for the solution of this constrained maximum. The steps involved in this method may be outlined as follows:

- Rewrite the constraint in the form,

  $(q_1P_1 + q_2P_2 + \ldots + q_n P_n - Y) = 0$

- Multiply the constraint by a constant A, which is the Lagrangian multiplier,

  $\lambda (q_1P_1 + q_2P_2 + \ldots + q_n P_n - Y) = 0$

- Subtract the above constraint from the utility function and obtain the 'composite function'.

  $\phi = U - \lambda (q_1P_1 + q_2P_2 + \ldots + q_n P_n - Y) = 0$

It can be shown that maximization of the 'composite' function implies maximization of the utility function.

The first condition for the maximization of a function is that its partial derivatives be equal to zero. Differentiating ϕ with respect to $q_1, \ldots, q_n$ and λ, and equating to zero we find:

$$\frac{\partial \phi}{\partial q_1} = \frac{\partial U}{\partial q_1} - \lambda(P_1) = 0$$

$$\frac{\partial \phi}{\partial q_2} = \frac{\partial U}{\partial q_2} - \lambda(P_2) = 0$$

$$\vdots \quad \vdots \quad \vdots \qquad \vdots$$

$$\frac{\partial \phi}{\partial q_n} = \frac{\partial U}{\partial q_n} - \lambda(P_n) = 0$$

$$\frac{\partial \phi}{\partial q_n} = -(q_1P_1 + q_2P_2 + \cdots + q_nP_n - Y) = 0$$

From these equations we obtain,

$$\frac{\partial U}{\partial q_1} = \lambda P_1$$

$$\frac{\partial U}{\partial q_2} = \lambda P_2$$

$$\vdots \quad \vdots \quad \vdots$$

$$\frac{\partial U}{\partial q_n} = \lambda P_n$$

But,

$$\frac{\partial U}{\partial q_1} = MU_1, \ \frac{\partial U}{\partial q_1} = MU_2, \ldots, \frac{\partial U}{\partial q_n} = MU_n$$

Substituting and solving for λ we find,

$$\lambda = \frac{MU_1}{P_1} = \frac{MU_2}{P_2} = \cdots = \frac{MU_n}{P_n}$$

Alternatively, we may divide the preceding equation corresponding to commodity x, by the equation which refers to commodity y, and obtain,

$$\frac{MU_x}{MU_y} = \frac{P_x}{P_y} = MRS_{x,y}$$

We observe that the equilibrium conditions are identical in the cardinalist approach and in the indifference-curves approach. In both theories we have,

$$\frac{MU_1}{P_1} = \frac{MU_2}{P_2} = \cdots = \frac{MU_x}{P_x} = \frac{MU_y}{P_y} = \cdots = \frac{MU_n}{P_n}$$

Thus, although in the indifference-curves approach cardinality of utility is not required, the MRS requires knowledge of the ratio of the marginal utilities; given that the first- order condition for any two commodities may be written as,

$$MU_x/MU_y = P_x/P_y = MRS_{x,y}$$

Hence the concept of marginal utility is implicit in the definition of the slope of the indifference curves, although its measurement is not required by this approach. What is needed is a diminishing marginal rate of substitution, which of course does not require diminishing marginal utilities of the commodities involved in the utility function.

Derivation of the Demand Curve using the Indifference-curves Approach

Graphical Derivation of the Demand Curve

As the price of a commodity, for example of x, falls, the budget line of the consumer shifts to the right, from its initial position (AB) to a new position (AB) due to the increase in the purchasing power of the given money income of the consumer. With more purchasing power in his possession the consumer can buy more of x (and more of y). The new budget line is tangent to a higher indifference curve (e.g. curve II). The new equilibrium occurs to the right of the original equilibrium (for normal goods) showing that as price falls more of the commodity will be bought.

If we allow the price of x to fall continuously and we join the points of tangency of successive budget lines and higher indifference curves we form the so-called price-consumption line, from which we derive the demand curve for commodity x. At point e_1 the consumer buys quantity x_1 at price y_1. At point e_2 the price, y_2, is lower than y_1, and the quantity demanded has increased to x_2, and so on. We may plot the price- quantity pairs defined by the points of equilibrium (on the price-consumption line) to obtain a demand curve, as shown in figure.

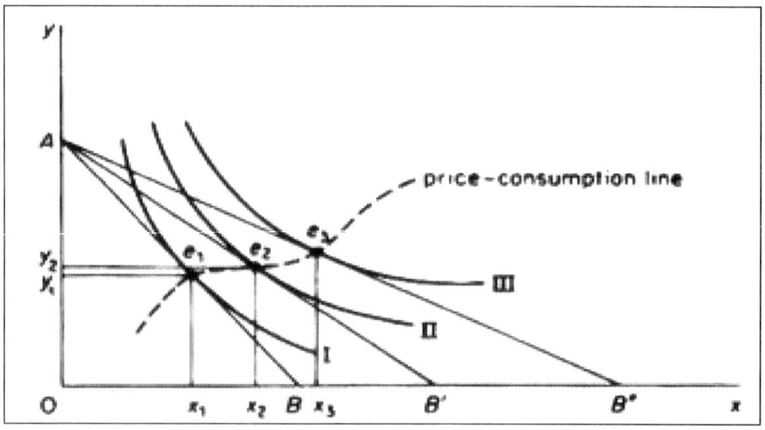

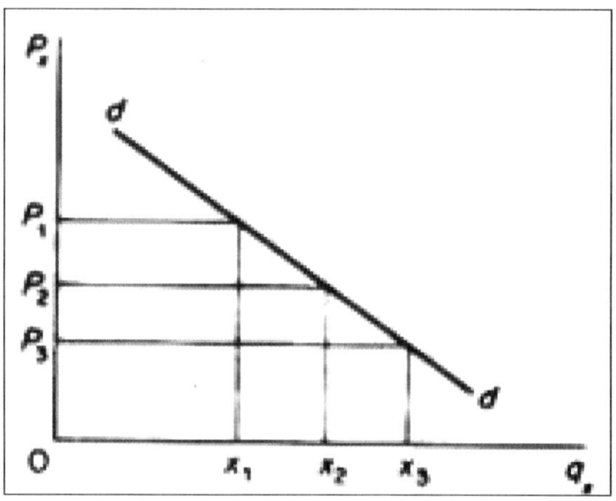

The demand curve for normal commodities will always have a negative slope, denoting the 'law of demand,' (the quantity bought increases as the price falls). In the indifference-curves approach the 'law of demand' is derived from what is known as Slutsky's theorem, which states that the substitution effect of a price change is always negative (relative to the price if the price increases, the quantity demanded decreases and vice versa). The formal proof of Slutsky's theorem involves sophisticated mathematics. However, we may show graphically the implications of this theorem.

We saw that a fall in the price of x from P_1 to P_2 resulted in an increase in the quantity demanded from x_1 to x_2. This is the total price effect which may be split into two separate effects, a substitution effect and an income effect. The substitution effect is the increase in the quantity bought as the price of the commodity falls, after 'adjusting' income so as to keep the real purchasing power of the consumer the same as before.

This adjustment in income is called compensating variation and is shown graphically by a parallel shift of the new budget line until it becomes tangent to the initial indifference curve. The purpose of the compensating variation is to allow the consumer to remain on the same level of satisfaction as before the price change. The compensated-budget line' will be tangent to the original indifference curve (I) at a point (e'_1) to the right of the original tangency (e_1), because this line is parallel to the new budget line which is less steep than the original one when the price of x falls. The movement from point e_1 to e'_1 shows the substitution effect of the price change the consumer buys more of x now that it is cheaper, substituting y for x.

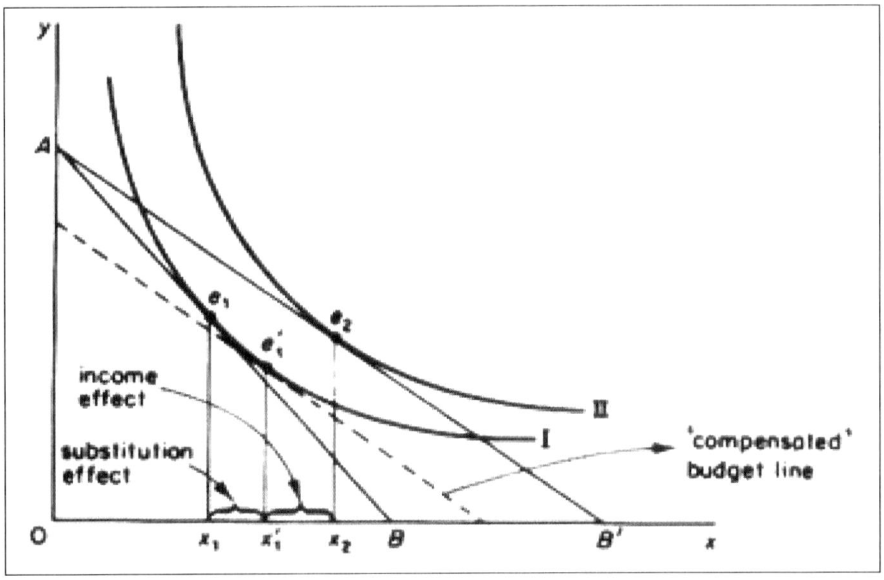

However, the compensating variation is a device which enables the isolation of the substitution effect, but does not show the new equilibrium of the consumer. This is defined by point e_2 on the higher indifference curve II. The consumer has in fact a higher purchasing power, and, if the commodity is normal, he will spend some of his increased real income on x, thus moving from x'_1 to x_2. This is the income effect of the price change.

The income effect of a price change is negative for normal goods and it reinforces the negative substitution effect. If, however, the commodity is inferior, the income effect of the price change will be positive: as the purchasing power increases, less of x will be bought. Still for most of the inferior goods the negative substitution effect will more than offset the positive income effect, so that the total price effect will be negative. Thus the negative substitution effect is in most cases adequate for establishing the law of demand.

(It is when the income effect is positive and very strong that the 'law of demand' does not hold. This is the case of the Giffen goods, which are inferior and their demand curve has a positive slope. Giffen goods are very rare in practice).

It should be noted that although Slutsky's theorem can be proved mathematically, its proof is based on the axiomatic assumption of the convexity of the indifference curves.

Mathematical derivation of the demand curve. The demand curve may be derived from the equilibrium condition,

$$\frac{MU_x}{P_x} = \frac{MU_y}{P_y} = \cdots = \frac{MU_n}{P}$$

and the budget constraint,

$$Y = \sum_{i=1}^{n} P_i q_i$$

For example, assume that there are only two commodities and that the total utility function is multiplicative of the form,

$$U = \frac{1}{4} q_x q_y$$

The marginal utilities of x and y are,

$$MU_x = \frac{\partial U}{\partial q_x} = \frac{1}{4} q_y$$

and

$$MU_y = \frac{\partial U}{\partial q_y} = \frac{1}{4} q_x$$

Substituting the marginal utilities in the equilibrium condition we obtain,

$$\frac{\left(\frac{1}{4}\right) q_y}{p_x} = \frac{\left(\frac{1}{4}\right) q_x}{p_y}$$

or

$$q_y P_y = q_x P_x$$

The equality of expenditures of the two commodities is not a general rule; the expenditures depend on the specific form of the utility function.

We may derive the demand for commodity x by substituting $q_y P_y$ in the budget constraint:

$$q_y P_y + q_x P_x = Y$$

$$2q_x P_x = Y$$

$$q_x = \frac{1}{2P_x} Y$$

Thus the demand for x is negatively related to its own price p_x and positively to income Y.

Similarly the demand for y is obtained by substituting $q_x p_x$ in the budget constraint.

$$q_y = 1/2p_y\ Y$$

In our particular example the demand curves are symmetric due to the particular multiplicative form of the consumer's utility function which we assumed.

Critique of the Indifference-curves Approach

The indifference-curves analysis has been a major advance in the field of consumer's demand. The assumptions of this theory are less stringent than for the cardinal utility approach. Only ordinality of preferences is required, and the assumption of constant utility of money has been dropped.

The methodology of indifference curves has provided a framework for the measurement of the 'consumer's surplus', which is important in welfare economics and in designing government policy.

Perhaps the most important theoretical contribution of this approach is the establishment of a better criterion for the classification of goods into substitutes and complements. Earlier theorists were using the total effect of a price change for this purpose, without compensating for the change in real income. The classification was based on the sign of the cross-elasticity of demand.

$$e_{yx} = \partial q_y / \partial p_x \cdot p_x / q_y$$

Where the total change in the quantity of y was considered as a result of a change in the price of x. A positive sign of the cross-elasticity implies that x and y are substitutes; a negative sign implies that the commodities are complements. This approach may easily lead to absurd classifications if the change in the price of x is substantial.

For example, if the price of beef is halved it is almost certain that both the consumption of beef and of pork will be increased, due to the increase of the real income of the consumer. This would imply a negative cross-elasticity for pork, and hence pork would be classified as a complementary commodity to beef.

Hicks' suggested measuring the cross-elasticity after compensating for changes in real income. Thus, according to Hicks, goods x and y are substitutes if, after compensating for the change in real income (arising from the change in the price of x) a decrease in the price of x leads to a decrease in the quantity demanded of y.

Although this criterion is theoretically more correct than the usual approach based on the total change in the quantity of y as a result of a change in the price of x, in practice its application is impossible because it requires knowledge of the individual preference functions, which cannot be statistically estimated. On the other hand, the usual approach of the total price effect is feasible be-cause it requires knowledge of the market demand functions which can be empirically estimated.

Although the advantages of the indifference-curves approach are important, the theory has indeed its own severe limitations. The main weakness of this theory is its axiomatic assumption of the existence and the convexity of the indifference curves. The theory does not establish either the existence or the shape of the indifference curves. It assumes that they exist and have the required shape of convexity.

Furthermore, it is questionable whether the consumer is able to order his preferences as precisely and rationally as the theory implies. Also the preferences of the consumers change continuously under the influence of various factors, so that any ordering of these preferences, even if possible, should be considered as valid for the very short run. Finally, this theory has retained most of the weaknesses of the cardinalist school with the strong assumption of rationality and the concept of the marginal utility implicit in the definition of the marginal rate of substitution.

Another defect of the indifference curves approach is that it does not analyze the effects of advertising, of past behaviour (habit persistence), of stocks, of the interdependence of the preferences of the consumers, which lead to behaviour that would be considered as irrational, and hence is ruled out by the theory. Furthermore speculative demand and random behaviour are ruled outlet these factors are very important for the pricing and output decisions of the firm.

Demand

Demand is an economic principle referring to a consumer's desire to purchase goods and services and willingness to pay a price for a specific good or service. Holding all other factors constant, an increase in the price of a good or service will decrease the quantity demanded, and vice versa. Market demand is the total quantity demanded across all consumers in a market for a given good. Aggregate demand is the total demand for all goods and services in an economy. Multiple stocking strategies are often required to handle demand.

Businesses often spend a considerable amount of money to determine the amount of demand the public has for their products and services. How much of their goods will they actually be able to sell at any given price? Incorrect estimations either result in money left on the table if demand is underestimated or losses if demand is overestimated. Demand is what helps fuel the economy, and without it, businesses would not produce anything.

Demand is closely related to supply. While consumers try to pay the lowest prices they can for goods and services, suppliers try to maximize profits. If suppliers charge too much, the quantity demanded drops and suppliers do not sell enough product to earn sufficient profits. If suppliers charge too little, the quantity demanded increases but lower prices may not cover suppliers' costs or allow for profits. Some factors affecting demand include the appeal of a good or service, the availability of competing goods, the availability of financing, and the perceived availability of a good or service.

Supply and Demand Curves

Supply and demand factors are unique for a given product or service. These factors are often summed up in demand and supply profiles plotted as slopes on a graph. On such a graph, the vertical axis denotes the price, while the horizontal axis denotes the quantity demanded or supplied. A demand curve slopes downward, from left to right. As prices increase, consumers demand less of a good or service. A supply curve slopes upward. As prices increase, suppliers provide more of a good or service.

Market Equilibrium

The point where supply and demand curves intersect represents the market clearing or market equilibrium price. An increase in demand shifts the demand curve to the right. The curves intersect at a higher price and consumers pay more for the product. Equilibrium prices typically remain in a state of flux for most goods and services because factors affecting supply and demand are always changing. Free, competitive markets tend to push prices toward market equilibrium.

Market Demand vs. Aggregate Demand

The market for each good in an economy faces a different set of circumstances, which vary in type and degree. In macroeconomics, we can also look at aggregate demand in an economy. Aggregate demand refers to the total demand by all consumers for all good and services in an economy across all the markets for individual goods. Because aggregate includes all goods in an economy, it is not sensitive to competition or substitution between different goods or changes in consumer preferences between various goods in the same way that demand in individual good markets can be.

Macroeconomic Policy and Demand

Fiscal and monetary authorities, such as the Federal Reserve, devote much of their macroeconomic policy making toward managing aggregate demand. If the Fed wants to reduce demand, it will raise prices by curtailing the growth of the supply of money and credit and increasing interest rates. Conversely, the Fed can lower interest rates and increase the supply of money in the system, therefore increasing demand. In this case, consumers and businesses have more money to spend. But in certain cases, even the Fed can't fuel demand. When unemployment is on the rise, people may still not be able to afford to spend or take on cheaper debt, even with low interest rates.

Elasticity of Demand

Elasticity of demand is an important variation on the concept of demand. Demand can be classified as elastic, inelastic or unitary.

An elastic demand is one in which the change in quantity demanded due to a change in price is large. An inelastic demand is one in which the change in quantity demanded due to a change in price is small.

The formula for computing elasticity of demand is:

$$\frac{(Q1-Q2)/(Q1+Q2)}{(P1-P2)/(P1+P2)}$$

If the formula creates a number greater than 1, the demand is elastic. In other words, quantity changes faster than price. If the number is less than 1, demand is inelastic. In other words, quantity changes slower than price. If the number is equal to 1, elasticity of demand is unitary. In other words, quantity changes at the same rate as price.

Elastic Demand

Elasticity of demand is illustrated in Figure. Note that a change in price results in a large change in quantity demanded. An example of products with an elastic demand is consumer durables. These are items that are purchased infrequently, like a washing machine or an automobile, and can be postponed if price rises. For example, automobile rebates have been very successful in increasing automobile sales by reducing price.

Close substitutes for a product affect the elasticity of demand. It another product can easily be substituted for your product, consumers will quickly switch to the other product if the price of your product rises or the price of the other product declines. For example, beef, pork and poultry are all meat products. The declining price of poultry in recent years has caused the consumption of poultry to increase, at the expense of beef and pork. So products with close substitutes tend to have elastic demand.

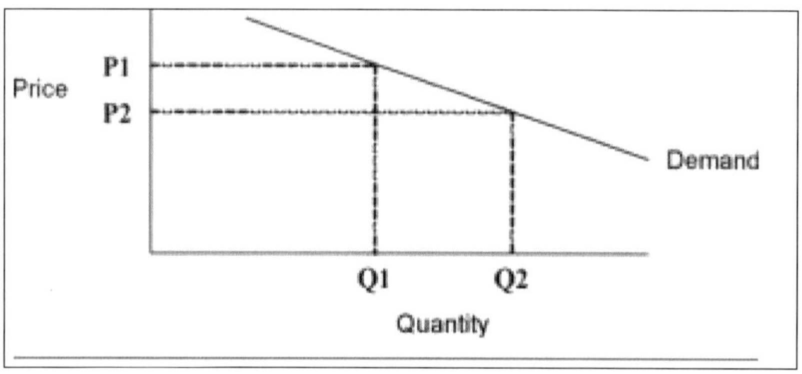

Elastic demand.

An example of computing elasticity of demand using the formula above is shown below. When the price decreases from $10 per unit to $8 per unit, the quantity sold increases from 30 units to 50 units. The elasticity coefficient is 2.25.

Elasticity example,

$P1 = \$10$

$P2 = \$8$

$Q1 = \$30$

$Q2 = \$50$

$$\frac{(Q1-Q2)/(Q1+Q2)}{(P1-P2)/(P1+P2)} = \frac{(50-30)/(50+30)}{(\$10-\$8)/(\$10+\$8)} = \frac{20/80}{\$2/\$18}$$

$$\frac{1/4}{1/9} = \frac{1\times 9}{4\times 1} = \frac{9}{4} = 2.25$$

Inelastic Demand

Inelastic demand is shown in figure. Note that a change in price results in only a small change in quantity demanded. In other words, the quantity demanded is not very responsive to changes in price. Examples of this are necessities like food and fuel. Consumers will not reduce their food purchases if food prices rise, although there may be shifts in the types of food they purchase. Also, consumers will not greatly change their driving behavior if gasoline prices rise.

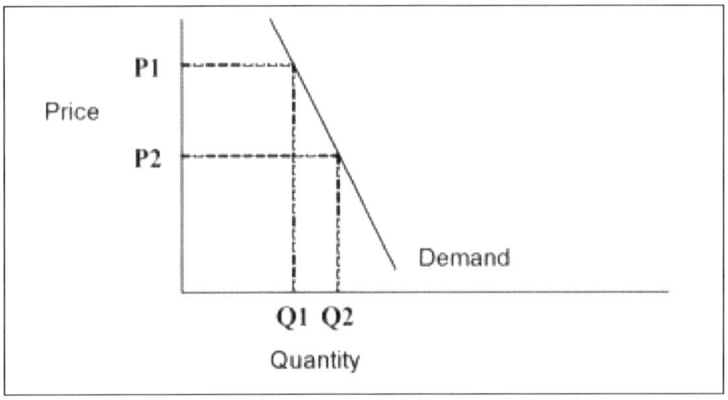

Inelastic demand.

An example of computing inelasticity of demand using the formula above is shown below. When the price decreases from \$12 to \$6 (50%), the quantity of demand increases from 40 to only 50 (25%). The elasticity coefficient is .33.

Inelasticity example,

$P1 = \$12$

$P2 = \$6$

$Q1 = \$40$

$Q2 = \$50$

$$\frac{(Q1-Q2)/(Q1+Q2)}{(P1-P2)/(P1+P2)} = \frac{(50-40)/(50+40)}{(\$12-\$6)/(\$12+\$6)} = \frac{10/90}{\$6/\$18}$$

$$\frac{1/9}{1/3} = \frac{1\times 3}{9\times 1} = \frac{3}{9} = .33$$

This does not mean that the demand for an individual producer is inelastic. For example, a rise in the price of gasoline at all stations may not reduce gasoline sales significantly. However, a rise of an individual station's price will significantly affect that station's sales.

Unitary Elasticity

If the elasticity coefficient is equal to one, demand is unitarily elastic as shown in Figure. For example, a 10% quantity change divided by 10% price change is one. This means that a one percent change in quantity occurs for every one percent change in price.

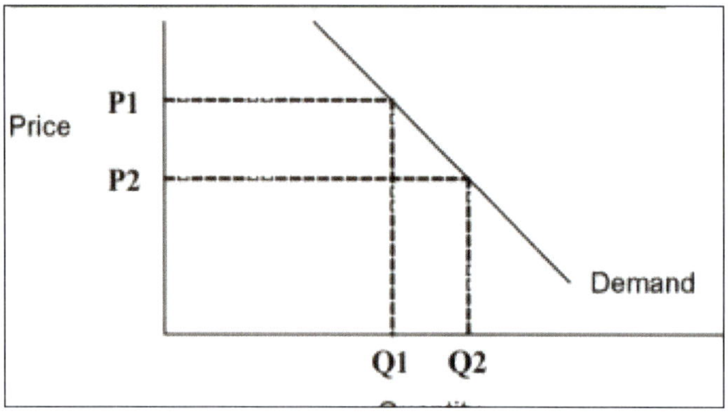

Unitary elasticity.

Demand Curve

The Demand Curve is a line that shows how many units of a good or service will be purchased at each possible price. The price is plotted on the vertical (Y) axis while the quantity is plotted on the horizontal (X) axis.

Demand curves are used to determine the relationship between price and quantity and follows the law of demand, which states that the quantity demanded will decrease as the price increases. In addition, demand curves are commonly combined with supply curves to determine the equilibrium price and equilibrium quantity of the market.

Drawing a Demand Curve

The demand curve is based on the demand schedule. The demand schedule shows exactly how many units of a good or service will be purchased at different price points.

For example, below is the demand schedule for high-quality organic bread:

Price	Quantity Demanded
$ 10.00	1000
$ 9.00	1200
$ 8.00	1400
$ 7.00	1700
$ 6.00	2000
$ 5.00	2400
$ 4.00	3000
$ 3.00	3700
$ 2.00	4500

It is important to note that as the price decreases, the quantity demanded increases. The relationship follows the law of demand. Intuitively, if the price for a good or service is lower, there would be a higher demand for it.

From the demand schedule above, the graph can be created:

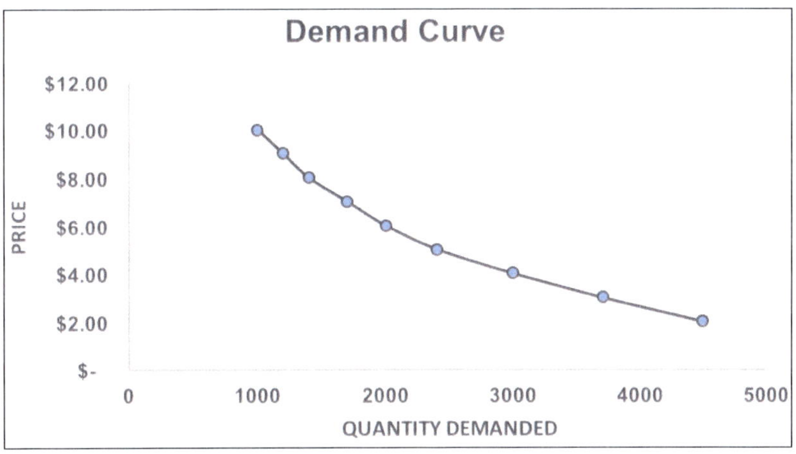

Through the demand curve, the relationship between price and quantity demanded is clearly illustrated. As the price for notebooks decreases, the demand for notebooks increases.

Shifts in Demand Curve

Shifts in the demand curve are strictly affected by consumer interest. Several factors can lead to a shift in the curve, for example:

Changes in income levels

If the good is a normal good, higher income levels would lead to an outward shift of the demand curve while lower income levels will lead to an inward shift. When income is increased, demand for normal goods or services will increase.

Changes in the Market's Size

A growing market results in an outward shift of the demand curve while a shrinking market results in an inward shift. A larger market size results from more consumers. Therefore, the demand (due to more consumers) will increase.

Changes in the Price of Related Goods and Services

When the price of complementary good decreases, the demand curve will shift outwards. Alternatively, if the price of complementary good increases, the curve will shift inwards. The opposite is true for substitute goods. For example, if the price for peanut butter goes down significantly, the demand for its complementary good – jelly – increases.

Example of a Shift in the Demand Curve

Recall the demand schedule for high-quality organic bread:

Price	Quantity Demanded
$ 10.00	1000
$ 9.00	1200
$ 8.00	1400
$ 7.00	1700
$ 6.00	2000
$ 5.00	2400
$ 4.00	3000
$ 3.00	3700
$ 2.00	4500

Assume that the price of a complementary good – peanut butter – decreases. How would this affect the demand curve for high-quality organic bread?

Since peanut butter is a complementary good to high-quality organic bread, a decrease in the price of peanut butter would increase the quantity demanded of high-quality organic bread. When consumers buy peanut butter, organic bread is also bought (hence, complementary). If the price of peanut butter decreases, more consumers would purchase peanut butter. Therefore, consumers would also purchase more high-quality organic bread as it is a complement to peanut butter.

Price	Quantity Demanded	New Quantity Demanded
$ 10.00	1000	1500
$ 9.00	1200	1700
$ 8.00	1400	1900

$ 7.00	1700	2300
$ 6.00	2000	2700
$ 5.00	2400	3300
$ 4.00	3000	4000
$ 3.00	3700	4800
$ 2.00	4500	5900

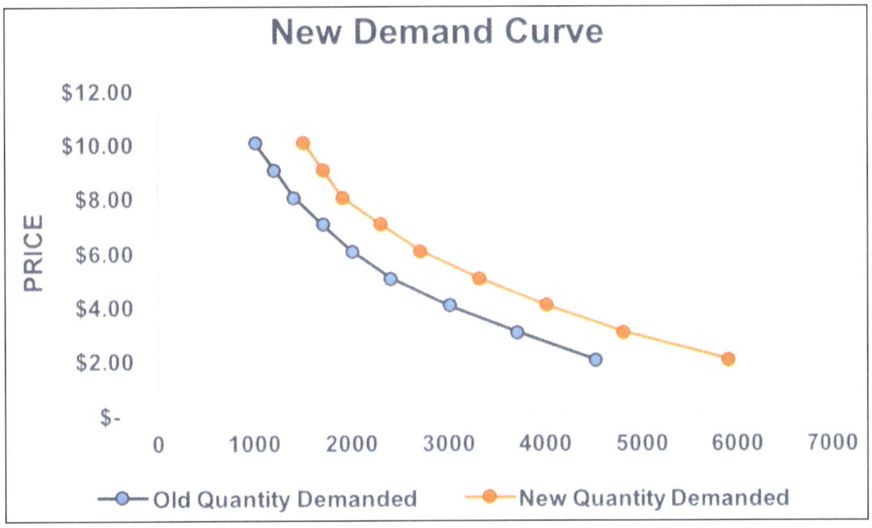

We can see from the chart above that a decrease in the price of a complementary good would increase the quantity demanded of high-quality organic bread.

Movements along the Demand Curve

Changes in price cause movements along the demand curve. Following the original demand schedule for high-quality organic bread, assume the price is set at P = $6. At this price, the quantity demanded would be 2000.

Price	Quantity Demanded
$ 10.00	1000
$ 9.00	1200
$ 8.00	1400
$ 7.00	1700
$ 6.00	2000
$ 5.00	2400
$ 4.00	3000
$ 3.00	3700
$ 2.00	4500

If the price were to change from P = $6 to P = $4, it would cause a movement along the demand curve as the new quantity demanded would be 3000.

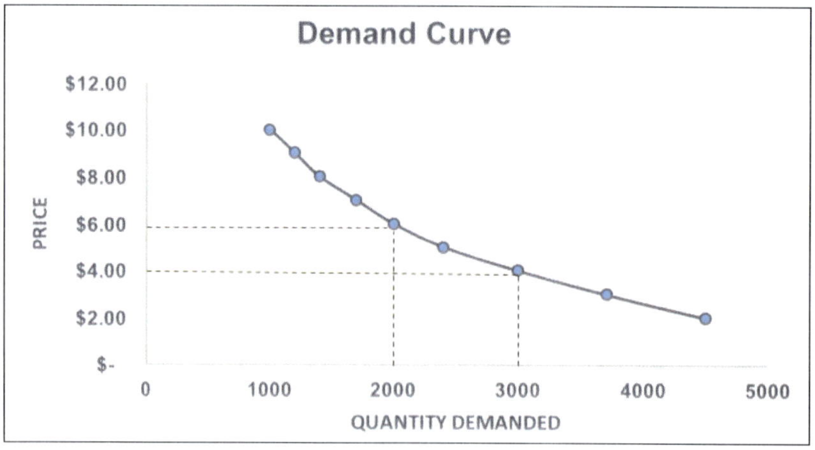

Supply

Supply is a fundamental economic concept that describes the total amount of a specific good or service that is available to consumers. Supply can relate to the amount available at a specific price or the amount available across a range of prices if displayed on a graph. This relates closely to the demand for a good or service at a specific price; all else being equal, the supply provided by producers will rise if the price rises because all firms look to maximize profits.

Supply and demand trends form the basis of the modern economy. Each specific good or service will have its own supply and demand patterns based on price, utility and personal preference. If people demand a good and are willing to pay more for it, producers will add to the supply. As the supply increases, the price will fall given the same level of demand. Ideally, markets will reach a point of equilibrium where the supply equals the demand (no excess supply and no shortages) for a given price point; at this point, consumer utility and producer profits are maximized.

The concept of supply in economics is complex with many mathematical formulas, practical applications and contributing factors. While supply can refer to anything in demand that is sold in a competitive marketplace, supply is most used to refer to goods, services, or labor. One of the most important factors that affects supply is the good's price. Generally, if a good's price increases so will the supply. The price of related goods and the price of inputs (energy, raw materials, labor) also affect supply as they contribute to increasing the overall price of the good sold.

The conditions of the production of the item in supply is also significant; for example, when a technological advancement increases the quality of a good being supplied, or if there is a disruptive innovation, such as when a technological advancement renders a good obsolete or less in demand. Government regulations can also affect supply, such as environmental laws, as well as the number of suppliers (which increases competition) and market expectations. An example of this is when environmental laws regarding the extraction of oil affect the supply of such oil.

Supply is represented in microeconomics by a number of mathematical formulas. The supply function and equation expresses the relationship between supply and the affecting factors, such as those mentioned above or even inflation rates and other market influences. A supply curve always describes the relationship between the price of the good and the quantity supplied. A wealth of information can be gleaned from a supply curve, such as movements (caused by a change in price), shifts (caused by a change that is not related to the price of the good) and price elasticity.

Elasticity of Supply

The price elasticity of supply is the measure of the responsiveness in quantity supplied to a change in price for a specific good.

In economics, elasticity is a summary measure of how the supply or demand of a particular good is influenced by changes in price. Elasticity is defined as a proportionate change in one variable over the proportionate change in another variable:

$$Elasticity = \frac{\%\,Change\,in\,quantity}{\%\,Change\,in\,price}$$

The price elasticity of supply (PES) is the measure of the responsiveness in quantity supplied (QS) to a change in price for a specific good (% Change QS/% Change in Price). There are numerous factors that directly impact the elasticity of supply for a good including stock, time period, availability of substitutes, and spare capacity. The state of these factors for a particular good will determine if the price elasticity of supply is elastic or inelastic in regards to a change in price.

The price elasticity of supply has a range of values:

- PES > 1: Supply is elastic.
- PES < 1: Supply is inelastic.
- PES = 0: The supply curve is vertical; there is no response of demand to prices. Supply is "perfectly inelastic".
- PES = ∞∞ (i.e., infinity): The supply curve is horizontal; there is extreme change in demand in response to very small change in prices. Supply is "perfectly elastic".

Inelastic goods are often described as necessities. A shift in price does not drastically impact consumer demand or the overall supply of the good because it is not something people are able or willing to go without. Examples of inelastic goods would be water, gasoline, housing, and food.

Elastic goods are usually viewed as luxury items. An increase in price for an elastic good has a noticeable impact on consumption. The good is viewed as something that individuals are willing to sacrifice in order to save money. An example of an elastic good is movie tickets, which are viewed as entertainment and not a necessity.

The price elasticity of supply is determined by:

- Number of producers: Ease of entry into the market.
- Spare capacity: It is easy to increase production if there is a shift in demand.

- Ease of switching: If production of goods can be varied, supply is more elastic.
- Ease of storage: When goods can be stored easily, the elastic response increases demand.
- Length of production period: Quick production responds to a price increase easier.
- Time period of training: When a firm invests in capital the supply is more elastic in its response to price increases.
- Factor mobility: When moving resources into the industry is easier, the supply curve in more elastic.
- Reaction of costs: If costs rise slowly it will stimulate an increase in quantity supplied. If cost rise rapidly the stimulus to production will be choked off quickly.

The result of calculating the elasticity of the supply and demand of a product according to price changes illustrates consumer preferences and needs. The elasticity of a good will be labelled as perfectly elastic, relatively elastic, unit elastic, relatively inelastic, or perfectly inelastic.

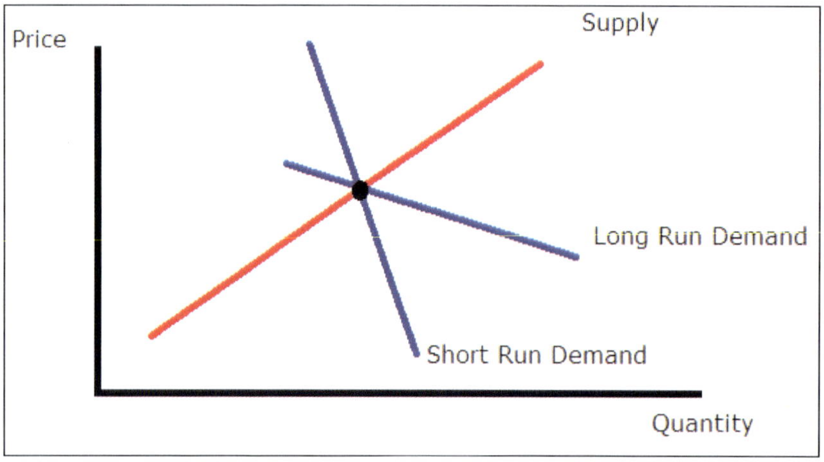

Price elasticity over time: This graph illustrates how the supply and demand of a product are measured over time to show the price elasticity.

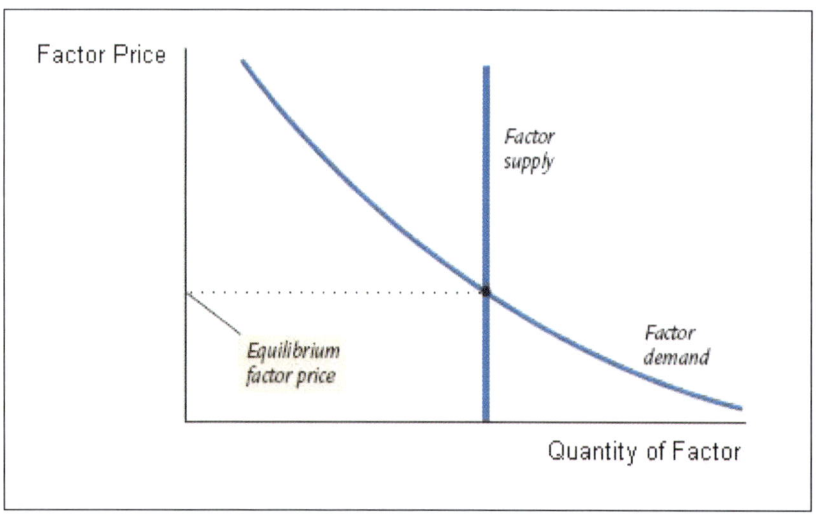

Perfectly inelastic supply: A graphical representation of perfectly inelastic supply.

Measuring the Price Elasticity of Supply

The price elasticity of supply is the measure of the responsiveness of the quantity supplied of a particular good to a change in price.

The price elasticity of supply (PES) is the measure of the responsiveness of the quantity supplied of a particular good to a change in price (PES = % Change in QS/% Change in Price). The intent of determining the price elasticity of supply is to show how a change in price impacts the amount of a good that is supplied to consumers. The price elasticity of supply is directly related to consumer demand.

Elasticity

The elasticity of a good provides a measure of how sensitive one variable is to changes in another variable. In this case, the price elasticity of supply determines how sensitive the quantity supplied is to the price of the good.

Calculating the PES

When calculating the price elasticity of supply, economists determine whether the quantity supplied of a good is elastic or inelastic. The percentage of change in supply is divided by the percentage of change in price. The results are analyzed using the following range of values:

- PES > 1: Supply is elastic.
- PES < 1: Supply is inelastic.
- PES = 0: Supply is perfectly inelastic. There is no change in quantity if prices change.
- PES = infinity: Supply is perfectly elastic. An decrease in prices will lead to zero units produced.

Factors that Influence the PES

There are numerous factors that impact the price elasticity of supply including the number of producers, spare capacity, ease of switching, ease of storage, length of production period, time period of training, factor mobility, and how costs react.

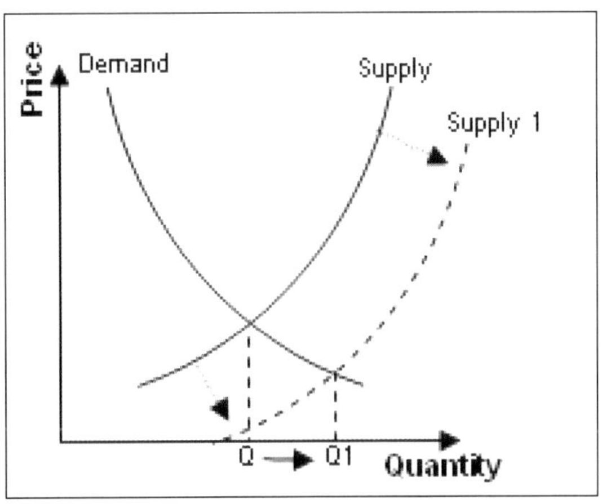

Supply and Demand Curves: A demand curve is used to graph the impact that a change in price has on the supply and demand of a good.

The price elasticity of supply is calculated and can be graphed on a demand curve to illustrate the relationship between the supply and price of the good.

Applications of Elasticities

In economics, elasticity refers to how the supply and demand of a product changes in relation to a change in the price.

In economics, elasticity refers to the responsiveness of the demand or supply of a product when the price changes.

The technical definition of elasticity is the proportionate change in one variable over the proportionate change in another variable. For example, to determine how a change in the supply or demand of a product is impacted by a change in the price, the following equation is used: Elasticity = % change in supply or demand/% change in price.

The price is a variable that can directly impact the supply and demand of a product. If a change in the price of a product significantly influences the supply and demand, it is considered "elastic". Likewise, if a change in product price does not significantly change the supply and demand, it is considered "inelastic".

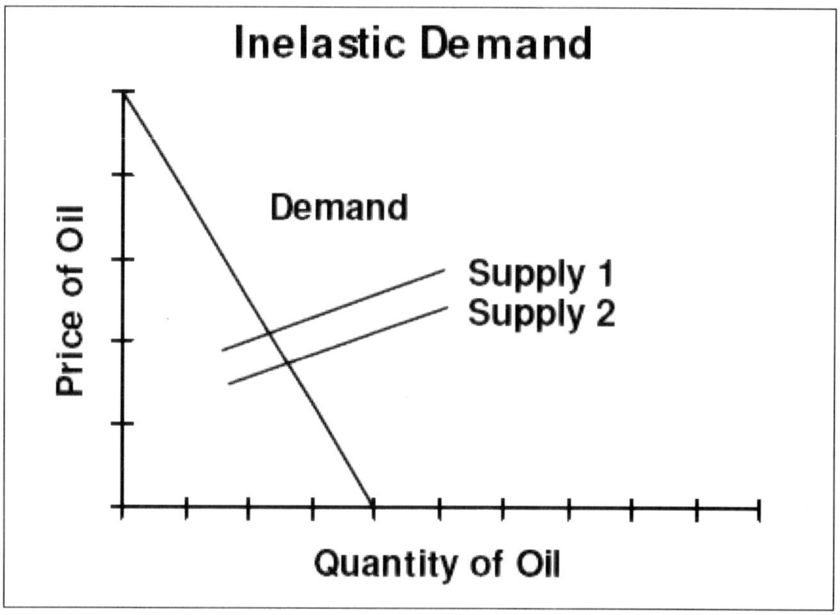

Inelastic Demand: For inelastic demand, when there is an outward shift in supply and prices fall, there is no substantial change in the quantity demanded.

For elastic demand, when the price of a product increases the demand goes down. When the price decreases the demand goes up. Elastic products are usually luxury items that individuals feel they can do without. An example would be forms of entertainment such as going to the movies or attending a sports event. A change in prices can have a significant impact on consumer trends as well as economic profits. For companies and businesses, an increase in demand will increase profit and revenue, while a decrease in demand will result in lower profit and revenue.

For inelastic demand, the overall supply and demand of a product is not substantially impacted by an increase in price. Products that are usually inelastic consist of necessities like food, water, housing, and gasoline. Whether or not a product is elastic or inelastic is directly related to consumer needs and preferences. If demand is perfectly inelastic, then the same amount of the product will be purchased regardless of the price.

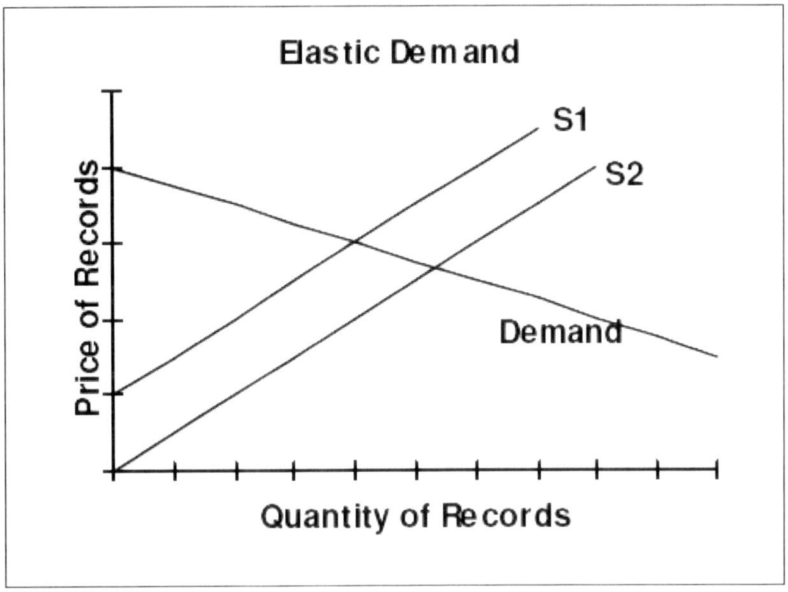

Elastic Demand: For elastic demand, when there is an outward shift in supply, prices fall which causes a large increase in quantity demanded.

Economists study elasticity and use demand curves in order to diagram and study consumer trends and preferences. An elastic demand curve shows that an increase in the supply or demand of a product is significantly impacted by a change in the price. An inelastic demand curve shows that an increase in the price of a product does not substantially change the supply or demand of the product.

References

- General-equilibrium-in-economics-meaning-assumptions-working-and-limitations- 28937: yourarticlelibrary.com, Retrieved 08 February, 2019
- Consumers-equilibrium-with-diagram, consumers-equilibrium- 25160: economicsdiscussion.net, Retrieved 05 May, 2019
- Theory-of-consumer-behaviour-indifference-curves, theory-of-demand- 4848: economicsdiscussion.net, Retrieved 25 August, 2019
- Demand-curve, resources/knowledge/economics: corporatefinanceinstitute.com, Retrieved 28 June, 2019
- Price-elasticity-of-supply, boundless-economics: courses.lumenlearning.com, Retrieved 19 April, 2019

4

Income and Employment

Income refers to the revenue earned from selling of the goods and services. Employment is defined as the relationship between employer and employee that are involved in the production, distribution and supply of goods and services. The topics elaborated in this chapter will help in gaining a better perspective about the aspects related to income and employment.

Income

Income is money (or some equivalent value) that an individual or business receives in exchange for providing a good or service or through investing capital. Income is used to fund day-to-day expenditures. Investments, pensions, and Social Security are primary sources of income for retirees. For individuals, income is most often received in the form of wages or salary.

In businesses, income can refer to a company's remaining revenues after paying all expenses and taxes. In this case, income is referred to as "earnings". Most forms of income are subject to taxation.

Understanding Income

Individuals receive income through earning wages by working and making investments into financial assets such as stocks, bonds, and real estate. For instance, an investor's stock holding may pay income in the form of an annual 5% dividend.

In most countries, earned income is taxed by the government before it is received. The revenue generated by income taxes finances government actions and programs as determined by federal and state budgets. The Internal Revenue Service (IRS) calls income from sources other than a job, such as investment income, "unearned income".

Taxable Income

Income from wages, salaries, interest, dividends, business income, capital gains, and pensions received during a given tax year are considered taxable income in the United States. Other taxable income includes annuity payments, rental income, farming, and fishing income, unemployment compensation, retirement plan distributions, and stock options. Lesser-known taxable income includes gambling income, bartending income, and jury duty pay.

The types of income listed above would be classified as ordinary income, which is composed mainly of wages, salaries, commissions, and interest income from bonds, and it is taxable using ordinary income rates. This type of income differs from capital gains or dividend income in that it can only be offset with standard tax deductions, while capital gains can only be offset with capital losses.

Tax-exempt and Tax-reduced Income

Types of income that may be tax-exempt include interest income from U.S. Treasury securities (which is exempt at the state and local levels), interest from municipal bonds (which is potentially exempt at the federal, state and local levels) and capital gains that are offset by capital losses.

Types of income taxed at lower rates include qualified dividends and long-term capital gains. Social Security income is sometimes taxable, depending on how much other income the taxpayer receives during the year.

Examples of Income

For private individuals, ordinary income is usually only made up of the salaries and wages they earn from their employers pretax. If, for example, a person works a customer service job at Target and earns $3,000 per month, his annual ordinary income would be $36,000, derived as $3,000 x 12. If he has no other income sources, this is the amount that would be taxed on his year-end tax return as gross income.

Additionally, if the same person also owned a rental property and earned $1,000 a month in rental income, his ordinary income would increase to $48,000 per year. If the same person earned $1,500 in qualified municipal bond interest payments, that portion of income would be tax-exempt.

For businesses, ordinary income is the pretax profit earned from selling its product or service. For example, the retailer, Target, had $69.5 million worth of total sales or revenue in the year ended in January 2017. The company had $48.9 million in costs of goods sold (COGS) and $15.6 million in total operating expenses. Target's ordinary income was $5 million, derived as follows:

- $69,500,000 - $48,900,000 - $15,600,000

This is the amount of income that would be taxed for the year. However, businesses are required to pay taxes quarterly.

Disposable and Discretionary Income

Disposable income is money that's remaining after paying taxes. Individuals spend disposable income on necessities, such as housing, food, and transportation. Discretionary income is the money that remains after paying all necessary expenses. People spend discretionary income on items like vacations, restaurant meals, cable television, and movies.

In a recession, individuals tend to be more prudent with their discretionary income. For example, a family may use their discretionary income to make extra payments on their mortgage or save it for an unexpected expense.

Disposable income is typically higher than discretionary income within the same household because expenses of necessary items are not removed from the disposable income. Both measures can be used to project the amount of consumer spending. However, either measure must also take into account the willingness of people to make purchases.

Economic Income

Economic income is the way for companies to account for changes in the value of a given asset in the market. It generally recognizes unrealized gains, in addition to recognizing realized gains.

A change in market value rather than cash received is the perfect example of an economic income. Economic income or loss recognizes all gains and losses whether realized or unrealized. This differs from accounting income which only recognizes realized gains: gains resulting from an actual business transaction. This defines the difference of accounting earnings vs economic earnings.

For income to be realized it must result from actual business transactions. A change in market value rather than cash received is economic income and not accounting income. When a gain or loss is unrealized it may or may not be accounted for in general. This depends on the placement of the gaining or losing asset in the balance sheet. Despite that this gain or loss may be accounted for, the fact that it is unrealized makes it an economic income or loss. The term economic income was born out of the need for financial accounting income vs economic income comparisons.

Economic Income and Time

Economic income assists companies in knowing the value of an asset if it was sold at a given time. Key to the economic income discussion is the current value of the asset. By then selecting a time period, research can estimate what price will be paid for the asset. This, as compared to estimations of market performance for the time period, can allow for projections of the market value of the asset in the future.

"If the current price of the land is $100,000 and we expect the market to increase by 10% next year, then the value of the land will be somewhere around $110,000 by the end of next year ($100k + $10k = $110k)".

These measurements allow projections which influence decisions of financing, cash flow, insurance, timing of the asset sale, and other important decisions. Including costs in the decision can expand further to allow for net accounting income vs net economic income comparisons.

Economic Income Example

A perfect example of economic income occurs every day. Realco is a company which sells land. Realco purchased, last year, a piece of land for $100,000. The following year Realco notices the land is selling for $110,000. What is Realco's economic income?

Realco has not sold the land. As a result it experienced an economic income of $10,000. This is proven by the fact that Realco did not have a transaction in which cash increased by $10,000. The economic income concept revolves around the recognition of income in spite of the fact that no sale has taken place.

If Realco sold the property, then it would have experienced an accounting income. Their land was sold for $10,000 more than initially worth. Thus, Realco has a realized gain of $10,000. The accounting earnings vs economic earnings calculation is the same: The difference is whether Realco gains $10,000 from the sale or not.

$110,000 (revenue from sale) – $100,000 (cost of land) = $10,000 (profit from sale)

```
economic income accounting income

$10,000                $10,000
```

In addition to monitoring market value changes, economic income provides a place holder for an asset in company financials. This allows for managerial accounting income vs economic income decisions. Without economic income, you would only account for an asset when sold or purchased. Economic income allows the monitoring of an asset between the transaction. At the time of accrual accounting income vs economic income evaluations are not the most important matter. They do form an important issue, however, with the natural business cycle changes that result from time.

National income means the value of goods and services produced by a country during a financial year. Thus, it is the net result of all economic activities of any country during a period of one year and is valued in terms of money. National income is an uncertain term and is often used interchangeably with the national dividend, national output, and national expenditure. We can understand this concept by understanding the national income definition.

The National Income is the total amount of income accruing to a country from economic activities in a years time. It includes payments made to all resources either in the form of wages, interest, rent, and profits.

The progress of a country can be determined by the growth of the national income of the country

There are two National Income Definition:

- Traditional Definition.
- Modern Definition.

Traditional

According to Marshall: "The labor and capital of a country acting on its natural resources produce annually a certain net aggregate of commodities, material and immaterial including services of all kinds. This is the true net annual income or revenue of the country or national dividend».

The definition as laid down by Marshall is being criticized on the following grounds.

Due to the varied category of goods and services, a correct estimation is very difficult.

There is a chance of double counting, hence National Income cannot be estimated correctly.

For example, a product runs in the supply from the producer to distributor to wholesaler to retailer and then to the ultimate consumer. If on every movement commodity is taken into consideration then the value of National Income increases.

Also, one other reason is that there are products which are produced but not marketed.

For example, In an agriculture-oriented country there are commodities which though produced but are kept for self-consumption or exchanged with other commodities. Thus there can be an underestimation of National Income.

Simon Kuznets defines national income as "the net output of commodities and services flowing during the year from the country's productive system in the hands of the ultimate consumers".

- GDP.
- GNP.

Gross Domestic Product

The total value of goods produced and services rendered within a country during a year is its Gross Domestic Product.

Further, GDP is calculated at market price and is defined as GDP at market prices. Different constituents of GDP are:

- Wages and salaries.
- Rent.
- Interest.
- Undistributed profits.
- Mixed-income.
- Direct taxes.
- Dividend.
- Depreciation.

Gross National Product

For calculation of GNP, we need to collect and assess the data from all productive activities, such as agricultural produce, wood, minerals, commodities, the contributions to production by transport, communications, insurance companies, professions such (as lawyers, doctors, teachers, etc). at market prices.

It also includes net income arising in a country from abroad. Four main constituents of GNP are:

- Consumer goods and services.
- Gross private domestic income.
- Goods produced or services rendered.
- Income arising from abroad.

GDP and GNP on the Basis of Market Price and Factor Cost

Market Price

The Actual transacted price including indirect taxes such as GST, Customs duty etc. Such taxes tend to raise the prices of goods and services in the economy.

Factor Cost

It Includes the cost of factors of production e.g. interest on capital, wages to labor, rent for land profit to the stakeholders. Thus services provided by service providers and goods sold by the producer is equal to revenue price.

Alternatively,

Revenue Price (or Factor Cost) = Market Price (net of) Net Indirect Taxes

Net Indirect Taxes = Indirect Taxes Net of Subsidies received,

Hence,

Factor Cost shall be equal to

(Market Price) LESS (Indirect Taxes ADD Subsidies).

Net Domestic Product

The net output of the country's economy during a year is its NDP. During the year a country's capital assets are subject to wear and tear due to its use or can become obsolete.

Hence, we deduct a percentage of such investment from the GDP to arrive at NDP.

So NDP=GDP at Factor Cost LESS Depreciation

The Accumulation of all factors of income earned by residents of a country and includes income earned from the county as well as from abroad.

Thus, National Income at Factor Cost shall be equal to NNP at Market Price LESS (Indirect Taxes ADD Subsidies).

Gross National Income

Gross national income is the value of all income (also called output or national output) produced by a country's residents (both citizens and foreign residents) within its geographical borders, plus net receipts of income (wages, salary, and property income) from abroad. In short, GNI is a measure of all money, goods, services, and investments that come into or stay in the country.

One caveat when these goods and services are tallied up is that only "final goods" are counted. This avoids double counting items. For instance, the value of a watermelon from the farm may be $1, then $5 at the grocery store. In this example, the watermelon's "final good" value is $5, and so the total value of the good would be counted in the country's income as $5.

How to Calculate Gross National Income

To calculate GNI for a country, add up the following:

- Consumption (C): Consumption (or personal consumption expenditure) is the value of all goods and services acquired and consumed by the country's households.
- Investment (I): This is any domestic capital spending by a country's citizen-run businesses.
- Government spending (G): This is all consumption and investments made by the government. Government spending does not include any transfer payments (such as social security paid to citizens), since they are not actually government spending, but a transfer of money.
- Net exports (X): This is the country's exports MINUS the country's imports. In order for this number to increase NNI, a country needs to export more than it imports.
- Net foreign factor income (NFFI): This is income that the country's citizens earn abroad MINUS the income that foreign residents earn in the country and send out of the country.

Formula for Gross National Income (GNI)

The formula for calculating GNI is often represented as: GNI = C + I + G + X + NFFI.

Calculate a Country's Gross National Income

Governments need to be well-informed about their own economies in order to implement effective fiscal policies. By tracking and analyzing countries' incomes, economists are able to recommend fiscal policies that will actually be effective in creating economic growth—fiscal policies like government stimulus packages, public works projects, and tax hikes or cuts.

Two specific ways to look at GNI data are GNI per country and GNI per capita.

What Is GNI per Country

Calculating GNI per country can provide reliable ways to look at a country's income in two ways:

- Entire income all at once: GNI is unique from other income calculations (like GDP) because it factors in net income from abroad, which is often a large part of a country's total income. Thus, it gives a more accurate picture of a country's income for countries that receive a lot of income from abroad.

- Income from year to year: Calculating GNI per country and looking at the growth or decline over a range of years measures an economy's ability to continue minimum production standards.

The World Bank, a prominent financial institution that collects economic data, collects data for GNI per country for countries all over the world, and it converts all data to the U.S. dollar for easy comparison. Rather than doing this conversion using the current exchange rate, the World Bank uses "purchasing power parity" (or PPP), which converts goods and services by comparing identical goods in each country and using that to determine what that good would cost in the United States. This is easy for goods like McDonald's hamburgers, but it can pose a problem for items not made or sold in the United States, such as yak carts.

However, calculating GNI per country is not an effective way to compare the economies of different countries. This is because GNI per country does not take into consideration the population of each country, so the numbers can be misleading when looking at countries with vastly different populations. For comparing economies of different countries, GNI per capita is much more effective.

GNI per Capita

GNI per capita is a way to look at the country's income divided by its population, and it is the clearest way to compare income per person in a country. GNI per capita is a strong indicator of the standard of living of an average citizen in the country, and higher GNI per capita numbers are correlated with things like:

- Higher literacy rates.
- Lower infant mortality.
- Better access to safe water.

The World Bank also collects this data, converts it to the U.S. dollar using the current exchange rate, and then applies the Atlas method, which uses average exchange rates over three years to even out any exchange-rate fluctuations.

Compare GNI to other National Income Calculations

Aside from gross national income, there are several other ways to calculate national income, including GDP, GNP, and NNI.

- Gross domestic product (GDP): GDP is an income calculation included within GNI. In fact, GNI can be represented as GDP + net foreign factor income. By comparing a country's GDP and GNI, we can determine how much foreign aid or foreign labor a country receives. Most countries have very little difference between their GDP and GNI—for instance, in 2016 the United States had a GNI only about 1.5 percent higher than its GDP. But in other cases, there is a large difference—if a country's GNI is mucher higher than their GDP, it means they receive a lot of foreign aid, whereas if their GDP is much higher than their GNI, it means that non-citizens make up a large portion of the country's production.

- Gross national product (GNP): GNP is very similar to GNI. However, there are a few small differences between them (for instance, GNP does not include subsidies receivable from abroad), and these differences have caused the World Bank to prefer GNI to GNP for income calculation.
- Net national income (NNI): NNI is GNI minus depreciation (of things like homes, buildings, and machinery). It is the most precise of the national accounting methods and can give the most accurate estimation of a country's total income and economic growth rate, as well as being the best measure for an economy's ability to continue minimum production standards—in other words, how well a country can keep up a consistent national output of goods and services.

Aggregates of National Income

In an economy, various goods and services are produced by different productive units during a period of one year. Such goods and services cannot be added together in terms of quantity (as we cannot add 5,000 tonnes of wheat + 10,000 mobile phones + 7,000 machines and so on). Therefore, these are expressed in terms of money.

There are many aggregates in national income to measure the value of goods and services in terms of money. Let us start with Gross Domestic Product at Market Price (GDP_{MP}).

Gross Domestic Product at Market Price (GDP_{MP})

It refers to gross market value of all final goods and services produced within the domestic territory of a country during a period of one year.

- 'Gross' in GDP_{MP} signifies that no provision has been made for depreciation, i.e. it includes depreciation.
- 'Domestic' in GDP_{MP} signifies that it includes goods and services produced by all units located within the domestic territory (irrespective of fact whether produced by residents or non-residents).
- 'Market Price' in GDP_{MF} signifies that it includes amount of indirect taxes paid and excludes amount of subsidy received, i.e. it shows that net indirect taxes (NIT) have been included.
- 'Product' in GDP_{MP} signifies that only final goods and services have to be included.

By making adjustments in GDP_{MP}, we can derive other aggregates.

Gross Domestic Product at Factor Cost (GDP_{FC})

It refers to gross money value of all the final goods and services produced within the domestic territory of a country during a period of one year.

$$GDP_{FC} = CDP_{MP} - \text{Net Indirect Taxes}$$

Net Domestic Product at Market Price (NDP_{MP})

It refers to net market value of all the final goods and services produced within the domestic territory of a country during a period of one year.

$NDP_{MP} = GDP_{MP}$ – Depreciation

Net Domestic Product at Factor Cost (NDP_{FC})

It refers to net money value of all the final goods and services produced within the domestic territory of a country during a period of one year.

$NDP_{FC} = GDP_{MP}$ – Net Indirect Taxes – Depreciation

NDP_{FC} is also known as Domestic Income or Domestic factor income.

Relationship between Four Domestic Concepts

GDP_{MP}, GDP_{FC}, NDP_{MP} and NDP_{FC} are four Domestic concepts. The term 'Domestic' signifies that contribution of only those producers (whether resident or non-resident) is to be included who are within the domestic territory of the country.

Gross National Product at Market Price (GNP_{MP})

It refers to gross market value of all the final goods and services produced by the normal residents of a country during a period of one year.

$GNP_{MP} = GDP_{MP}$ + Net factor income from abroad

It must be noted that GNP_{MP} can be less than GDP_{MP} when NFIA is negative. However, GNP_{MP} will be more than GDP_{MP} when NFIA is positive.

Gross National Product at Factor Cost (GNP_{FC})

It refers to gross money value of all the final goods and services produced by the normal residents of a country during a period of one year.

$GNP_{FC} = GNP_{MP}$ – Net Indirect Taxes

Net National Product at Market Price (NNP_{MP})

It refers to net market value of all the final goods and services produced by the normal residents of a country during a period of one year. $NNP_{MP} = GNP_{MP}$ – Depreciation.

Net National Product at Factor Cost (NNP_{FC})

It refers to net money value of all the final goods and services produced by the normal residents of a country during a period of one year.

$NNP_{FC} = GNP_{MP}$ – Net Indirect Taxes – Depreciation.

It must be noted that NNP_{FC} is also known as National Income.

Relationship between Four National Concepts

GNP_{MP}, GNP_{FC}, NNP_{MP} and NNP_{FC} are four National concepts. The term National' signifies that production of only normal residents of the country is to be included even if they are outside the domestic territory of the country.

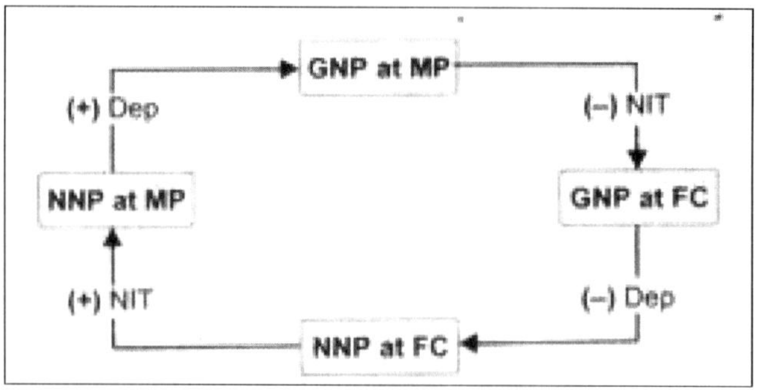

Multiplier and the Determination of National Income

One of the central concepts of modern macroeconomics is the multiplier. The Keynesian income determination model shows how the interaction of consumption and investment spending determines the level of national output.

Clearly, an increase in investment will increase the level of output and employment. Thus, an investment boom may bring a nation out of a deep or mild depression—by having a higher C + I schedule cut the 45° line at a higher level of equilibrium GNP.

Keynes realised that an increase in investment will increase the level of income and employment. He has also shown that an increase in investment will increase national income by a multiplied amount – by an amount greater than itself.

The multiplier is the number by which change in autonomous investment has to be multiplied to find out the resulting change in income. This amplified effect of investment on income is known as the 'multiplier'.

Keynes pointed out that an increase in private investment will cause output and employment to expand; a decrease in investment will cause them to contract, through the investment multiplier.

The reason is simple enough. Since investment is one part of GNP, when it rises in value, the whole will also increase in value.

The Keynesian model of income determination shows that an increase in investment will increase GNP by an amplified or multiplied amount – by an amount greater than itself. This is so because investment spending is high-powered spending.

Assumptions of the Multiplier

The Keynesian concept of multiplier is based on the following assumptions.

Autonomous Investment

The Keynesian multiplier comes into operation for any autonomous (income-independent) change in spending.

Lump-sum Taxes

The multiplier is derived on the assumption that taxes are lump-sum (once-for-all) only. If part of economy's extra income is taxed away by the government, total leakages (i.e., the withdraws from the income flow) would rise and the value of the multiplier would be smaller.

Closed Economy

It is also assumed that the economy is closed. The multiplier ignores all external economic transactions that could be significant for a country with a foreign sector.

Availability of Consumption Goods

The process of income propagation is largely conditioned by a steady flow of mass consumption goods.

Continuity of Investment

For the realisation of the full effect of the multiplier it is absolutely essential that the various increments in investment are repeated at periodic intervals.

Positive Net Investment

For realising the full value of the multiplier it is not enough for gross investment to be positive. Gross investment to the extent of depreciation always take place in an economy. But net investment or net addition to society's stock of capital has to be positive.

Stability of MPC

For the concept of the multiplier to be meaningful it is also necessary to argue that there is no change in MPC at frequent intervals, i.e., at least during the process of income generation.

No Time Lag between Successive Expenditures on Consumption Goods

It is argued that income changes are immediately reflected in consumption changes. There is no lag between receipt of income and expenditure on consumption.

Unemployed Resources

Finally, Keynes argued that the multiplier principle becomes effective only when there are unemployed resources in the economy. In other words, there must exist involuntary idleness of resources including manpower.

In short, the greater the extra consumption re-spending, the larger the value of multiplier. The greater the MPS "leakage" into extra saving at each round of spending, tire smaller the numerical value of the multiplier.

Limitations of (and leakages from) the Multiplier

Anything that leads to a fall in national income through the multiplier is to be considered as a leakage.

There are Three Such Leakages

- Savings,
- Taxes, and
- Imports.

The most important leakages from the circular flow of income are the following.

Saving

It is the most important leakage. If MPC = 1 and MPS = 0, the numerical value of the multiplier would approach infinity. This means that if the entire new income created by an act of investment at each stage of the income generation process were spent by the people on buying consumer goods, then even a once-for-all increase in investment would go on creating extra income until the economy reached the stage of full employment, But MPC is rarely equal to 1.

In practice, people hardly spend their entire income on consumption goods. They save a certain portion. The portion they save (i.e., do not spent) disappears from the circular flow, thus reducing the value of the multiplier. Thus, the stronger the MPS of the people, the smaller will be the value of the investment multiplier.

Debt Repayment

James Duesenberry has pointed out people do not spent their entire extra income on consumption goods. They use a part of it to repay their past debt. As a result, the value of tire multiplier gets reduced.

Accumulation of Idle Cash Balances

People often save money by keeping idle cash balances in banks. This idle money does not come into circulation and is unlikely to lead to an increase in consumption spending.

Stock Exchange Transactions

It is often observed that a major portion of the new income generated in the economy is utilised to buy old bonds and securities from others. Most people sell these long-term credit instruments when in distress and incur capital losses. So, such transactions are unlikely to raise society's total consumption appreciably.

Imports

No country in the world is self-sufficient. Therefore, a country has to spend some money on imports. However, imports do not add to domestic expenditure and is unlikely to have any income and employment effect.

To the extent we spend a certain portion of our new income on imported goods, money leaks out of the country. In other words, the value of imports peters out of the income-stream, thus limiting the value of the multiplier.

Price Inflation

During inflation money income may rise but real income falls. Thus, real consumption spending (which determines the value of the multiplier) will fall. In other words, a major portion of increased money income will be neutralised by price inflation, instead of stimulating consumption and creating jobs and incomes in the process.

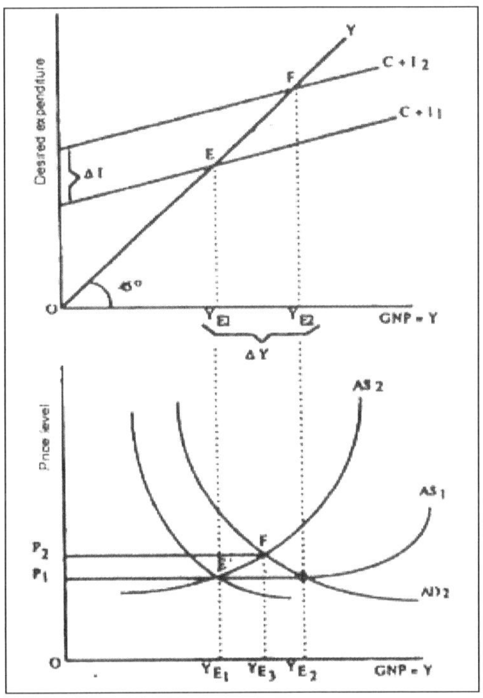

The effect of price change.

The equilibrium value of GNP (or national income) in the typical Keynesian income-expenditure or 45° diagram framework is related to the aggregate supply- aggregate- demand model in figure However, the Keynesian framework depicted in the top half of the diagram completely neglects price-level consideration.

Instead, the Keynesian approach is based on the assumption that the relevant portion of the nation's AS curve is horizontal, implying that the additional demand for goods and services is fully reflected in increased real output rather than partially reflected in higher prices. Figure shows that when investment spending increases, the desired expenditure line shifts upward from $C + I_1$ to $C + I_2$.

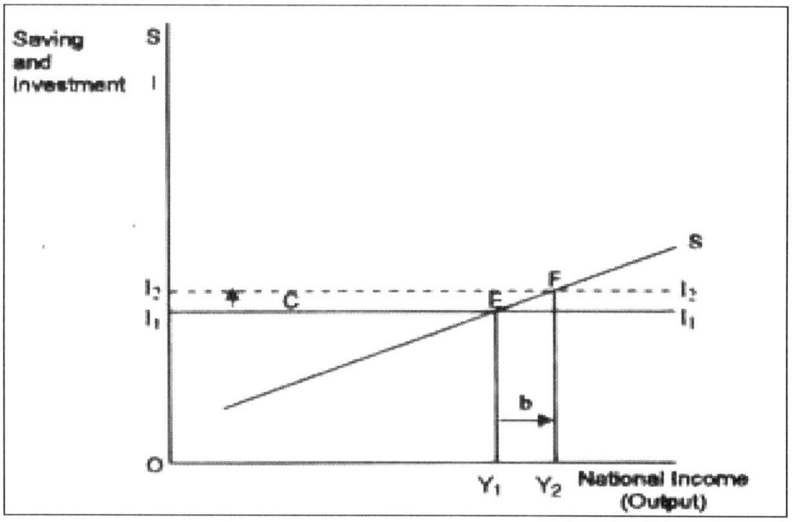

Income determination by Saving and Investment.

This, in its turn, leads to a multiple increase in national income (from OY_{E1} to OY_{E2}). In the bottom half of the diagram, the AD curve shifts horizontally by the same magnitude ($OY_{E2} - OY_{E1}$). This means that if the AS curve is completely elastic, (i.e., a horizontal straight line) upto a certain level of output (OY_{E2}), equilibrium value of GNP will increase from OY_{E1} to OY_{E2} in the bottom half of the diagram.

This is shown by point G. But there is no rise in the general price level (which is P_1). However, the AS curve normally slopes upward from left to right. In fact, beyond a certain level of output (OY_{E1}) the AS curve slopes upward as is indicated by the curve AS_2.

In such a situation, equilibrium output and price both rise in the event of an increase in government expenditures, as is indicated by point F. Thus, in reality a part of the increased expenditure is manifested in higher prices rather than in higher real GNP.

As commented by Regan and Thomas, "The extent to which the initial increase in spending is dissipated in higher prices instead of greater real output depends on the state of the economy at a time the stimulus occurs. When the economy is initially operating far below capacity with considerable unemployment, the aggregate supply curve is quite flat and almost all the increased spending results in increased real output. When the economy is initially operating fairly close to full capacity, the aggregate supply curve is quite steep. In this event much of the increase in spending is reflected in higher prices".

Taxes

If the government taxes away a certain portion of the extra income generated in the economy the value of the multiplier will fall. So, like savings, taxes also act as a leakage from the circular flow. Taxes are contractionary in their effects inasmuch as they reduce real consumption spending by reducing disposable income.

All modern economies rely on progressive income taxes for raising revenue and reducing income inequality. Thus, as GNP begins to rise because of a shift in spending, part of the extra GNP is taken away by the government in the form of income taxes.

Hence, a rise in GNP is not reflected in a corresponding (equivalent) increase in disposable income. If a representative Indian is in a 40 percent marginal tax bracket, a one-rupee increase in gross income yields to just 60 paise increase in (personal) disposable income.

Given an MPC of 0.8 the individual adds only 48 paise to national income (GNP) through his secondary consumption spending (0.8 x 60). Thus, James F. Ragan and L.B. Thomas have rightly commented: "The effective MPC out of GNP is reduced by the existence of income taxes, and the true multiplier is reduced considerably relative to a society with no income taxes".

Corporate Savings

Moreover, companies do not always distribute their entire net profit (gross profits less corporation tax) as dividend. They retain a certain portion for expansion and diversification. To the extent they follow the policy of saving a certain portion of their net profits, the consumption spending of shareholders fails to increase correspondingly. Therefore, the value of the multiplier will be less than otherwise.

Effects on Investment Spending

Again, there is the indirect effect on investment of a rise in the rate of interest by raising GNP. Let us assume that consumer spending or government expenditure increases. This will immediately lead to an increase in GNP. This, in turn, is likely to induce an increase in the desire to borrow (although Keynes ignored induced investment and considered only autonomous investment).

The increased demand for loanable funds will raise the rate of interest and choke off investment demand. This is known as the crowing-out effect, i.e., the shortage of investment in the private sector and the consequent rise in the rate of interest.

Thus, "the initial expansion of consumption or government spending, by driving up GNP and interest rates, may crowd out some investment spending. If so, part of the extra GNP (in the form of government goods and consumption goods) is offset by the reduced output of investment goods. In this event, the true multiplier is not as the simple multiplier".

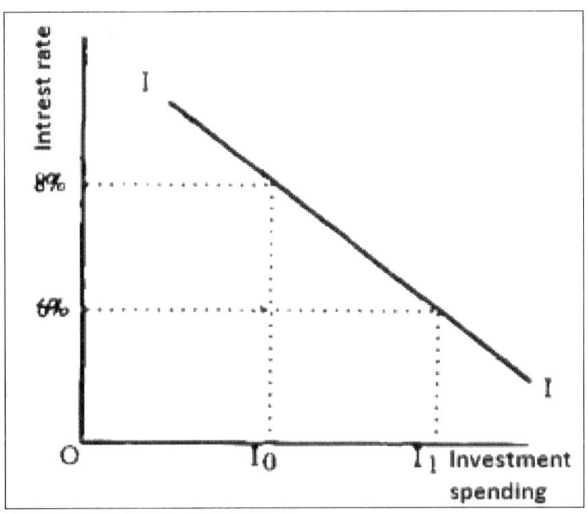

In practice, however, things are not that simple. Figure is a typical investment demand schedule indicating the relationship between interest rates and investment spending, when all other factors influencing investment are assumed to remain unchanged.

However, with an increase in GNP in response to the initial increase in spending, the business outlook tends to improve and the rate of utilisation of existing capacity also increases. These factors will shift the investment demand curve of figure to the right. This means that investment spending may increase in spite of the higher interest rates.

Thus, instead of crowding out, spending crowding in effect may be observed. This refers to a favourable response of investment spending to the initial increase in spending. The actual income generated by an increase in spending depends partly on the state of the economy when the increase in spending occurs and partly on the steepness of the investment demand curve of figure. Thus, the fact is that "the true multiplier is likely to differ from the simple multiplier as a result of induced effects of investment spending".

Employment

Full employment refers to a situation in which every able bodied person who is willing to work at the prevailing rate of wages is, infact, employed. Alternatively, it is a situation when there is no involuntary unemployment.

As production requires working time and human capital, firms and other organizations pay people, providing them with a key component of their income.

Particularly low national employment rates may signal a long-lasting depression and underdevelopment.

The kind of job of a person is one of the determinants of his belonging to social groups.

Composition

Employment can be expressed in number of people working or in total working hours. A mixed measure is the number of hours divided by standard working hours to give a full-time equivalence to jobs.

If considered in terms of the number of people, employment is purposefully divided along principal 8 axes:

- Economic activity, like agriculture, mining, manufacturing, services.
- Occupation, as with workers, clerks, managers, self-employed;
- Institutional sector (public, private, cooperatives,);
- Dimension of the employing organization (small, medium, large firms);
- Kind of legal contract, with its clauses regarding durability over time, method of remuneration, guarantees;
- Level of wages and other remunerations;

- Age;
- Gender;
- Education and skill level and horizontal differentiation.

Along their professional life, people are hired, change job (internally or externally to their organization) and finish their career. In many countries, they thus become pensioners and receive pensions from Social Security or private funds. Accordingly, important events for employment dynamics are hiring, firing and retirement, which in turn means that labour market economic models should include routines for hiring, firing and retirement. Dysfunctional mechanisms may lead to long and uncertain transition from school to work and from one workplace to another, with long spells of unemployment.

It's also important to monitor whether groups of workers face unhealthy conditions, too long working hours, sexual harrassment, and other humiliating conditions.

Changes in the composition of employment can happen even if the total remains unchanged.

Determinants

In a macroeconomic perspective, levels of employment depend on levels of economic activity (broadly measured by GDP) and on intensity of labour per unit of product (productivity).

An important role is played by institutional arrangements (as laws, contracts and collective negotiations) on how to react to slow-downs in GDP.

Employment in a certain activity may be ceiled up by the number of employable skilled people and by timing, contents, and effectiveness of vocational training. Job openings signal to external population that a jobplace is available, either because of a previous co-worker's fireing/retiring/moving along or away the career ladder or because of the addition of a new jobplace (for higher production or a new production).

General population dynamics is a very broad framework for employment and should not be used as a proxy for its dynamics, since demographic variables are extremely slow in changes, whereas employment reacts to economic climate.

The relationship with wages is two fold: Higher wages may reduce the incentive for firms to employ but, conversely, high employment may give more power to employees in wage negotiations, thus increasing their remuneration.

Employment creation happens both in the private and the public sector, while policies and rules on the labour market and the general economy exert an impact on both. Politicians promising job creation may mean to foster public expenditure for goods and services produced in the private sector, thus increasing the number of jobs there.

Impact on other Variables

High levels of employment rate and longer working hours mean, also at the same wages, a larger income for employee. Income distribution gets more equitable with a sharp reduction of poverty. On-the-job training raise skills.

Working conditions usually improve and people have confidence in maintaining their jobs and even getting better ones. This perspective is conducive to investment in human capital.

In this environment it is likely an increase of wages. Consumption of employee will be boasted but global consumption may follow a slower path if reduction in other income source takes place. Global consumption depends on consumption/saving attitude of different social groups and their income share.

Happiness at the individual level is linked to fair working conditions, in terms of stability, personal relationships with colleagues, suppliers and clients, as well as of the pay and the actual content of operations.

The willingness of voters to confirm the current government can be influenced by the labour market conditions. In particular, a rising unemployment can make the voters less likely to support it, with growing anger and anxiety. Jobless recovery makes the incumbent particularly vulnerable, because GDP rise would authorise to boast success, whereas people will be unwilling to recognize it because of the difficulties in finding jobs.

Long-term Trends

Employment has always grown, but at a very different pace according to countries. Where its growth has been the highest, reduced productivity growth have usually kept GDP dynamics low (often from an already low level). Where its growth has been the lowest, productivity has usually (but not always) been high with a relatively good GDP performance (often from an already high level). In between these two extremes, employment growth has been matched with any other situation.

In many countries, employment has followed short-term GDP dynamics, especially in prolonged recessions when a fall in employment takes place, with more moderate growth than GDP along growth path in the long-term, because of increases in productivity.

In other countries, employment has been static at the same level for some decades, with GDP dynamics mirroring itself only on productivity.

It is expected that "green jobs" in environment-related clean sectors will play an important role in overcoming the present crisis linked to climate change and that innovative economic policies should maximise the co-benefit of employment and environment protection.

Business Cycle Behaviour

At the beginning of recession, overhead hours usually fall, reducing average received wages because overhead are typically much better paid than normal hours. Employment is static for a more or less long period after recession has begun, because of institutional arrangements (as contracts) and of the fact that firms forecast that the recession will be short: they are unwilling to dismiss people since they will soon need the same workers in the future, the more so as these employees have firm-specific and task-specific skills that would be necessary to build up if a completely new personnel would be hired.

As recession hits harder, perspectives gloom, and strategic decisions on restructuring take places: the number of firing rises dramatically. It first touch weak workers in the firm hierarchy, but then extend to mid-management.

It is often in this case that a fall in employee consumption is not counterbalanced by an increase of other groups' consumption, since also they are touched by recession. Through the Keynesian multiplier, recession worsen.

This overall bad condition is conducive to changes in government composition and its policies, possibly with the introduction of pro-growth packages of measures.

With recovery, firms exploit better their production capacity and personnel, thus GDP can growth without new employees and machines ("jobless recovery"). This is particularly true if recovery was achieved by a fall in wages, a rise in profits and a more un-equal income distribution, so that GDP growth is led by a small number of purchase of higher-quality goods purchased by the rich.

Employment starts growing during expansion, when the perspective of growth are consolidated, limits to overheads are reached, and firms urgently need new personnel, possibly in connection with new investments (both requiring new skills and widening the number of people with the same skills).

At peaks, in many activity branches, a shortage of personnel may be felt and employment increases less than it could otherwise. Fims become less selective in their hiring, which is particularly favourable for discriminated categories. Minorities, young, women and immigrants see their employment opportunities steeply rising.

Importance of Employment in Economics

As economies develop, employment moves from the primary to the secondary and then the tertiary sector. In the Netherlands, for instance, most workers (74%) are employed in the tertiary sector whereas in Vietnam, the majority of workers (60%) are employed in the primary sector.

Within any country at any particular time, some industries will be expanding and some will be contracting. For instance, employment in textiles is declining whilst it is increasing in ICT and software. This change requires workers to be occupationally and geographically mobile.

Full and Part Time Work

Most workers work full time. Some, however, work part time. Some opt to work part time, as it may fit in with their children's school hours, enable them to look after elderly relatives or pursue other interests. Other people are forced to work part time because they are not able to find full time jobs.

Employed and Self-employed

In some countries, including the UK, USA and most of Europe, most people work for someone else – i.e. they are employees. The number of self-employed workers is, however, rising. In other countries, a high proportion of people are already self-employed and many of them work in the unorganised sector.

Organised and Unorganised Sectors

The unorganised sector covers workers who do not have the same access to the social security benefits, employment protection and rights as organised labour. For instance, whilst a country may operate a minimum wage, unorganised labour may be paid below it.

The unorganised sector does not include unions and so the workers cannot bargain collectively, to improve their conditions. Some of those working in the unorganised sector are self-employed, some are migratory workers and some are casual workers. Most of them do not pay income tax.

Workers in the unorganised sector tend to have lower productivity, lower levels of training and lower wages than workers of organised sector. A growth in the organised sector tends to raise the quality of employment and labour productivity.

In 2005 more than 90% of the country's labour forces (423m out of 470m workers) were employed in the unorganised sector. In rural areas, mobile casual workers constitute most of the unorganised labour whereas in urban areas, it is contract and sub-contract migratory workers, maids, mechanics in small-scale garages and street stall holders. The average productivity of workers in the private organised sector in the country is six times higher than that of those working in the unorganised sector.

High and Low Quality Employment

High quality employment is skilled work which is interesting and which provides workers with the opportunity to progress, access to training, good working conditions and a relatively high degree of job security. In contrast, low quality employment is unskilled work which often does not require or provides training and does not provide good working conditions.

Private and Public Sector Employment

The proportion of workers employed in the public and private sectors varies from country to country and time to time. In the UK, in 2005, 80% of workers were employed in the public sector while 20% were employed in the private sector.

A major reason for the reduction in the proportion of population, employed in the public sector, in a number of countries in recent years, has been privatization. This involves the sale of state owned enterprises to the private sector. For instance, fewer workers are now employed in the public sector in Poland than twenty years ago.

Workers in the public sector often have more job security and higher non-wage benefits. In some cases, however, their productivity is lower than that of workers in the private sector.

Flexible Employment

Global competition is putting pressure on firms to ensure that their labour force is flexible. A flexible labour force is one which adjusts quickly and smoothly to changes in market conditions. This flexibility can take a number of different forms. One is in terms of the number of workers employed.

The easier it is to hire and fire workers, the more able firms are in adjusting their output in line with consumer demand. Such flexibility, which can be called numerical flexibility, can increase workers' sense of job insecurity but it can also raise employment. This is because firms may be more willing to take on more workers when demand for their products rises if they know they can let them go, should demand fall.

Other forms of flexibility are temporal flexibility (the ability to change the number of hours, people work), location flexibility (the ability to change the location, where workers work), functional flexibility (the ability to change the tasks, workers perform) and wage flexibility (the ability to raise or lower wages).

Changes in Employment and Unemployment

A rise in employment may reduce unemployment if it is the unemployed who fill at least some of the extra jobs. It is, however, possible that both employment and unemployment increase. This will occur if the labour force grows faster than the number of jobs available. It is also possible for unemployment to fall without an increase in employment.

This is because, finding a job is not the only reason why people stop being unemployed. Some unemployed people may reach retirement age, some may go into full time education and some may emigrate while some may just stop searching for work.

Unemployment

Unemployment, also referred to as joblessness, occurs when people are without work and actively seeking employment. Unemployment, also referred to as joblessness, occurs when people are without work and are actively seeking employment. During periods of recession, an economy usually experiences high unemployment rates. There are many proposed causes, consequences, and solutions for unemployment.

There are several types of unemployment, each one defined in terms of cause and severity.

Cyclical Unemployment

Cyclical unemployment exists when individuals lose their jobs as a result of a downturn in aggregate demand (**AD**). If the decline in aggregate demand is persistent, and the unemployment long-term, it is called either *demand deficient*, *general*, or ***Keynesian*** unemployment. For example, unemployment levels of 3 million were reached in the UK in the last two recessions, between 1980 and 1982, and between 1990 and 1992. In the most recent recession of 2008-2010, unemployment levels rose to 2.4m in the last quarter of 2009, and are likely to peak at over 2.5m during 2010.

Demand Deficient Unemployment

This is caused by a lack of aggregate demand, with insufficient demand to generate full employment.

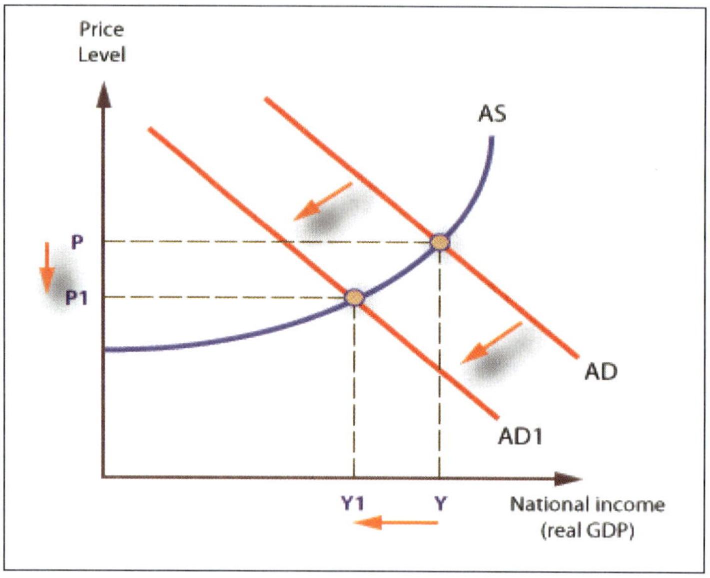

Structural Unemployment

Structural unemployment occurs when certain industries decline because of long term changes in market conditions. For example, over the last 20 years UK motor vehicle production has declined while car production in the Far East has increased, creating structurally unemployed car workers. Globalisation is an increasingly significant cause of structural unemployment in many countries.

Regional Unemployment

When structural unemployment affects local areas of an economy, it is called 'regional' unemployment. For example, unemployed car workers in the Midlands and Essex add to regional unemployment in these areas. In the UK, the further we move away from the affluent South East the greater the unemployment rate. Geographical immobility makes regional differences more extreme.

Classical Unemployment

Classical unemployment is caused when wages are 'too' high. This explanation of unemployment dominated economic theory before the 1930s, when workers themselves were blamed for not accepting lower wages, or for asking for too high a wage. Classical unemployment is also called *real wage* unemployment.

Seasonal Unemployment

Seasonal unemployment exists because certain industries only produce or distribute their products at certain times of the year. Industries where seasonal unemployment is common include farming, tourism, and construction.

Frictional Unemployment

Frictional unemployment, also called *search unemployment*, occurs when workers lose their current job and are in the process of finding another one. There may be little that can be done to reduce this type of unemployment, other than provide better information to reduce the search time. This suggests that *zero unemployment* is impossible at any one time because some workers will always be in the process of changing jobs.

Voluntary Unemployment

Voluntary unemployment is defined as a situation when workers choose not to work at the current equilibrium wage rate. For one reason or another, workers may elect not to participate in the labour market. There are several reasons for the existence of voluntary unemployment including excessively generous welfare benefits and high rates of income tax. Voluntary unemployment is likely to occur when the equilibrium wage rate is below the wage necessary to encourage individuals to supply their labour.

The Natural Rate of Unemployment

This is a term associated with new Classical and monetarist economists. It is defined as the rate of unemployment that still exists when the labour market it in equilibrium, and includes seasonal, frictional and voluntary unemployment. The US economist Milton Friedman first used the concept to help explain the connection between unemployment and inflation. Friedman argued that if unemployment fell below the *natural rate* there would be an increase in the rate of inflation.

The different types of unemployment can be illustrated through the AJ-LF model.

Over the last 30 years, employment in the service sector has increased to over 70% of total employment, while employment in manufacturing has decreased to under 20%. Since the 1940s employment in the primary sector, including agriculture, has been less that 3% of the workforce.

Recent changes have created *two speed economy*, with a relatively buoyant service sector and a declining manufacturing one.

The main reasons are:

- Globalisation and the rise of new 'low cost' overseas competitor countries.
- Increased competition within the domestic product market.
- The increasing comparative advantage as an international supplier of financial services.

Structural Unemployment and Labour Mobility

Labour immobility is likely to increase structural unemployment. This is because those industries that are growing and need labour, often called *sunrise industries*, are not necessarily able to employ the same workers who have been displaced in the declining, *sunset industries*.

There are three types of labour immobility.

Geographical Immobility

Geographical immobility occurs when workers are not willing or able to move from region to region, or town to town. Geographical mobility is made worse by immense house price variation between regions. It may be extremely difficult for workers in Yorkshire to sell their home and buy an equivalent one in London.

Other factors also contribute to geographical immobility, such as strong social and family ties, and parents being unwilling to disrupt their children's education by changing schools. The stresses of moving home can also be a deterrent to mobility for some.

Industrial Immobility

Industrial immobility occurs when workers do not move between industries, such as moving from employment in motor industry to employment in the insurance industry. Industrial immobility has affected ndustrial countries, as the growth of service industries, and the decline of manufacturing industries, has increased the need for mobility.

Occupational Immobility

Occupational immobility occurs when workers find it difficult to change jobs within an industry. For example, it may be very difficult for a doctor to retrain to be a dentist.

Industrial and occupation immobility are most likely to happen when skills are not transferable between industry and job.

Information failure also contributes to labour immobility because workers may be immobile because they do not know where all the suitable jobs for them are.

A resulting problem with labour market immobility is that it can create regional unemployment, which is a type of structural unemployment. This means that a change in the structure of industry leaves some people unable to respond by changing job, industry, or location and as a result, they remain temporarily or permanently unemployed.

Immobility can also lead to rising labour costs, as firms have to increase wages to encourage workers to relocate.

New classical economists would tend to see structural unemployment as an example of government failure. Labour markets do not clear, they argue, because wages are not allowed to adjust effectively, and the price mechanism is distorted. By removing distortions and imperfections in the labour market workers would move more quickly from job to job.

For example, by keeping welfare benefits to a minimum there is an incentive to retrain and look for paid work. Welfare benefits can trap individuals into a life of unemployment because of the effects of moral hazard and the disincentive effect it creates. This increases labour immobility, and hence contributes to structural unemployment.

However, labour immobility can also be addressed from the perspective of labour market failure. Training and re-training are regarded as merit goods, where individuals under perceive the long term benefit to themselves. They also fail to appreciate the positive externalities that training and re-training generate for the wider community. This means that there is a significant role for the state in providing free or subsidised training and retraining programmes.

In addition, there is the potential situation of labour market poaching. Why should a firm in the booming service sector provide free training to a displaced worker from the manufacturing sector if the worker will leave for another job shortly after training? Why should firms do any training at all if they believe that workers will be poached by higher wages? The poacher can, of course, afford to pay higher wages because of savings in training costs.

References

- Economic-income-definition: strategiccfo.com, Retrieved 09 April, 2019
- Concept-of-national-income, fundamentals-of-economics-and-management: toppr.com, Retrieved 19 May, 2019
- What-is-gross-national-income-definition-and-formula-for-gni-how-does-gni-compare-to-other-national-income-calculations: masterclass.com, Retrieved 18 January, 2019
- Aggregates-of-national-income-to-measure-the-value-of-goods-and-services, macro-economics/national-income-macro-economics- 30282: yourarticlelibrary.com, Retrieved 05 August, 2019
- Multiplier-and-the-determination-of-national-income, national-income/determination- 26044: economicsdiscussion.net, Retrieved 29 June, 2019
- Importance-of-employment-in-economics- 32872: yourarticlelibrary.com, Retrieved 10 April, 2019
- Unemployment-types-and-causes, Managing-the-economy: economicsonline.co.uk, Retrieved 23 July, 2019

5

Aggregate Demand, Inflation and Deflation

Aggregate demand refers to the final goods and services that are demanded in an economy at a particular period of time. Inflation is defined as the rise in the price of goods and services. Deflation is defined as the fall in the price of goods and services. This chapter discusses in detail about aggregate demand, inflation and deflation.

Aggregate Demand

Aggregate demand refers to the total demand for final goods and services in the economy.

Since aggregate demand is measured by total expenditure of the community on goods and services, therefore, aggregate demand is also defined as 'total amount of money which all sectors (households, firms, government) of the economy are ready to spend on purchase of goods and services.

Alternatively, it is the total expenditure which the community intends to incur on purchase of goods and services. Thus, aggregate demand is synonymous with aggregate expenditure in the economy. If the total intended (i.e., ex-ante) expenditure on buying all the output is larger than before, this shows a higher aggregate demand.

On the contrary, if the community decides to spend less on the available output, it shows a fall in the aggregate demand. In simple words, aggregate demand is the total expenditure on consumption and investment. It should be noted that determination of output and employment in Keynesian framework depends mainly on the level of aggregate demand in short period.

Components of AD

Thus, the main components of aggregate demand (aggregate expenditure) in a four sector economy are:

- Household (or private) consumption demand (C).
- Private investment demand (I).
- Government demand for goods and services (G).
- Net export demand (X-M).

Thus,

$$AD = C + I + G + (X - M)$$

Mind, all the variables represent planned (ex-ante) and not actual (ex-post).

Household (or Private) Consumption Demand (C)

It is defined as 'Value of goods and services that households are able and willing to buy.' Alternatively, it refers to ex-ante (planned) consumption expenditure to be incurred by all households on purchase of goods and services. For instance, households' demand for food, clothing, housing, books, furniture, cycles, radios, TV sets, educational and medical services will be called household consumption demand. Consumption (C) is a function (f) of disposable income (Y), i.e., C = J(Y).

As disposable income increases, consumption expenditure also increases but by how much? It depends upon propensity to consume. The relationship between income and consumption is called 'propensity to consume' or consumption function. Consumption function is represented by the equation.

Private Investment Demand (I)

This refers to planned (ex-ante) expenditure on creation of new capital assets like machines, buildings and raw materials by private entrepreneurs. Remember, investment in Keynesian sense does not imply purchase of existing shares or securities but means expenditures on creation of new capital assets such as plants and equipment, inventories, construction works, etc. that help in production. Investment is made not only to maintain present level of production, but also to increase production capacity in future.

An economy grows through investment. Among three categories of investment, namely, purchase of new buildings, addition to stock and investment in fixed plant or machinery, the investment demand is focussed on last category, i.e., machinery.

The relationship between investment demand and rate of interest is called investment demand function. There is inverse relationship between rate of interest and investment demand. Investment is of two types—Autonomous and Induced but all private investment expenditure is assumed as induced investment.

What determines investment in private enterprise economy? Just as household consumption demand depends on disposable income of households, investment demand in private enterprise economy depends mainly on two factors, namely, MEI {Marginal Efficiency of Investment) and Rate of Interest. In other words, the investors Judge whether the expected rate of return on new investment is equal to or greater than or less than the market rate of interest.

Suppose a businessman makes an additional investment by taking loan. He has to pay interest on it which is his expenditure on new investment. Before making investment, he would compare the interest he has to pay on loan and the profit he is expected to get on this investment. According to Keynes, the net return expected from a new unit of investment is called Marginal Efficiency of Investment (MEI).

Thus, three elements which are important in understanding investment are:

- Revenue (i.e., rate of return on new investment).
- Cost (i.e., rate of interest).
- Expectations (of profit).

Investment Demand Function

Of the three elements which affect investment, rate of interest is the most important. The relationship between investment demand and rate of interest is called investment demand function. There is inverse relationship between the rate of interest and investment demand, i.e., higher the rate of interest, the lower will be the investment demand.

Government Demand for Goods and Services (G)

It refers to government planned (ex-ante) expenditure on purchase of consumer and capital goods to fulfill common needs of the society. The level of government expenditure is determined by government policy Present-day states are by and large welfare states wherein government participation in economic welfare of the people has increased manifold.

Government demand may be for satisfying public needs for roads, schools, hospitals, water works, railway transport or for infrastructure (like roads, bridges, airports), maintenance of law and order and defence from external aggression. Investment can be induced and autonomous.

It needs to be noted that whereas investment in private sector is made with profit motive and, therefore, called induced investment, government investment is guided by people's welfare motive and, therefore, called autonomous investment. Since investment expenditure is assumed to be autonomous, graphically investment curve is a horizontal line parallel to x-axis as shown as RI in figure.

Net Exports (Exports-imports) Demand

Net export is the difference between export of goods and services and import of goods and services during a given period. Net exports reflect the demand of foreign countries for our goods and services over our demand for foreign countries' goods and services. Thus, net exports show expected (ex-ante) net foreign demand.

This strengthens the income, output and employment process of our economy. As against it, imports from abroad drive out the earning of the economy and, therefore, they do not encourage domestic output and employment.

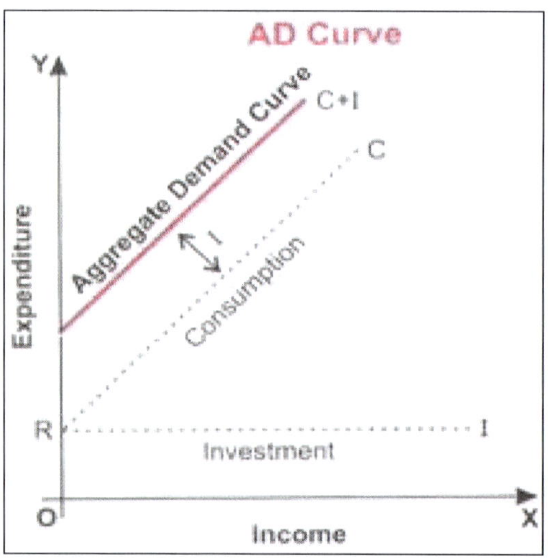

There are many factors which influence the volume of net foreign demand such as foreign exchange rates, terms of trade, trade policy of the importing and exporting countries, relative prices of goods, incomes of the nations, balance of payment position, types of exchange control, etc. Since net exports or foreign expenditure on our goods and services constitute a small proportion of the total expenditure (or aggregate demand), this constituent of net exports is usually ignored.

In sum, aggregate demand is the sum of the above- mentioned four types of demand (expenditure), i.e., AD = C + 1 + G + (X-M). Since determination of income (output) and employment is to be studied in the context of a two sector (Household and Firm) economy we shall, therefore, include in aggregate demand (AD) only two broad components of demand such as consumption demand (C) and investment demand (I). Put in symbols:

$$AD = C + I$$

This has been depicted in figure. Aggregate demand curve has been shown as sum of consumption (C) and investment (I).

Following are noteworthy points of the diagram:

- AD curve has a positive slope which means when income increases, AD (expenditure) also increases.
- AD curve does not originate at point O which shows that even at zero level of income, some minimum level of consumption is essential.
- Investment curve is a straight line parallel to X-axis because according to Keynes, level of investment remains constant at all levels of income during short period.

Inflation

Inflation is often defined in terms of its supposed causes. Inflation exists when money supply exceeds available goods and services. Or inflation is attributed to budget deficit financing. A deficit budget may be financed by the additional money creation. But the situation of monetary expansion or budget deficit may not cause price level to rise. Hence the difficulty of defining 'inflation'.

Inflation may be defined as 'a sustained upward trend in the general level of prices' and not the price of only one or two goods. G. Ackley defined inflation as 'a persistent and appreciable rise in the general level or average of prices'. In other words, inflation is a state of rising prices, but not high prices.

It is not high prices but rising price level that constitute inflation. It constitutes, thus, an overall increase in price level. It can, thus, be viewed as the devaluing of the worth of money. In other words, inflation reduces the purchasing power of money. A unit of money now buys less. Inflation can also be seen as a recurring phenomenon.

While measuring inflation, we take into account a large number of goods and services used by the people of a country and then calculate average increase in the prices of those goods and services over a period of time. A small rise in prices or a sudden rise in prices is not inflation since they may reflect the short term workings of the market.

It is to be pointed out here that inflation is a state of disequilibrium when there occurs a sustained rise in price level. It is inflation if the prices of most goods go up. Such rate of increases in prices may be both slow and rapid. However, it is difficult to detect whether there is an upward trend in prices and whether this trend is sustained. That is why inflation is difficult to define in an unambiguous sense.

Let's measure inflation rate. Suppose, in December 2007, the consumer price index was 193.6 and, in December 2008, it was 223.8. Thus, the inflation rate during the last one year was,

223.8- 193.6/193.6 x 100 = 15.6

As inflation is a state of rising prices, deflation may be defined as a state of falling prices but not fall in prices. Deflation is, thus, the opposite of inflation, i.e., a rise in the value of money or purchasing power of money. Disinflation is a slowing down of the rate of inflation.

Types of Inflation

As the nature of inflation is not uniform in an economy for all the time, it is wise to distinguish between different types of inflation. Such analysis is useful to study the distributional and other effects of inflation as well as to recommend anti-inflationary policies. Inflation may be caused by a variety of factors. Its intensity or pace may be different at different times. It may also be classified in accordance with the reactions of the government toward inflation.

Thus, one may observe different types of inflation in the contemporary society:

On the Basis of Causes

Currency Inflation

This type of inflation is caused by the printing of currency notes.

Credit Inflation

Being profit-making institutions, commercial banks sanction more loans and advances to the public than what the economy needs. Such credit expansion leads to a rise in price level.

Deficit-induced Inflation

The budget of the government reflects a deficit when expenditure exceeds revenue. To meet this gap, the government may ask the central bank to print additional money. Since pumping of additional money is required to meet the budget deficit, any price rise may the be called the deficit-induced inflation.

Demand-pull Inflation

An increase in aggregate demand over the available output leads to a rise in the price level. Such inflation is called demand-pull inflation (henceforth DPI). But why does aggregate demand rise? Classical economists attribute this rise in aggregate demand to money supply. If the supply of money in an economy exceeds the available goods and services, DPI appears. It has been described by Coulborn as a situation of "too much money chasing too few goods".

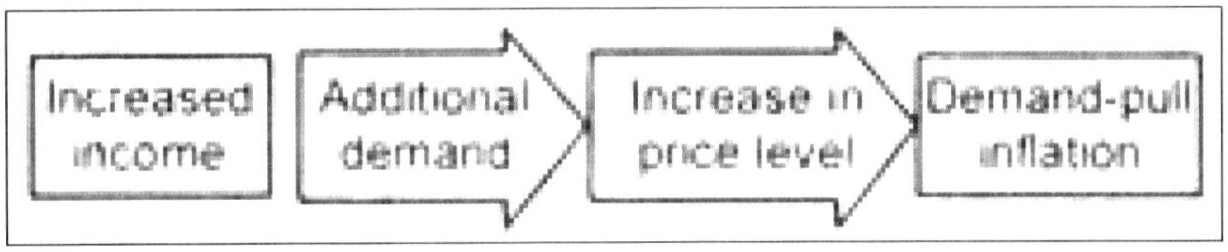

Keynesians hold a different argument. They argue that there can be an autonomous increase in aggregate demand or spending, such as a rise in consumption demand or investment or government spending or a tax cut or a net increase in exports (i.e., C + I + G + X – M) with no increase in money supply. This would prompt upward adjustment in price. Thus, DPI is caused by monetary factors (classical adjustment) and non-monetary factors (Keynesian argument).

DPI can be explained in terms of Fig., where we measure output on the horizontal axis and price level on the vertical axis. In Range 1, total spending is too short of full employment output, YF. There is little or no rise in the price level. As demand now rises, output will rise. The economy enters Range 2, where output approaches towards full employment situation. Note that in this region price level begins to rise. Ultimately, the economy reaches full employment situation, i.e., Range 3, where output does not rise but price level is pulled upward. This is demand-pull inflation. The essence of this type of inflation is that "too much spending chasing too few goods".

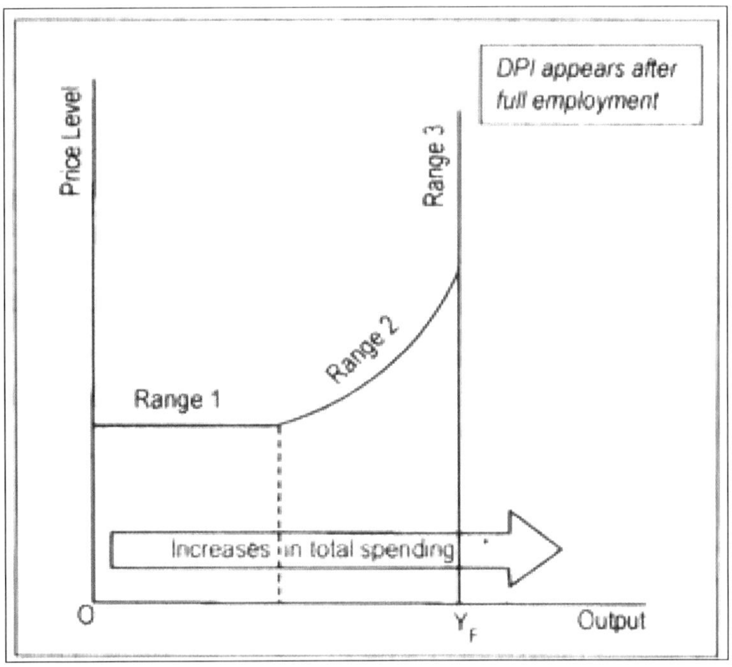

Cost-push Inflation

Inflation in an economy may arise from the overall increase in the cost of production. This type of inflation is known as cost-push inflation (henceforth CPI). Cost of production may rise due to an increase in the prices of raw materials, wages, etc. Often trade unions are blamed for wage rise since wage rate is not completely market-determinded. Higher wage means high cost of production. Prices of commodities are thereby increased.

A wage-price spiral comes into operation. But, at the same time, firms are to be blamed also for the price rise since they simply raise prices to expand their profit margins. Thus, we have two important variants of CPI wage-push inflation and profit-push inflation.

Anyway, CPI stems from the leftward shift of the aggregate supply curve:

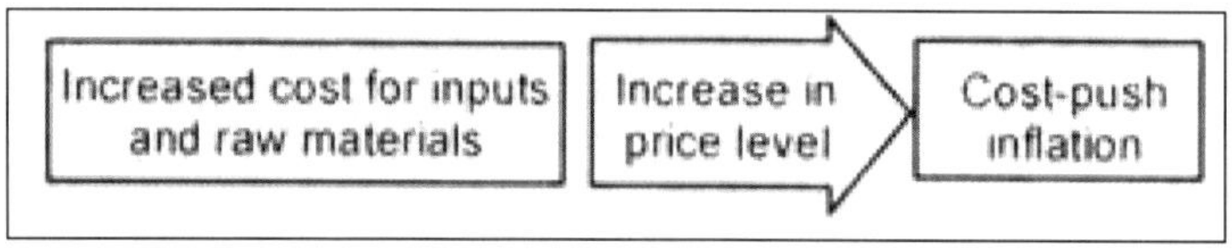

On the Basis of Speed or Intensity

Creeping or Mild Inflation

If the speed of upward thrust in prices is slow but small then we have creeping inflation. What speed of annual price rise is a creeping one has not been stated by the economists. To some, a creeping or mild inflation is one when annual price rise varies between 2 p.c. and 3 p.c. If a rate of price rise is kept at this level, it is considered to be helpful for economic development. Others argue that if annual price rise goes slightly beyond 3 p.c. mark, still then it is considered to be of no danger.

Walking Inflation

If the rate of annual price increase lies between 3 p.c. and 4 p.c., then we have a situation of walking inflation. When mild inflation is allowed to fan out, walking inflation appears. These two types of inflation may be described as 'moderate inflation'.

Often, one-digit inflation rate is called 'moderate inflation' which is not only predictable, but also keep people's faith on the monetary system of the country. Peoples' confidence get lost once moderately maintained rate of inflation goes out of control and the economy is then caught with the galloping inflation.

Galloping and Hyperinflation

Walking inflation may be converted into running inflation. Running inflation is dangerous. If it is not controlled, it may ultimately be converted to galloping or hyperinflation. It is an extreme form of inflation when an economy gets shattered". Inflation in the double or triple digit range of 20, 100 or 200 p.c. a year is labelled "galloping inflation".

Government's Reaction to Inflation

Inflationary situation may be open or suppressed. Because of anti-inflationary policies pursued by the government, inflation may not be an embarrassing one. For instance, increase in income leads to an increase in consumption spending which pulls the price level up.

If the consumption spending is countered by the government via price control and rationing device, the inflationary situation may be called a suppressed one. Once the government curbs are lifted, the suppressed inflation becomes open inflation. Open inflation may then result in hyperinflation.

Causes of Inflation

Inflation is mainly caused by excess demand decline in aggregate supply or output. Former leads to a rightward shift of the aggregate demand curve while the latter causes aggregate supply curve to shift leftward. Former is called demand-pull inflation (DPI), and the latter is called cost-push inflation (CPI). Before describing the factors, that lead to a rise in aggregate demand and a decline in aggregate supply, we like to explain "demand-pull" and "cost-push" theories of inflation.

Demand-pull Inflation Theory

There are two theoretical approaches to the DPI—one is classical and other is the Keynesian.

According to classical economists or monetarists, inflation is caused by an increase in money supply which leads to a rightward shift in negative sloping aggregate demand curve. Given a situation of full employment, classicists maintained that a change in money supply brings about an equiproportionate change in price level.

That is why monetarists argue that inflation is always and everywhere a monetary phenomenon. Keynesians do not find any link between money supply and price level causing an upward shift in aggregate demand.

According to Keynesians, aggregate demand may rise due to a rise in consumer demand or investment demand or government expenditure or net exports or the combination of these four components of aggreate demand. Given full employment, such increase in aggregate demand leads to an upward pressure in prices. Such a situation is called DPI. This can be explained graphically.

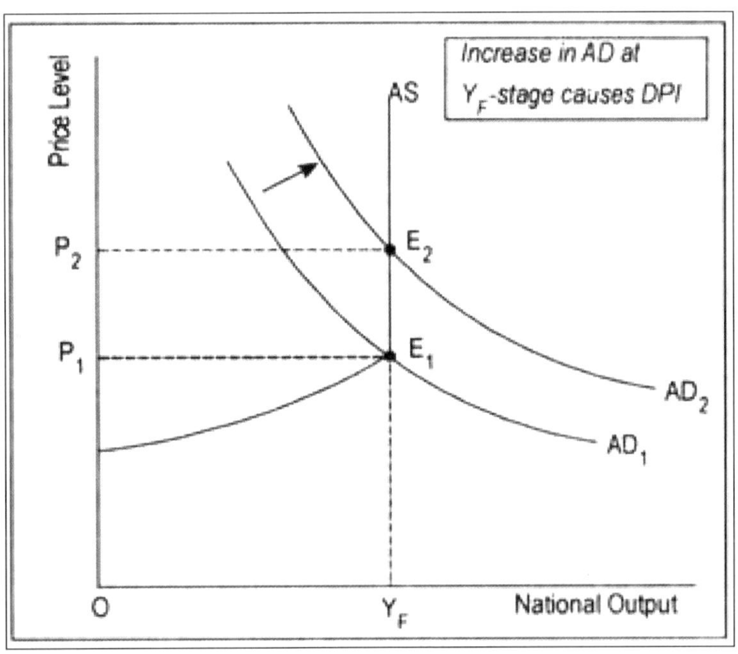

DPI: Shifts in AD Curve.

Just like the price of a commodity, the level of prices is determined by the interaction of aggregate demand and aggregate supply. In figure., aggregate demand curve is negative sloping while aggregate supply curve before the full employment stage is positive sloping and becomes vertical after the full employment stage is reached. AD_1 is the initial aggregate demand curve that intersects the aggregate supply curve AS at point E_1.

The price level, thus, determined is OP_1. As aggregate demand curve shifts to AD_2, price level rises to OP_2. Thus, an increase in aggregate demand at the full employment stage leads to an increase in price level only, rather than the level of output. However, how much price level will rise following an increase in aggregate demand depends on the slope of the AS curve.

Causes of Demand-pull Inflation

DPI originates in the monetary sector. Monetarists' argument that "only money matters" is based on the assumption that at or near full employment excessive money supply will increase aggregate demand and will, thus, cause inflation.

An increase in nominal money supply shifts aggregate demand curve rightward. This enables people to hold excess cash balances. Spending of excess cash balances by them causes price level to rise. Price level will continue to rise until aggregate demand equals aggregate supply.

Keynesians argue that inflation originates in the non-monetary sector or the real sector. Aggregate demand may rise if there is an increase in consumption expenditure following a tax cut. There may be an autonomous increase in business investment or government expenditure. Government expenditure is inflationary if the needed money is procured by the government by printing additional money.

In brief, increase in aggregate demand i.e., increase in (C + I + G + X – M) causes price level to rise. However, aggregate demand may rise following an increase in money supply generated by the printing of additional money (classical argument) which drives prices upward. Thus, money plays a vital role. That is why Milton Friedman argues that inflation is always and everywhere a monetary phenomenon.

There are other reasons that may push aggregate demand and, hence, price level upwards. For instance, growth of population stimulates aggregate demand. Higher export earnings increase the purchasing power of the exporting countries. Additional purchasing power means additional aggregate demand. Purchasing power and, hence, aggregate demand may also go up if government repays public debt.

Again, there is a tendency on the part of the holders of black money to spend more on conspicuous consumption goods. Such tendency fuels inflationary fire. Thus, DPI is caused by a variety of factors.

Cost-push Inflation Theory

In addition to aggregate demand, aggregate supply also generates inflationary process. As inflation is caused by a leftward shift of the aggregate supply, we call it CPI. CPI is usually associated with non-monetary factors. CPI arises due to the increase in cost of production. Cost of production may rise due to a rise in cost of raw materials or increase in wages.

However, wage increase may lead to an increase in productivity of workers. If this happens, then the AS curve will shift to the right- ward not leftward—direction. We assume here that productivity does not change in spite of an increase in wages.

Such increases in costs are passed on to consumers by firms by raising the prices of the products. Rising wages lead to rising costs. Rising costs lead to rising prices. And, rising prices again prompt trade unions to demand higher wages. Thus, an inflationary wage-price spiral starts. This causes aggregate supply curve to shift leftward.

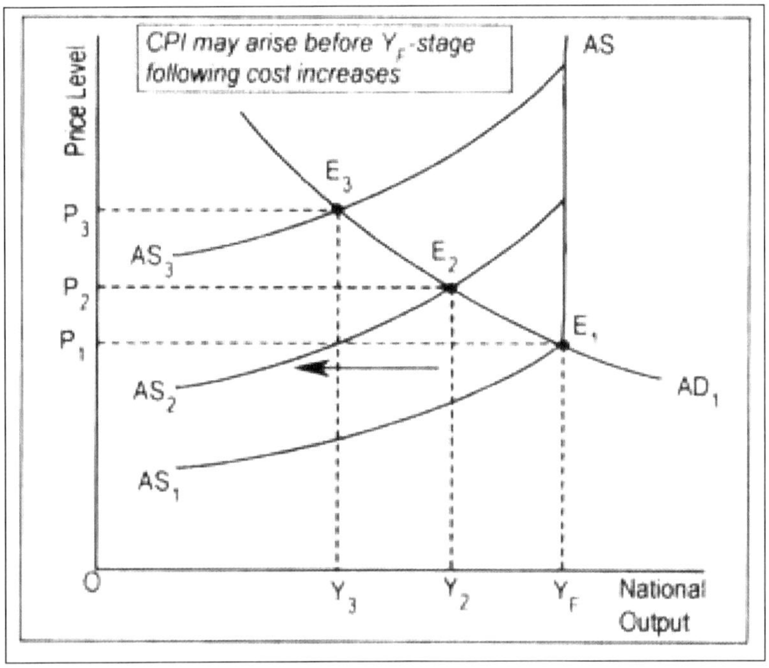

CPI: Shifts in AS Curve.

This can be demonstrated graphically where AS_1 is the initial aggregate supply curve. Below the full employment stage this AS curve is positive sloping and at full employment stage it becomes perfectly inelastic.

Intersection point (E_1) of AD_1 and AS_1 curves determine the price level (OP_1). Now there is a left-ward shift of aggregate supply curve to AS_2. With no change in aggregate demand, this causes price level to rise to OP_2 and output to fall to OY_2. With the reduction in output, employment in the economy declines or unemployment rises. Further shift in AS curve to AS_3 results in a higher price level (OP_3) and a lower volume of aggregate output (OY_3). Thus, CPI may arise even below the full employment (Y_F) stage.

Causes of Cost-push Inflation

It is the cost factors that pull the prices upward. One of the important causes of price rise is the rise in price of raw materials. For instance, by an administrative order the government may hike the price of petrol or diesel or freight rate. Firms buy these inputs now at a higher price. This leads to an upward pressure on cost of production.

Not only this, CPI is often imported from outside the economy. Increase in the price of petrol by OPEC compels the government to increase the price of petrol and diesel. These two important raw materials are needed by every sector, especially the transport sector. As a result, transport costs go up resulting in higher general price level.

Again, CPI may be induced by wage-push inflation or profit-push inflation. Trade unions demand higher money wages as a compensation against inflationary price rise. If increase in money wages exceed labour productivity, aggregate supply will shift upward and leftward. Firms often exercise power by pushing prices up independently of consumer demand to expand their profit margins.

Fiscal policy changes, such as increase in tax rates also leads to an upward pressure in cost of production. For instance, an overall increase in excise tax of mass consumption goods is definitely inflationary. That is why government is then accused of causing inflation.

Finally, production setbacks may result in decreases in output. Natural disaster, gradual exhaustion of natural resources, work stoppages, electric power cuts, etc., may cause aggregate output to decline. In the midst of this output reduction, artificial scarcity of any goods created by traders and hoarders just simply ignite the situation.

Inefficiency, corruption, mismanagement of the economy may also be the other reasons. Thus, inflation is caused by the interplay of various factors. A particular factor cannot be held responsible for any inflationary price rise.

Effects of Inflation

People's desires are inconsistent. When they act as buyers they want prices of goods and services to remain stable but as sellers they expect the prices of goods and services should go up. Such a happy outcome may arise for some individuals; "but, when this happens, others will be getting the worst of both worlds".

When price level goes up, there is both a gainer and a loser. To evaluate the consequence of inflation, one must identify the nature of inflation which may be anticipated and unanticipated. If inflation is anticipated, people can adjust with the new situation and costs of inflation to the society will be smaller.

In reality, people cannot predict accurately future events or people often make mistakes in predicting the course of inflation. In other words, inflation may be unanticipated when people fail to adjust completely. This creates various problems.

One can study the effects of unanticipated inflation under two broad headings

- Effect on distribution of income and wealth;
- Effect on economic growth.

Effects of Inflation on Distribution of Income and Wealth

During inflation, usually people experience rise in incomes. But some people gain during inflation at the expense of others. Some individuals gain because their money incomes rise more rapidly than the prices and some lose because prices rise more rapidly than their incomes during inflation. Thus, it redistributes income and wealth.

Though no conclusive evidence can be cited, it can be asserted that following categories of people are affected by inflation differently.

Creditors and Debtors

Borrowers gain and lenders lose during inflation because debts are fixed in rupee terms. When debts are repaid their real value declines by the price level increase and, hence, creditors lose. An individual may be interested in buying a house by taking loan of Rs. 7 lakh from an institution for 7 years.

The borrower now welcomes inflation since he will have to pay less in real terms than when it was borrowed. Lender, in the process, loses since the rate of interest payable remains unaltered as per agreement. Because of inflation, the borrower is given 'dear' rupees, but pays back 'cheap' rupees. However, if in an inflation-ridden economy creditors chronically loose, it is wise not to advance loans or to shut down business.

Never does it happen. Rather, the loan-giving institution makes adequate safeguard against the erosion of real value. Above all, banks do not pay any interest on current account but charges interest on loans.

Bond and Debenture-holders

In an economy, there are some people who live on interest income—they suffer most. Bondholders earn fixed interest income: These people suffer a reduction in real income when prices rise. In other words, the value of one's savings decline if the interest rate falls short of inflation rate. Similarly, beneficiaries from life insurance programmes are also hit badly by inflation since real value of savings deteriorate.

Investors

People who put their money in shares during inflation are expected to gain since the possibility of earning of business profit brightens. Higher profit induces owners of firm to distribute profit among investors or shareholders.

Salaried People and Wage-earners

Anyone earning a fixed income is damaged by inflation. Sometimes, unionised worker succeeds in raising wage rates of white-collar workers as a compensation against price rise. But wage rate changes with a long time lag. In other words, wage rate increases always lag behind price increases. Naturally, inflation results in a reduction in real purchasing power of fixed income-earners.

On the other hand, people earning flexible incomes may gain during inflation. The nominal incomes of such people outstrip the general price rise. As a result, real incomes of this income group increase.

Profit-earners, Speculators and Black Marketers

It is argued that profit-earners gain from inflation. Profit tends to rise during inflation. Seeing inflation, businessmen raise the prices of their products. This results in a bigger profit. Profit margin, however, may not be high when the rate of inflation climbs to a high level.

However, speculators dealing in business in essential commodities usually stand to gain by inflation. Black marketers are also benefited by inflation.

Thus, there occurs a redistribution of income and wealth. It is said that rich becomes richer and poor becomes poorer during inflation. However, no such hard and fast generalisation can be made. It is clear that someone wins and someone loses during inflation.

These effects of inflation may persist if inflation is unanticipated. However, the redistributive burdens of inflation on income and wealth are most likely to be minimal if inflation is anticipated by the people. With anticipated inflation, people can build up their strategies to cope with inflation.

If the annual rate of inflation in an economy is anticipated correctly people will try to protect them against losses resulting from inflation. Workers will demand 10 p.c. wage increase if inflation is expected to rise by 10 p.c.

Similarly, a percentage of inflation premium will be demanded by creditors from debtors. Business firms will also fix prices of their products in accordance with the anticipated price rise. Now if the entire society "learn to live with inflation", the redistributive effect of inflation will be minimal.

However, it is difficult to anticipate properly every episode of inflation. Further, even if it is anticipated it cannot be perfect. In addition, adjustment with the new expected inflationary conditions may not be possible for all categories of people. Thus, adverse redistributive effects are likely to occur.

Finally, anticipated inflation may also be costly to the society. If people's expectation regarding future price rise become stronger they will hold less liquid money. Mere holding of cash balances during inflation is unwise since its real value declines. That is why people use their money balances in buying real estate, gold, jewellery, etc. Such investment is referred to as unproductive investment. Thus, during inflation of anticipated variety, there occurs a diversion of resources from priority to non-priority or unproductive sectors.

Effect on Production and Economic Growth

Inflation may or may not result in higher output. Below the full employment stage, inflation has a favourable effect on production. In general, profit is a rising function of the price level. An inflationary situation gives an incentive to businessmen to raise prices of their products so as to earn higher volume of profit. Rising price and rising profit encourage firms to make larger investments.

As a result, the multiplier effect of investment will come into operation resulting in a higher national output. However, such a favourable effect of inflation will be temporary if wages and production costs rise very rapidly.

Further, inflationary situation may be associated with the fall in output, particularly if inflation is of the cost-push variety. Thus, there is no strict relationship between prices and output. An increase in aggregate demand will increase both prices and output, but a supply shock will raise prices and lower output.

Inflation may also lower down further production levels. It is commonly assumed that if inflationary tendencies nurtured by experienced inflation persist in future, people will now save less and consume more. Rising saving propensities will result in lower further outputs.

One may also argue that inflation creates an air of uncertainty in the minds of business community, particularly when the rate of inflation fluctuates. In the midst of rising inflationary trend, firms cannot accurately estimate their costs and revenues. That is, in a situation of unanticipated inflation, a great deal of risk element exists.

It is because of uncertainty of expected inflation, investors become reluctant to invest in their business and to make long-term commitments. Under the circumstance, business firms may be deterred in investing. This will adversely affect the growth performance of the economy.

However, slight dose of inflation is necessary for economic growth. Mild inflation has an encouraging effect on national output. But it is difficult to make the price rise of a creeping variety. High rate of inflation acts as a disincentive to long run economic growth. Hyper-inflation discourages savings.

A fall in savings means a lower rate of capital formation. A low rate of capital formation hinders economic growth. Further, during excessive price rise, there occurs an increase in unproductive investment in real estate, gold, jewellery, etc. Above all, speculative businesses flourish during inflation resulting in artificial scarcities and, hence, further rise in prices.

Again, following hyperinflation, export earnings decline resulting in a wide imbalances in the balance of payment account. Often galloping inflation results in a 'flight' of capital to foreign countries since people lose confidence and faith over the monetary arrangements of the country, thereby resulting in a scarcity of resources. Finally, real value of tax revenue also declines under the impact of hyperinflation. Government then experiences a shortfall in investible resources.

Thus economists and policymakers are unanimous regarding the dangers of high price rise. But the consequence of hyperinflation are disastrous. In the past, some of the world economies (e.g., Germany after the First World War, Latin American countries in the 1980s) had been greatly ravaged by hyperinflation.

The German Inflation of 1920s was also Catastrophic

During 1922, the German price level went up 5,470 per cent. In 1923, the situation worsened; the German price level rose 1,300,000,000 (1.3 billion) times. By October of 1923, the postage in the lightest letter sent from Germany to the United States was 200,000 marks. Butter cost 1.5 million marks per pound, meat 2 million marks, a loaf of bread 200,000 marks, and an egg 60,000 marks. Prices increased so rapidly that waiters changed the prices on the menu several times during the course of a lunch. Sometimes, customers had to pay the double price listed on the menu when they observed it first. A photograph of the period shows a German housewife starting the fire in her kitchen stove with paper money and children playing with bundles of paper money tied together into building blocks.

Demand Pull Inflation

Demand Pull Inflation is defined as an increase in the rate of inflation caused by the Aggregate Demand curve. It is the most common cause of inflation.

Demand Pull Inflation involves inflation rising as real Gross Domestic Product rises and unemployment falls, as the economy moves along the Phillips Curve. Demand Pull Inflation is commonly described as "too much money chasing too few goods".

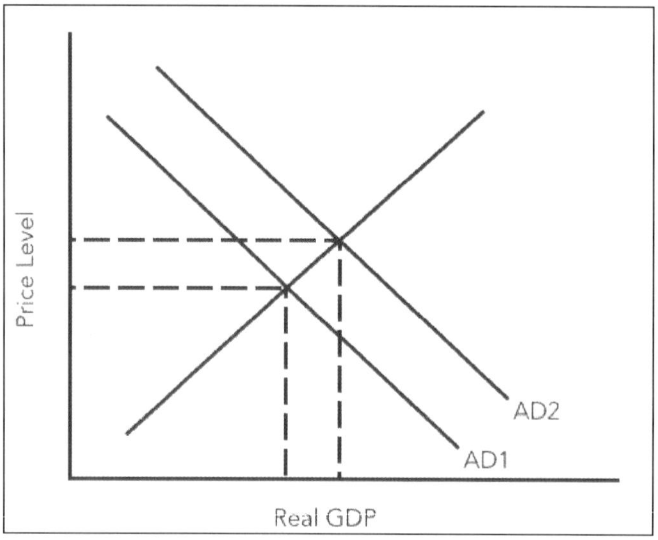

Demand pull inflation graph.

More accurately, it should be described as involving "too much money spent chasing too few goods," since only money that is spent on goods and services can cause inflation. This rise in price level is not expected to happen unless the economy is already at a full-employment level. The term demand-pull inflation is mostly associated with Keynesian economics.

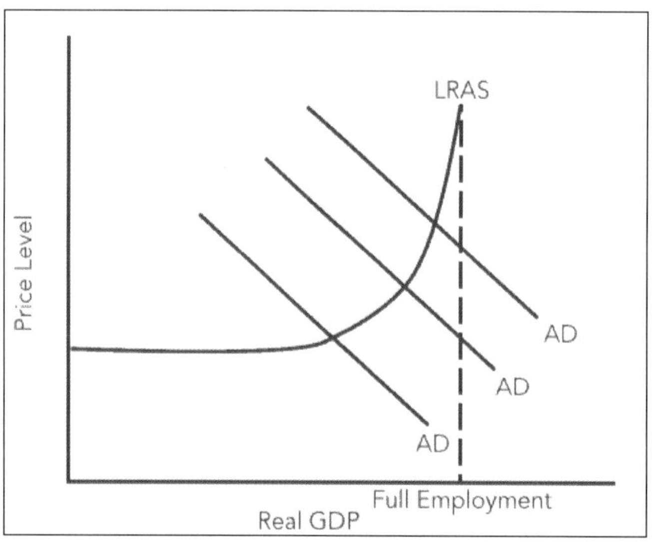

For example, if aggregate demand is rising at 3%, but the productive capacity is only rising at 2%.

Thus, firms will see that demand is outstripping supply and will respond by increasing prices. As firms produce more, they will hire more workers. This hiring spree will cause a fall in unemployment. This increased demand for workers puts upward pressure on wages, leading to wage-push inflation. Finally, higher wages increase the disposable income of employees, leading to a rise in consumer spending.

The effect of inflation will depend on how steep the Aggregate Supply curve is, as in how close it is to full employment. The closer it is, the higher the rise in inflation. This effect can be seen more clearly in the Keynesian Aggregate Demand curve.

Six Causes of Demand Pull Inflation

Consumption

If there is a sharp increase in consumption and investment along with extremely positive businesses atmosphere, then there will be a rise in Aggregate Demand.

Exchange Rate

A depreciation of the exchange rate increases the price of imports and reduces the price of a country's exports. Consumers will buy fewer imports, while exports grow. There will be an increase in Aggregate Demand.

Government Spending

An enormous increase in government spending will drive up Aggregate Demand.

Expectations

The expectation that inflation will rise often leads to a rise in inflation. Workers and firms will raise their prices to 'catch up' to inflation.

Monetary Growth

If there is excessive monetary growth – when they are too much money in the system chasing too few goods. The 'price' of a goodwill thus increase.

Example of Demand Pull Inflation

We can take an example of a small country named Staples with a landmass of just 100 square miles. Despite its historically impressive growth rate, Staples now faces an aging workforce and declining infrastructure. A few years ago, the inflation rate was 3%. However, the data now suggest that the country is falling behind on its growth target.

The central bank of Staples is eager to maintain the growth rate. The central banks decide to enact an aggressive expansionary monetary policy. It decreased the discount rate to push interest rates down, purchased government bonds, decreased required reserve ratios, and let the commercial banks loosen credit standards. These policies resulted in a massive increase in consumption. The country's demand for cars and refrigerators increased to 5,000 vehicles per month and 3,000 refrigerators per quarter, respectively. However, the country could only produce 2,000 cars per month and 1,500 refrigerators per quarter.

Staples is now experiencing Demand Pull inflation. The decline in growth rate was due to an aging population and decaying infrastructure. The problem could only be solved by improving the skills of the workforce and by investing in the infrastructure. By employing an expansionary monetary policy, the excess money increased demand, without increasing the capacity.

Countering Demand Pull Inflation

To counter demand pull inflation, governments, and central banks would have to implement a tight monetary and fiscal policy. Examples include increasing the interest rate or lowering government spending or raising taxes. An increase in the interest rate would make consumers spend less on durable goods and housing. It would also increase investment spending by firms and businesses. In demand pull inflation, Aggregate Demand D is rising too fast, so these contractionary policies would lower the rise, meaning inflation would still occur but at a lower rate.

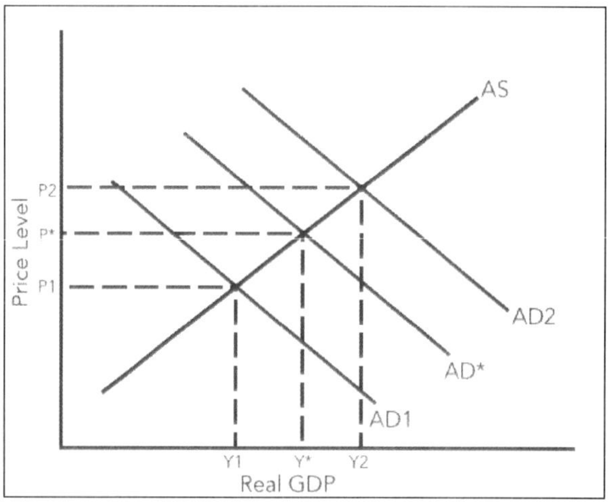

In the diagram above, with a tight monetary and fiscal policy, Aggregate Demand shifts from AD1 to AD*, instead of AD2 (a higher rate of inflation). This leads to an equilibrium price level of P* and output Y*, instead of P2 and Y2.

Cost Push Inflation

Cost-push inflation is a situation where even though there is no increase in aggregate demand, but there is an increase in input prices like raw material and wages.

- The primary driver of cost-push inflation increase is the cost of production factor that results in a decrease of aggregate supply, i.e. total production of goods, in the economy.
- However, demand for these goods remains steady despite the weakening supply scenario that eventually gives way to the increase in the prices of the goods (inflation).

Causes of Cost-push Inflation

Three of the major causes for the increase in costs that generate cost-push inflation are the following:

Wage Push Inflation

One of the causes of cost-push inflation is when the increase in the wages of labor is more than the increase in their productivity at work. Since the labors have to be paid more, the producers increase the price of finished goods to pass on the hike in production cost that eventually results in inflation. This type of inflation is usually seen when there is a strong labor union.

Let us take the example of a company wherein the workers are producing 100 units annually and their wages are fixed at $20 per hour. Now, let us assume that the labor union has demanded a hike in the wage by 25% and consequently the company has increased the wage to $25 per hour. However, the production output has increased from 100 units to 110 units annually. As such, there is a difference between the rise in production output (10%) and a rise in wages (25%) which is known as wage-push inflation.

Profit Push Inflation

The causes of cost-push inflation are when entrepreneurs or producers increase the prices of goods and services more than the popular expectation in order to garner a higher profit margin that again leads to inflationary conditions.

Let us take an example where the senior management of a company has decided to increase the price of its product from $200 to $230 although there is no corresponding increase in the price of inputs and wages. It can be seen that there is a 15% rise in profit leading to inflation and as such this type of inflation is known as profit-push inflation.

Material

Another major cause of cost-push inflation is when there is an increase in the prices of some key materials (such as steel, energy, oil, etc.) which are used, either directly or indirectly, in almost the entire economy. Consequently, an increase in the prices of such material significantly influences the cost structure of all industries and eventually the economy ends up in the clutches of inflation.

The supply shock created by the Organization of the Petroleum Exporting Countries (OPEC) four decades ago is a classic example of material cost-push inflation. The organization intended to decrease the global oil supply by raising the prices that resulted in a sharp increase in inflation that eventually led to a supply shock.

Besides, some other causes of inflation can be natural disasters and government regulations. A good example of inflation caused by the natural disaster is the Hurricane Katrina that created havoc in the US in the year 2005 as the storm destroyed oil refineries that led to soaring of gas prices. On the other hand, an example of inflation due to government regulation is a tax on cigarettes and alcohol which leads to the increased price of these products and hence inflation.

Effects

It is important to understand that inflation per se is not such a bad thing. However, the inflation caused by cost-push inflation is somewhat the wrong kind of inflation. Cost-push inflation is characterized by rising prices and falling real GDP. The fall in real GDP despite an increase in the overall price level is indicative of the fact that the productivity level of the economy is deteriorating. Further, cost-push inflation also affects employment as the decline in real GDP results in decreased demand for goods and services that then compels firms to lay off workers and decreasing the employment. As such, this type of inflation results in a fall in living standards.

Measures to Control Cost-push Inflation

Most often governments intend to implement a deflationary fiscal policy such as higher taxes, lower spending etc. while central banks tend to increase the interest rates. Both the measures are expected to increase the cost of borrowing which is then likely to cut down consumer spending and investment. However, the problem with higher interest rates is that even though it is likely to reduce the inflation rate, it has the potential to result in a big fall in the GDP.

As such, a better long term solution to cost-push inflation can be an implementation of improved supply-side policies that is expected to increase productivity. However, the problem with this solution is that such policies are likely to take a long time to have any effect on the economy.

Measures for Controlling Inflation

It is not easy to control inflation by using a particular measure or instrument.

The main aim of every measure is to reduce the inflow of cash in the economy or reduce the liquidity in the market.

The different measures used for controlling inflation are shown in figure.

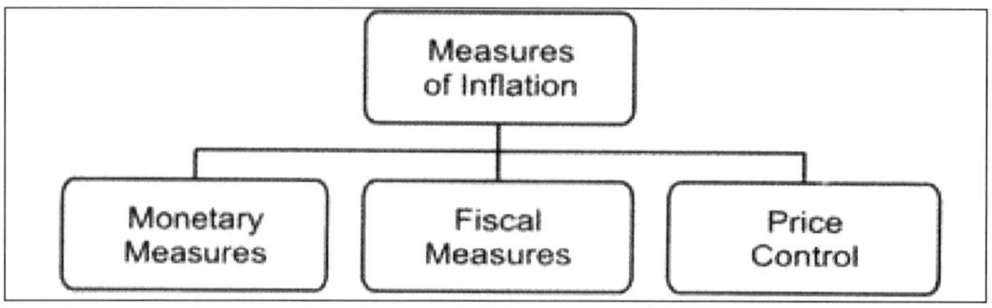

Different Measures for Controlling Inflation.

Monetary Measures

The government of a country takes several measures and formulates policies to control economic activities. Monetary policy is one of the most commonly used measures taken by the government to control inflation.

In monetary policy, the central bank increases rate of interest on borrowings for commercial banks.

As a result, commercial banks increase their rate of interests on credit for the public. In such a situation, individuals prefer to save money instead of investing in new ventures.

This would reduce money supply in the market, which, in turn, controls inflation. Apart from this, the central bank reduces the credit creation capacity of commercial banks to control inflation.

The monetary policy of a country involves the following:

Rise in Bank Rate

Refers to one of the most widely used measure taken by the central bank to control inflation.

The bank rate is the rate at which the commercial bank gets a rediscount on loans and advances by the central bank. The increase in the bank rate results in the rise of rate of interest on loans for the public. This leads to the reduction in total spending of individuals.

The main reasons for reduction in total expenditure of individuals are as follows;

Making the Borrowing of Money Costlier

Refers to the fact that with the rise in the bank rate by the central bank increases the interest rate on loans and advances by commercial banks. This makes the borrowing of money expensive for general public.

Consequently, individuals postpone their investment plans and wait for fall in interest rates in future. The reduction in investments results in the decreases in the total spending and helps in controlling inflation.

Creating Adverse Situations for Businesses

Implies that increase in bank rate has a psychological impact on some of the businesspersons. They consider this situation adverse for carrying out their business activities. Therefore, they reduce their spending and investment.

Increasing the Propensity to Save

Refers to one of the most important reason for reduction in total expenditure of individuals. It is a well-known fact that individuals generally prefer to save money in inflationary conditions. As a result, the total expenditure of individuals on consumption and investment decreases.

Direct Control on Credit Creation

Constitutes the major part of monetary policy.

The central bank directly reduces the credit control capacity of commercial banks by using the following methods:

Performing Open Market Operations (OMO)

Refers to one of the important method used by the central bank to reduce the credit creation capacity of commercial banks. The central bank issues government securities to commercial banks and certain private businesses.

In this way, the cash with commercial banks would be spent on purchasing government securities. As a result, commercial bank would reduce credit supply for the general public.

Changing Reserve Ratios

Involves increase or decrease in reserve ratios by the central bank to reduce the credit creation capacity of commercial banks. For example, when the central bank needs to reduce the credit creation capacity of commercial banks, it increases Cash Reserve Ratio (CRR). As a result, commercial banks need to keep a large amount of cash as reserve from their total deposits with the central bank. This would further reduce the lending capacity of commercial banks. Consequently, the investment by individuals in an economy would also reduce.

Fiscal Measures

Apart from monetary policy, the government also uses fiscal measures to control inflation. The two main components of fiscal policy are government revenue and government expenditure. In fiscal policy, the government controls inflation either by reducing private spending or by decreasing government expenditure, or by using both.

It reduces private spending by increasing taxes on private businesses. When private spending is more, the government reduces its expenditure to control inflation. However, in present scenario, reducing government expenditure is not possible because there may be certain on-going projects for social welfare that cannot be postponed.

Besides this, the government expenditures are essential for other areas, such as defense, health, education, and law and order. In such a case, reducing private spending is more preferable rather than decreasing government expenditure. When the government reduces private spending by increasing taxes, individuals decrease their total expenditure.

For example, if direct taxes on profits increase, the total disposable income would reduce. As a result, the total spending of individuals decreases, which, in turn, reduces money supply in the market. Therefore, at the time of inflation, the government reduces its expenditure and increases taxes for dropping private spending.

Price Control

Another method for ceasing inflation is preventing any further rise in the prices of goods and services. In this method, inflation is suppressed by price control, but cannot be controlled for the long term. In such a case, the basic inflationary pressure in the economy is not exhibited in the form of rise in prices for a short time. Such inflation is termed as suppressed inflation.

The historical evidences have shown that price control alone cannot control inflation, but only reduces the extent of inflation. For example, at the time of wars, the government of different countries imposed price controls to prevent any further rise in the prices. However, prices remain at peak in different economies. This was because of the reason that inflation was persistent in different economies, which caused sharp rise in prices. Therefore, it can be said inflation cannot be ceased unless its cause is determined.

Deflation

Deflation is the reduction of prices of goods, and although deflation may seem like a good thing when you're standing at the checkout counter, it's not. Rather, deflation is an indication that economic conditions are deteriorating. Deflation is usually associated with significant unemployment, which is only corrected after wages drop considerably. Furthermore, businesses' profits drop significantly during periods of deflation, making it more difficult to raise additional capital to expand and develop new technologies.

"Deflation" is often confused with "disinflation". While deflation represents a decrease in the prices of goods and services throughout the economy, disinflation represents a situation where inflation increases at a slower rate. However, disinflation does not usually precede a period of deflation. In fact, deflation is a rare phenomenon that does not occur in the course of a normal economic cycle, and therefore, investors must recognize it as a sign that something is severely wrong with the state of the economy.

Causes of Deflation

Deflation can be caused by a number of factors, all of which stem from a shift in the supply-demand curve. Remember, the prices of all goods and services are heavily affected by a change in the supply and demand, which means that if demand drops in relation to supply, prices will have to drop accordingly. Also, a change in the supply and demand of a nation's currency plays an instrumental role in setting the prices of the country's goods and services.

Although there are many reasons why deflation may take place, the following causes seem to play the largest roles:

Change in Structure of Capital Markets

When many different companies are selling the same goods or services, they will typically lower their prices as a means to compete. Often, the capital structure of the economy will change and companies will have easier access to debt and equity markets, which they can use to fund new businesses or improve productivity.

There are multiple reasons why companies will have an easier time raising capital, such as declining interest rates, changing banking policies, or a change in investors' aversion to risk. However, after they have utilized this new capital to increase productivity, they are going to have to reduce their prices to reflect the increased supply of products, which can result in deflation.

Increased Productivity

Innovative solutions and new processes help increase efficiency, which ultimately leads to lower prices. Although some innovations only affect the productivity of certain industries, others may have a profound effect on the entire economy.

For example, after the Soviet Union collapsed in 1991, many of the countries that formed as a result struggled to get back on track. In order to make a living, many citizens were willing to work for very low prices, and as companies in the United States outsourced work to these countries, they were able to significantly reduce their operating expenses and bolster productivity. Inevitably, this increased the supply of goods and decreased their cost, which led to a period of deflation near the end of the 20th century.

Decrease in Currency Supply

As the currency supply decreases, prices will decrease so that people can afford goods. How can currency supplies decrease? One common reason is through central banking systems.

For instance, when the Federal Reserve was first created, it considerably contracted the money supply of the United States. In the process, this led to a severe case of deflation in 1913. Also, in many economies, spending is often completed on credit. Clearly, when creditors pull the plug on lending money, customers will spend less, forcing sellers to lower their prices to regain sales.

Austerity Measures

Deflation can be the result of decreased governmental, business, or consumer spending, which means government spending cuts can lead to periods of significant deflation. For example, when Spain initiated austerity measures in 2010, preexisting deflation began to spiral out of control.

Deflationary Spiral

Once deflation has shown its ugly head, it can be very difficult to get the economy under control for a number of reasons. First of all, when consumers start cutting spending, business profits decrease. Unfortunately, this means that businesses have to reduce wages and cut their own purchases. In turn, this short-circuits spending in other sectors, as other businesses and wage-earners have less money to spend. As horrible as this sounds, it continues to get worse and the cycle can be very difficult to break.

Effects of Deflation

Deflation can be compared to a terrible winter: The damage can be intense and be experienced for many seasons afterwards. Unfortunately, some nations never fully recover from the damage caused by deflation. Hong Kong, for example, never recovered from the deflationary effects that gripped the Asian economy in 2002.

Deflation may have any of the following impacts on an economy:

Reduced Business Revenues

Businesses must significantly reduce the prices of their products in order to stay competitive. Obviously, as they reduce their prices, their revenues start to drop. Business revenues frequently fall and recover, but deflationary cycles tend to repeat themselves multiple times.

Unfortunately, this means businesses will need to increasingly cut their prices as the period of deflation continues. Although these businesses operate with improved production efficiency, their profit margins will eventually drop, as savings from material costs are offset by reduced revenues.

Wage Cutbacks and Layoffs

When revenues start to drop, companies need to find ways to reduce their expenses to meet their bottom line. They can make these cuts by reducing wages and cutting positions. Understandably, this exacerbates the cycle of inflation, as more would-be consumers have less to spend.

Changes in Customer Spending

The relationship between deflation and consumer spending is complex and often difficult to predict. When the economy undergoes a period of deflation, customers often take advantage of the substantially lower prices. Initially, consumer spending may increase greatly; however, once businesses start looking for ways to bolster their bottom line, consumers who have lost their jobs or taken pay cuts must start reducing their spending as well. Of course, when they reduce their spending, the cycle of deflation worsens.

Reduced Stake in Investments

When the economy goes through a series of deflation, investors tend to view cash as one of their best possible investments. Investors will watch their money grow simply by holding onto it. Additionally, the interest rates investors earn often decrease significantly as central banks attempt to fight deflation by reducing interest rates, which in turn reduces the amount of money they have available for spending.

In the meantime, many other investments may yield a negative return or are highly volatile, since investors are scared and companies aren't posting profits. As investors pull out of stocks, the stock market inevitably drops.

Reduced Credit

When deflation rears its head, financial lenders quickly start to pull the plugs on many of their lending operations for a variety of reasons. First of all, as assets such as houses decline in value, customers cannot back their debt with the same collateral. In the event a borrower is unable to make their debt obligations, the lenders will be unable to recover their full investment through foreclosures or property seizures.

Also, lenders realize the financial position of borrowers is more likely to change as employers start cutting their workforce. Central banks will try to reduce interest rates to encourage customers to borrow and spend more, but many of them will still not be eligible for loans.

Tools to Fix Deflation

Fortunately, it is possible to reduce the impact of deflation. However, fighting deflation requires a disciplined approach, as it will not fix itself. Prior to the Great Depression, it was commonly believed that deflation would eventually run its course. However, economists suggested government intervention was necessary to break a deflationary spiral.

During the Great Depression, the government attempted different methods to fight deflation, most of which proved ineffective. For example, President Franklin D. Roosevelt believed that deflation was caused by an oversupply of goods and services, so he attempted to reduce the supply of resources on the market. One way he tried to do this was to purchase farmland so farmers could not produce as many crops to sell in the marketplace. However, these kinds of "solutions" only further damaged the economy, possibly worsening the deflationary spiral.

Central banks have a considerable influence over the direction of inflation and deflation by changing the nation's monetary supply. For example, the Federal Reserve has engaged in quantitative easing as a means to prevent deflation. Although increasing the nation's monetary supply too much could create excessive inflation, a moderate expansion in the nation's monetary base could be an effective means of fighting deflation.

The central banks' efforts to fight deflation are effective in some instances, but not in others. The biggest limitation with central bank policies is that they can only decrease interest rates until they are near 0%. After reducing interest as much as possible, central banks no longer have a large bevy of solutions available to them. In fact, there still exists no clear-cut, foolproof way to address deflation.

Examples of Deflation

Although deflation is a rare occurrence in the course of an economy, it is a phenomenon that has occurred a number of times throughout history. Among others, these are incidences in which deflation has occurred:

Expansion of Industrial Revolution

During the late 19th century, manufacturers took advantage of new technology that allowed them to increase their productivity. As a result, the supply of goods in the economy increased substantially, and consequently, the prices of those goods decreased. Although the increase in the level of productivity after the Industrial Revolution was a positive development for the economy, it also led to a period of deflation.

Great Depression

The Great Depression was the most financially trying time in American history. During this dark era in history, unemployment spiked, the stock market crashed, and consumers lost much of their savings. Also, employees in high production industries such as farming and mining were producing a great amount, but not getting paid accordingly. As a result, they had less money to spend and were unable to afford basic commodities, even in spite of how much vendors were forced to reduce prices.

Depression of 1920-1921

About eight years prior to the onset of the Great Depression, the United States underwent a shorter depression while recovering from the aftermath of World War I. During this time, a million members of the Armed Forces returned to civilian life, and employers hired a number of returning troops at reduced wages. The labor market was already very tight before they returned, and due to the expansion in the workforce, unions lost much of their bargaining power and were unable to demand higher wages, which resulted in reduced spending.

European Debt Crisis

The debt crisis in Europe is causing a number of complications for the global economy. In response to this crisis, governments have implemented austerity measures, such as cutting government assistance to needy families. However, these measures have reduced GDP considerably. Also, the banks have contracted their credit, which has reduced the money supply within the country. As a result, Europe is undergoing massive deflation.

Debt Deflation

Debt deflation is a theory based on the principle of the correlation between the debt burden and the price level in a country. Deflation has the effect of significantly reducing the debt burden. Conversely, a price increase leads to an increase in the debt burden. This is the theory put forward by its creator Irving Fisher in 1933. In his opinion, debt deflation explains all major economic crises.

Mechanism of Debt Deflation

When a country has economic growth, the confidence of economic agents (households, companies, the State, etc.) is high. Households consume more and part of their consumption is financed by debt. At the corporate level, this growth drives investment financed by debt. The stronger the (GDP) growth, the more willing the agents are to go into debt.

At first, debt fuels growth, it helps to accelerate it. But in the long term, this excessive debt drives prices down and leads to deflation. Effectively, by repaying their debts, economic agents gradually lose purchasing power. Cases of over-indebtedness are more and more frequent and there is a desire to reduce debt. Household consumption ends up gradually decreasing. With lower demand for goods and services, prices fall. This is the mechanism of Fisher's debt deflation.

Debt Deflation and Unemployment

Debt deflation is a dangerous mechanism.

Faced with the decline in activity, companies do not react immediately. It may take several months for the productive system to adapt to the drop in demand. During this time, companies see their inventories increase. They lower their prices to sell off their stocks, which reduces their margins and therefore their profits.

If demand remains low, companies must adapt and reduce their costs. This requires a reduction in wages and numerous redundancies. Debt deflation therefore leads to an increase in unemployment.

Deflation and the Debt Burden

When there is deflation in a country, its currency gains value. A smaller amount of money is needed to buy goods and services, as prices are falling. From a debt perspective, deflation is beneficial for lenders and penalizing for borrowers. For borrowers, debt repayment becomes increasingly expensive, as money gains value over time. They need to pay back more than before.

For economic agents, deflation therefore has a strong impact on their debt level. This forces some agents to sell some of their assets to cover this increase in the cost of debt. The massive sale of assets lowers their prices and fuels deflation. This is an additional loss for economic agents. Deflation is self-sustaining and that is why it is very difficult to get out of it.

For Fisher, this theory of debt deflation explains all economic crises.

Methods to Control Deflation

Currency Expansion

Deflation can be controlled though currency expansion. The central bank can issue new notes to increase the supply of currency in the country. The new money is injected into the economy. The people get more income. They spend more on goods and services. The demand increases, which raises the level of production. In this way deflation is driven out of the economy and the rate of growth can maintained.

Credit Expansion

Credit expansion is a method to control deflation. The central bank can ask commercial banks to expand the volume of credit in the country. The rate of interest is lowered. The business activities go up and the period of deflation comes to an end.

Low Bank Rate

Deflation may be controlled by lowering the bank rate. The central bank can lower the bank rate to provide more funds to commercial banks. The lower bank rate is an indication for the banks that there is less money supply in the economy. In order to meet the business requirements the banks provide more loans. In case of need, they can get money from the central bank. The low bank rate helps to combat deflation.

Low Reserve Ratio

The low reserve ratio is a tool to control the deflation. As per law commercial banks are bound to deposit **5 %** of their demand and time deposits with the central bank. The decrease in reserve ratio encourages commercial banks to provide more loans. When there is shortage of funds, the banks can borrow from central bank. The increasing rate of loan is another step to kill the evil forces of deflation.

Consumer Credit

Deflation is controllable by means of consumer credit. The loans must be provided to consumers for the purchase of household assets. Te number of installments can be increased to provide relief to the borrowers. In this way more money remains in the business. The additional money helps the people to expand business activities. The consumer's credit is one of the methods to eradicate the germs of deflation.

Tax Decrease

Deflation can be controlled though tax decrease. The rate of tax may be reduced and that personal income may increase. The saved amount can be used for purchase of goods and services. The demand for goods goes up. The businessmen try to raise the level of production. The market forces work for improving the rate of economic growth.

Public Debt Payment

The government can repay public debt as a tool to control deflation. The debt can be returned by the government in order to increase the supply of money. The amount can be used for other purposes. The business persons can obtain more loans than before. The liberal loan policy at concessional rates is helpful for the business. The banks are able to earn income. In this way deflation is negated.

Public Works

The government can start public works programmed to eliminate the deflation. The construction of roads, dams, bridges, hospitals, schools and power projects is possible. The amount is transferred from government to general public. The incomes of people go up. The demand for goods increases and there is improvement in production. The public works programmed is another way to eliminate the deflation.

New Investment

Deflation can be controlled though new investment. The investment can be used to setup new factors and mills. The money is transferred from idle hands to productive hands. The production and employment increase due to new investment. The flow of money from idle hands to productive hands raises the level of growth. The economy moves in the right direction for the welfare of the people by overcoming deflation.

Production Control

The control over production can help to control deflation. The producers can fix production quota for each. The control over supply is necessary to maintain the price level. The association of producers may be asked to take steps for reasonable and quality output. The demand can be noted and supply must be released to the market. This method is also one of the ways to control deflation.

References

- Aggregate-demand-its-meaning-and-components-economics-721: economicsdiscussion.net, Retrieved 23 January, 2019
- Inflation-types-causes-and-effects-with-diagram-6401: economicsdiscussion.net, Retrieved 03 July, 2019
- Demand-pull-inflation: intelligenteconomist.com, Retrieved 15 August, 2019
- Cost-push-inflation: wallstreetmojo.com, Retrieved 19 May, 2019
- Deflation-definition-causes-effects: moneycrashers.com, Retrieved 29 April, 2019
- Methods-to-control-deflation, banking-finance: businessstudynotes.com, Retrieved 16 March, 2019

6

Government Budget and Economic Policy

Government budget is an annual financial statement that estimates government expenditure and revenue for the coming financial year. The policy that falls under the domain of taxation, money supply, government budgets, labor market, etc. is termed as economic policy. This chapter closely examines the concepts of government budget and economic policy to provide an extensive understanding of the subject.

The government budget is an annual financial statement showing item wise estimates of expected revenue and anticipated expenditure during a fiscal year. Just as your household budget is all about what you earn and spend, in the same way the government budget is a statement of its income and expenditure. In the beginning of every year the government presents before the Lok Sabha an estimate of its receipts and expenditure for the coming financial year. It plans its expenditure according to its objectives and then tries to raise the resources to meet the proposed expenditure.

The main objectives of a government budget:

- Economic growth: To promote rapid and balanced economic growth so as to improve living standard of the people.
- Reduction of poverty and unemployment: to eradicate mass poverty and unemployment by creating employment opportunities and providing maximum social benefits to the poor.
- Reduction of inequalities: Inequalities of income and wealth are reduced through levying taxes and granting subsidies. Government levies high rate of tax on rich people and lower rate in the lower income group and also provides the latter with subsidies and amenities. Economic progress in itself is not a sufficient goal but the goal must be equitable progress.
- Reallocation of resources: The reallocation of resources is necessary in order to achieve social and economic objectives. The government allocate resources into areas where private initiative is absent such as public sanitation, education, health etc.
- Price stability: To maintain price stability and correct business cycles involving depression characterized by falling output, prices and increasing unemployment.
- Management of public enterprises: To manage public enterprises which are of nature of national monopolies like railways, electricity etc.

Government Deficit

A deficit is an amount by which the expenditures in a budget exceed the income. A Government Deficit is the amount of money in the set budget by which the government expenditure exceeds the government income amount. This deficit provides an indication of the financial health of the economy. To reduce the deficit or the gap between the expenditures and income, the government may cut back on certain expenditures and also increase revenue-generating activities.

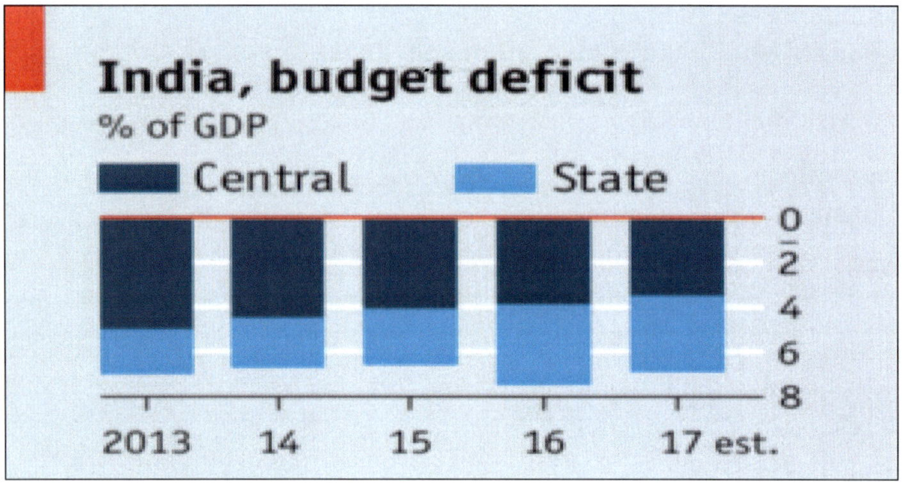

Types of Government Deficit

Revenue Deficit

The shortfall between the total revenue received to the total revenue expenditure is revenue deficit.

Revenue deficit = Total revenue expenditure – Total revenue receipts

This deficit only includes current income and current expenses. A high value of deficit indicates that the government should cut down on its expenditures. The government may increase its revenue receipts by increasing tax income. Disinvestment which means selling off assets is another remedial measure to reduce revenue deficit.

Fiscal Deficit

A fiscal deficit is a gap by which government's total expenditures exceed the government's total generated revenue. This, however, does not include the government borrowings.

Fiscal deficit = Total expenditure – Total receipts excluding borrowings

Fiscal deficit indicates the amount of money that the government will need to borrow during the financial year. A greater deficit implies more borrowing by the government and the extent of the deficit indicates the amount of expense for which the money is borrowed.

A huge disadvantage or implication of fiscal deficit is it may lead to a debt trap. Also, it may lead to unnecessary and wasteful expenditure by the government. Increased fiscal deficit leads to uncontrolled inflation. Borrowing is one way to reduce fiscal deficit. Another way is deficit financing.

Deficit financing refers to the printing of new notes to increase cash flow in the system. The fiscal deficit is a positive outcome if it leads to the creation of assets. It is detrimental to the economic condition of the nation if it is used to simply cover revenue deficit.

Primary Deficit

A primary deficit is the amount of money that the government needs to borrow apart from the interest payments on the previously borrowed loans.

Primary deficit = Fiscal deficit – Interest payments on previous loans

Measures to Reduce Government Deficit

- Increased emphasis on tax-based revenues and appropriate measures to reduce tax evasion.
- Disinvestment should be done where assets are not being used effectively
- Reduction in subsidies by the government will also help reduce the deficit.
- Try and avoid unplanned expenditures.
- Borrowing from domestic sources.
- Borrowing from external sources.
- A broadened tax base may also help in reducing the government deficit.

To summarize, a government deficit is a condition where the budget expenditure exceeds the budget revenue receipts. This could be due to a sudden shift in budget requirements. A controlled deficit situation causes an economy to grow.

An uncontrolled government deficit may lead to deterioration in the financial health of the economy. The agenda of the government should be to plan the revenues and expenditures such that the economy moves towards a balanced budget situation.

Government Revenue refers to the revenue of the government finance by means of participating in the distribution of the social products, which is the financial resources for ensuring the government to function. The contents of government revenue have been changed several times. Now it includes the following main items:

- Various tax revenues, including value added tax, business tax, consumption tax, land value added tax, tax on city maintenance and construction, resources tax, tax on use of urban land, enterprise income tax, personal income tax, tariff, stamp tax on security transactions, tax on purchase of motor vehicles, tax on agriculture and animal husbandry and tax on occupancy of cultivated land, etc.
- Special revenues, including revenues from the fee on sewage treatment, fee on urban water resources, fee for the compensation of mineral resources and extra-charges for education, etc.
- Other revenues, including revenue from interest, revenue from the repayment of capital construction loan, revenue from capital construction projects, and donations and grants.

- Subsidies for the losses of the state-owned enterprises. This is an item of negative revenue, consisting of subsidies to industrial, commercial and grain purchasing and supply enterprises.

Government Expenditure refers to the distribution and use of the funds the government finance has raised, so as to meet the needs of economic construction and various causes. It includes the following main items:

- Expenditure for capital construction: It refers to the non-gratuitous use and appropriation of funds for capital construction in the range of capital construction, outlay of capital as well as the loans on capital construction approved by the government for special purpose or policy purpose and the expenditure with discount paid in an overall way within the amount of the funds appropriated to the departments for capital construction.

- Innovation funds of the enterprises: They refer to the funds appropriated from the government budget for the enterprises to tap the latent power, upgrade the technology and carry out innovation, including the innovation fund of the departments, loan of the enterprises for innovation, subsidies on the innovation of the small fertilizer plant, small cement plant, small coal mines, small machinery plant and small steel plant, the expenditure of interest for the loan for innovation.

- Geological prospecting expenses: They refer to the expenses appropriated from the government budget to the geological prospecting units for the expenditure of the prospecting work, including the expenditures of the administrative agencies for geological prospecting and their institutional units as well as the geological prospecting expenditure.

- Expenditures for science and technology promotion: They refer to the expenses appropriated from the government budget for the scientific and technological expenditure, including new products development expenditure, expenditure for intermediate trial and subsidies on important scientific researches.

- Expenditure for supporting rural production: It refers to the expenditures appropriated from the government budget for supporting the various expenditures of the rural collective units or households for production, including the subsidies to the small water conservancy projects and well drilling, sprinkling irrigation projects run by the villages; subsidies on the rural water and soil conserving measures; subsidies to the small power stations run by the villages; subsidies to the expenditure for fighting against particularly severe draughts; subsidies on the rural waste land exclamation; fund for supporting the township enterprises; fund for supporting rural cooperative production organizations, subsidies to the expenditure for popularization of the agricultural technologies and plant protection in the rural areas; subsidies to the expenditure for the protection of grasslands and cattle and fowls; subsidies on afforestation and forest protection in rural areas; subsidies on the rural aquatic products industry; special fund for developing grain production.

- Operating expenses of the departments of farming, forestry, water conservancy and meteorology etc. They refer to the expenses appropriated from the government budget for the expenditures of agricultural exclamation, farms, agriculture, animal husbandry, agricultural machinery, forestry, timber industry, water conservancy, aquatic products industry, meteorology, technology popularization in township enterprises, popularization (demonstration) of improved varieties, plant (cattle and fowls, forest) protection, water quality monitoring, prospecting and designing, resources investigation, cadres training, subsidies to horticulture gardens, expenditure of specialized secondary schools, subsidies on the experiments of sowing herbage seeds by flights, expenditures of afforestation agencies and meteorology agencies, expenses for fishery administration and operating expenses for agricultural administration, etc.

- Operating expenses of the departments of industry, transport and commerce: They refer to the expenses appropriated from the government budget to cover the expenditure on salaries and operational expenditure of the departments of industry, transport and commerce for the expenditure of business development, including expenses for prospecting and designing, expenditures of specialized secondary schools, expenditures of the technical training schools and expenditures for cadres training, etc.
- Operating expenses of the departments of culture, education, science and public health: They refer to the expenses appropriated from the government budget for the expenditures on salaries and operational expenditure of the causes of culture, publication, cultural relics, education, public health, traditional Chinese medical science, free medical services, sports, archives, earthquake, ocean, communications, broadcasting, film and television, family planning; expenditure for training of cadres of government, party and mass organization; expenditures for natural sciences, social sciences, associations for science and technology and the special expenditure for the high-tech researches. They include mainly wages, extra wages, welfare funds, pension for the retirees, stipend, expenses for official business, expenses for equipment purchases, expenses for repairs, business expenses and subsidies to the units which are unable to support their expenditures by their own earnings.
- Pension for the disabled or for the families of the bereaved and relief funds for social welfare: They refer to the funds appropriated from the government budget for the expenditures of pension for the disabled or for the families of the bereaved and relief funds for social welfare, including the lump-sum or regular pension paid by the departments of civil affairs to the members of martyrs families and families of those who died for the public interest, pension to the revolutionary disabled, subsidies for permanent disability of various kinds, subsidies to the military martyrs dependents and the demobilized servicemen, expenditure for settling down the demobilized servicemen, operating expenses of the consoling institutions, expenses for management and repair of the commemorative buildings for the martyrs, the expenses managed by the departments of civil affairs for the retirees and those who have quitted their work, expenses for social relief in rural and urban areas, operating expenses for providing relief to the areas of natural calamity and subsidies on the reconstruction after the particularly severe natural calamities, etc.
- Expenditure on retirees: It refers to the expenditure on retirees of government agencies and institutions that are covered by the state budget.
- Expenses on subsidies to social security system: It refers to expenditure from the state

budget for subsidies to social security system, including subsidies to the social insurance fund, subsidies to promoting employment, subsidies to laid-off workers of state-owned enterprises, supplement to national social security funds, etc.

- Expenditures for national defence: They refer to the funds appropriated from the government budget for the expenditures for building up national defence and safeguarding national security, including expenses of national defence, expenses of scientific researches on national defence, expenses for building up peoples militia and expenditure for special projects, etc.

- Administrative expenses: They include expenditure for administration, subsidies to the parties and mass organizations, diplomatic expenditure, expenditure for public security, judicial expenditure, law court expenditure, procuratorial expenditure and subsidies to the expenses for treating the cases by the public security departments, procuratorial organs and law courts.

- Expenditure on policy-related subsidies: It refers to the expenditure appropriated, with the approval of the government, from the state budget for price subsidies on such products as grain, cotton and edible oil. More specifically, it includes subsidies to the difference between the selling prices and purchasing prices of grains, cotton and edible oil, subsidies for curtaining prices and for sugar reserve, subsidies to the difference between the selling prices and purchasing prices of means pf agricultural production, risk fund for grains, risk fund for non-staple food, risk fund for local production of coal, etc.

- Expenditure on interest of debts: It refers to expenses from the state budget on paying interest of domestic and foreign debts.

Revenue of the central government and revenue of the local governments: refers to the revenue of the central government and that of the local governments as defined by the decentralized taxation system starting from 1994. In accordance with this system, the revenue of the central government includes tariff, consumption tax and value added tax levied by the customs, consumption tax, income tax of the enterprises subordinate to the central government, income taxes of the local banks, foreign-funded banks and non-bank financial institutions, business tax and profits of railways, head offices of banks, head office of insurance company, which are handed over to the government in a centralized way, tax on city maintenance and construction, tax on purchasing motor vehicles, tonnage tax of ships, 75% of the value added tax, 94% of the tax on stock dealing (stamp tax), interest income tax in the personal income tax, proportion of the personal income tax (other that interest income tax) to be shared by the central government, and tax on ocean petroleum resources,. The revenue of the local governments includes business tax, income tax of the enterprises subordinate to the local government, proportion of the personal income tax (other that interest income tax) to be shared by the central government, tax on the use of urban land, tax on the adjustment of the investment in fixed assets, tax on town maintenance and construction, tax on real estates, tax on the use of vehicles and ships, stamp tax, slaughter tax, tax on agriculture and animal husbandry, tax on special agricultural products, tax on the occupancy of cultivated land, contract tax, value-added tax on land, income from charges on use of state-owned land, 25% of the value added tax, 6% of the tax on stock dealing (stamp tax) and tax on resources other than the ocean petroleum resources.

Expenditure of the central government and expenditure of the local governments: according to the different functions of the central government and local governments in the economic and social activities, the rights of affairs administration are classified between the central government and local governments; and the classification of the expenditure between the central government and local governments are made on the basis of the classification of the rights of affairs administration between them. The expenditure of the central government includes the expenditure for national defence, expenditure for armed police forces, the administrative expenses and various operating expenses at the level of central government, expenditure for key projects and the expenditure of the central government for adjusting the national economic structure, coordinating the development among different regions and exercising the macro-economic regulation and control. The expenditure of the local governments includes mainly the administrative expenses and various operating expenses at the level of local governments, the expenditure for capital construction and technological innovation with the funds raised by the local government, expenditure for supporting rural production, expenditure for city maintenance and construction and expenditure for price subsidies, etc.

Extra-budgetary revenue and expenditure: Extra-budgetary fund refers to financial fund of various types not covered by the regular government budgetary management, which is collected, allocated or arranged by government agencies, institutions and social organizations while performing duties delegated to them or on behalf of the government in accordance with laws, rules and regulations. It mainly covers following items: administrative and institutional fees, governmental funds and extra charges that are stipulated by laws and regulations; administrative and institutional fees approved by the State Council and provincial governments and their financial and planning (price management) departments; governmental funds and extra charges established by the State Council and the Ministry of Finance; funds turned over to competent departments by their subordinate institutions; self-raised and collected funds by township governments for their own expenditure; and other financial funds that are not covered in budgetary management. Social security funds are treated as extra-budget fund and managed for its exclusive use, given the circumstance that separate government budgetary system for social security is yet to be designed. Special accounts are opened by the financial departments in banks for the management of revenue and expenditure of extra-budgetary fund. Extra-budgetary revenue and expenditure is managed separately, namely, revenue of institutions and departments must enter into the special accounts of the financial departments at the same administrative level, and their extra-budgetary expenditure is arranged in line with the extra-budget plans and appropriated from these accounts.

Revenue from debts refers to fund raised by the state in credit forms, including various domestic government bonds issued by the Ministry of Finance to commercial banks and other investors, bonds in foreign currencies issued by the Ministry of Finance at the international capital market, and other foreign debts borrowed and to be repaid centrally by the government finance.

Expenditure on repayment of principal of debts refers to the expenditure from government finance on the repayment of principal of domestic and foreign debts.

Deficit of central government finance refers to the difference between the total expenditure and the total revenue of the central government.

Government Economic Policy

Government economic policy is a measure by which a government attempts to influence the economy. The national budget generally reflects the economic policy of a government, and it is partly through the budget that the government exercises its three principal methods of establishing control: the allocative function, the stabilization function, and the distributive function.

Over time, there have been considerable changes in emphasis on these different economic functions of the budget. In the 19th century, government finance was primarily concerned with the allocative function. The job of government was to raise revenue as cheaply and efficiently as possible to perform the limited tasks that it could do better than the private sector. As the 20th century began, the distribution function acquired increased significance. Social welfare benefits became important, and many countries introduced graduated tax systems. In the later interwar period, and more especially in the 1950s and 60s, stabilization was central, although equity was also a major concern in the design of tax systems. In the 1970s and 80s, however, the pendulum swung back. Once more, allocative issues came to the fore, and stabilization and distribution became less significant in government finance.

The Allocative Function

The allocative function in budgeting determines on what government revenue will be spent. Because a high proportion of national income is now devoted to public expenditure, allocation decisions become more significant in political and economic terms. At all times and in all countries the calls for expenditure on specific services or activities, or for more generous transfer payments, will always exceed the amount that can reasonably be raised in taxation or by borrowing. The debate about how these scarce resources should be allocated has continued for hundreds of years, and, although numerous methods of deciding on priorities have emerged, it has never been satisfactorily resolved. In practice, most democracies contain a number of different factions that disagree on the proper allocation of resources and indeed the proper level of public sector involvement in the economy; the frequent change of national governments is related to the constant search for the right answers.

Public Goods

Economists have sought to provide objective criteria for public expenditures through the so-called theory of public goods. It is generally recognized that some goods needed by the public cannot be provided through the private market. Lighthouses are a classic example. The costs of a lighthouse are such that no one shipowner will want to finance it; on the other hand, if a lighthouse is provided for one shipowner, it can be made available to all for no additional cost. Indeed it must be available to all, since there is no practical means of excluding ships from using the facility provided by the lighthouse, even if their owners have refused to pay for it. The only practical method of providing such services is by collective action.

If goods are to be provided in this way, rather than through the private market, it is immediately necessary to confront the twin problems of deciding how much to provide and who should pay for that provision. Even if all individuals wanted the service equally—as, perhaps, with lighthouses—their views on the extent of the service would be influenced by the allocation of the costs. Where different households may have different preferences and some may not want the service at all—as, for example, with defense by nuclear weapons—these difficulties are compounded. Economists have tried to devise abstract voting schemes that would reconcile these difficulties, but these appear to have little practical application.

Moreover, others would challenge this whole approach to the problem. It would be absurd to say that the consumer has a taste for national defense and that it is the job of the government to satisfy it. The task of national leaders is to evolve a defense policy and persuade the public to accept it. Similarly, conservationists must attempt to awaken the public to the importance of parks and wildlife. In the context of public policy, the efficient allocation of resources consists not merely of distributing funds in the pursuit of given objectives but also involves determining the objectives themselves.

Genuine public goods pose severe problems for the national budget; it is very difficult to decide how far particular goods—the arts, national parks, even defense—should be supplied, and therefore no formal procedure of determination is likely to evolve. What should be given to each will continue to be the subject of intense political debate, with allocation changing as the government changes.

Merit Goods

The concept of merit goods assists governments in deciding which public or other goods should be supplied. Merit goods are commodities that the public sector provides free or cheaply because the government wishes to encourage their consumption. Goods such as subsidized housing or social services, which predominantly help the poor, or health care services, which help the poor and elderly, are generally regarded as having considerable merit and therefore have a strong claim on government resources. Other examples include the provision of retraining schemes or urban regeneration programs.

Cost-benefit Analysis

Once decisions have been made on how the limited national budget should be divided between different groups of activities, or even before this, public authorities need to decide which specific projects should be undertaken. One method that has been used is cost-benefit analysis. This attempts to do for government programs what the forces of the marketplace do for business programs: to measure, and compare in terms of money, the discounted streams of future benefits and future costs associated with a proposed project. If the ratio of benefits to costs is considered satisfactory, the project should be undertaken. "Satisfactory" means, among other things, that the project is superior to any available public or private alternative. Or, if funds are limited, public investment projects may be assigned priorities according to their cost-benefit ratios.

One difficulty with cost-benefit analysis is that every government agency has an incentive to estimate favourable ratios for its own projects. It must, after all, compete with other agencies for funds. No one can be certain as to the returns to be expected from an irrigation canal or a highway. Private investors have also been known to exaggerate their claims in appealing to stockholders, but they are generally subject to market sanctions that encourage them to err on the side of caution.

In addition to the possibility that cost-benefit analysis may be biased by the preformed views of those commissioning the study, there are other, more fundamental difficulties. Almost all proposals have effects that are difficult to value in monetary terms. The siting of a new airport brings problems of noise and property blight to local people and increases the risk that civilians may die in an accident. Putting a sensible value on human life has been a continuing difficulty for those carrying out cost-benefit analyses, even though every project does in fact affect probabilities of life and death. These problems are, of course, not confined to cost-benefit analysis. Additional expenditure on health service or on road safety or better housing or heating old people's homes in winter all affect the number of people who die prematurely. The failure of cost-benefit analysis to provide answers to the problems of valuing life, or the quality of life, is a reflection of the wider problem confronting all decisions on public expenditure: the influence of subjective judgment.

Public Ownership and Privatization

Until the mid-1970s the proportion of economic activity controlled by the government and the share of taxes in national income tended to increase in most countries. Since then, however, challenges to this growth in the role of government have become increasingly influential, and moves to privatization have been common.

There are several types of privatization. One involves the sale to private owners of state-owned assets, and this is most correctly called privatization. Publicly owned houses may be sold to their occupants. Commodity stockpiles may be reduced or disbanded. Increasingly, however, attention has been turned to the sale of publicly owned industries, thus reversing the move to nationalization that occurred, particularly in western Europe, around and after World War II.

Where the privatized industry operates in a competitive environment, no new problems arise. Singapore has privatized its airline system, for example, which now competes with a mixture of privately and publicly owned international airlines. Where privatization occurs but monopoly continues, however, there are new difficulties. Both Japan and the United Kingdom have privatized their telecommunications networks. Although, in certain limited areas of telecommunications, competition is possible—and has been allowed to develop in both the United States and Britain—technical and legal restrictions inhibit competition in many sectors of the industry.

Regulation is necessary, therefore, to restrict the freedom of privatized monopolies, or near monopolies, to raise prices and to exploit consumers in other ways. In the United States, which has by far the longest history of regulating private utilities, such regulation has normally limited the rate of return that they earn to what is considered a fair level. A disadvantage of this is that it may give the industry no greater incentive to increased efficiency than would exist in public ownership, since higher costs can be passed directly onto consumers. There have been experiments, therefore, with other forms of regulation, which seek to strike a balance between incentives for better performance and the ability to exploit consumers.

A further problem for such regulation is that utilities and similar industries normally operate in both competitive and monopoly markets. They may be inclined to use their monopoly power in some areas to gain unfair competitive advantages in others. Despite these difficulties, an increasingly wide range of industries, ranging from water supply to airports, are now considered candidates for privatization.

Privatization can also mean the dismantling of existing statutory restrictions on competition. State activities are often protected by legal prohibitions on competing private enterprise. German railways, for example, are entirely state-owned, and the law not only prevents competing railroads but severely restricts coach services and limits competitive trucking. The dismantling of such restrictions is seen as one method of improving the efficiency of state concerns.

Another demand of privatization is the contracting out of publicly provided services. U.S. municipalities have often entrusted activities such as refuse collection, and in some cases even fire service, to private contractors, and European countries are increasingly experimenting with similar schemes. These possibilities demonstrate that a service may be government-financed but not necessarily provided by the government; if extended more widely, the concept could yield a different view of the economic role of the state.

While the objective of privatization is often to increase the efficiency of government activities, its implementation may also have important effects on government revenue. Any savings that result from lower costs lead directly to lower tax rates. Where budgeting procedures do not distinguish between capital and current transactions, the proceeds of privatization sales provide a once-and-for-all boost to revenues. The availability of this source of funding for state activity has given an artificial attractiveness to privatization, especially in the United Kingdom. If an industry is sold for the present value of its expected earnings and if these earnings are the same in public and private ownership, privatization should have no net impact on public finances. If it is expected to be more efficient in the private sector, government finance, on balance, gains. If it is sold for less than the maximum revenue that would be obtained—and this is often the case, either because of the difficulty of selling assets as large as nationalized industries or because the government wishes to secure a wide dispersion of share ownership—the impact is likely to be negative.

Other forms of Government Intervention

Government spending is not the only way in which government allocates resources. Its regional policies will determine whether domestic and overseas investors build factories in particular places, while its taxation policies will determine whether they build them at all. Government competition and merger policies affect the structure of industry and commerce, while regulatory activities—setting the number of hours shops may be open or who may buy cigarettes—have profound effects on commercial activities.

Government also affects allocations by setting the legal and administrative framework within which the economy functions. It may specify minimum wage levels or control the siting of new ventures and the activities of existing ones. Such activities of government profoundly affect the allocation of resources, but they are rarely monitored or subject to serious control.

The Stabilization Function

Stabilization of the economy (e.g., full employment, control of inflation, and an equitable balance of payments) is one of the goals that governments attempt to achieve through manipulation of fiscal and monetary policies. Fiscal policy relates to taxes and expenditures, monetary policy to financial markets and the supply of credit, money, and other financial assets.

Stabilization Theory

The new stabilization policy needed a theoretical rationale if it was ever to win general acceptance from the leaders of public opinion. The main credit for providing this belongs to Keynes. In his General Theory of Employment, Interest and Money he endeavoured to show that a capitalist economy with its decentralized market system does not automatically generate full employment and stable prices and that governments should pursue deliberate stabilization policies. There has been much controversy among economists over the substance and meaning of Keynes's theoretical contribution. Essentially, he argued that high levels of unemployment might persist indefinitely unless governments took monetary and fiscal action. At that time he believed that fiscal action was likely to be more effective than monetary measures. In the deep depression of the 1930s, interest rates had ceased to exert much influence on the ways in which owners of wealth disposed of their funds; they might choose to hold larger cash balances instead of spending more money as the traditional theory had suggested. Nor were investors inclined to take advantage of low interest rates if they could not find profitable uses for borrowed funds, particularly if their firms were already suffering from excess capacity. Keynes's pessimistic view of monetary policy had a strong influence on economists and governments during and immediately after World War II, with the result that monetary policy was not tried very much during the 1940s. It was often forgotten during the policy discussions of the time that Keynes's views on the efficacy of monetary policy were related to the particular situation of the 1930s.

Another influential idea embodied in Keynes's writing was that of economic stagnation. He suggested that in the advanced industrial countries people tended to save more as their incomes grew larger and that private consumption tended to be a smaller and smaller part of the national income. This implied that investment would have to take a continually larger share of the national income in order to maintain full employment. Since he doubted that investment would rise sufficiently to do this, Keynes was rather pessimistic about the possibility of achieving full employment in the long run. He thus suggested that there might be some permanent tendency to high levels of unemployment. This also had considerable influence on economic policy during the early postwar period; it was some time before those in decision-making positions realized that inflation, rather than stagnation and unemployment, was to be the main problem confronting them.

The desirability of pursuing policies to maintain high levels of employment was generally accepted in most industrial countries after the war. In 1944 the British government stated in its White Paper on Employment Policy that "the government accept as one of their primary aims and responsibilities the maintenance of a high and stable level of employment after the war". One of the most influential British economists at this time was Sir William Beveridge, whose book Full Employment in a Free Society had a strong impact on general thinking. Similar ideas were expressed in the United States in the Employment Act of 1946, which stated: "The Congress hereby declares that it is the continuing policy and responsibility of the Federal Government to promote maximum employment, production and purchasing power". The Employment Act was less specific as to policy than the British government's White Paper, but it established a council of economic advisers to assist the president and called upon him to present to every regular session of Congress a report on the state of the economy. The president was also required to present a program showing "ways and means of promoting a high level of employment and production". Similar programs were adopted in other countries. In Sweden in 1944 the Social Democrats published a document somewhat similar to the British White Paper, and other such declarations were made in Canada and Australia.

Stabilization Policy Problems

A broad distinction may be made between two types of stabilization policies: discretionary and automatic. Discretionary policies involve deliberate actions taken by the authorities, such as open market operations, changes in discount rates and reserve requirements, and changes in tax rates or government expenditures. Automatic policies put reliance on built-in stabilizers that function without any deliberate intervention by the authorities. In the monetary field, for example, an increase in commodity prices tends to reduce the real value of financial assets, and if the government does nothing to offset this by increasing the volume of financial assets in the system, private spending will tend to decline. On the fiscal side, the main automatic stabilizer is the relation between tax revenues and cyclical changes in the economy. During booms, tax revenues rise and the need for expenditures on unemployment compensation decreases, channeling a larger proportion of the national income into government coffers; these effects are accentuated if the tax system is progressive because tax revenues rise more rapidly than money incomes. Provided that the government does not raise its expenditures along with the increased revenues, the budget tends to have a braking effect on private expenditure in boom times and an expansionary effect in times of recession.

The Problem of Time Lags

There has been much discussion over the merits of discretionary policies as against automatic stabilizers. One advantage of automatic stabilizers is that the effects occur without the necessity of government action, which means that there is no delay, or lag, because of political controversies, administrative problems, or difficulties in determining whether the time has come to act. There are three types of lag in economic policy: the recognition lag, the decision lag, and the effect lag.

The recognition lag is the time it takes for the authorities to discover the need to make a change in economic policy. The reasons for this type of lag are that statistical information is often somewhat behind the event and that it is sometimes difficult to distinguish between random fluctuations and fundamental shifts in economic trends. Governments prefer to wait until there is certainty that, say, an increase in unemployment is not a passing thing.

The decision lag is the period between the time when the need for action is recognized and the time when action is taken. Although the recognition lag is presumably of about the same duration for both monetary and fiscal policies, the decision lag is usually considerably shorter for monetary policy than for fiscal policy. The central bank can change monetary policy almost overnight, whereas a change in fiscal policy is more complex, both politically and administratively. In many countries changes in income taxes, for example, can be made only at the beginning of a calendar year; such changes are often complicated by political discussions in the legislative body.

The effect lag is the amount of time between the time action is taken and an effect is realized. Monetary policy involves longer delays than fiscal policy; the time between a change in monetary policy and its ultimate effect on private investment may be between one and two years.

Some economists argue that the sum of all the lags is so long and uncertain that the best strategy is not to take any action; by the time the effects occur the economic situation may be radically different. Some countries have tried to shorten the lags in fiscal and monetary policy. One way to reduce the recognition lag is to improve the forecasting techniques, for example, by using sophisticated questionnaires or computerized econometric models.

In order to reduce the decision lag in fiscal policy, some countries have given the authorities power to take limited action without the prior consent of the legislature. In the United Kingdom the government introduced a regulation that allowed it to make immediate changes in tax policy. In Belgium and West Germany the governments also have some discretionary powers to change tax rates without first asking the legislature. In most countries, however, the legislative bodies have been reluctant to give up control of the budget, and increasing skepticism about the effectiveness of stabilization policy has led to a retreat from frequent small adjustments to fiscal policy.

Attempts to shorten the effect lag of fiscal policy have produced new policy tools. Some countries now use systems of taxes or subsidies to influence business investment within a relatively short time. Attempts have also been made to reduce the effect lag in monetary policy. Some countries have tried using various tools of credit rationing rather than relying on traditional measures such as open market operations. But the effect lag is still a serious problem for monetary policy.

Conflicts Among Goals

Perhaps the most serious unsolved problem of stabilization policy is the multiplicity of goals that policymakers must consider. Every government has aims other than stabilizing the economy. First, it must stay in power—a need that is likely to limit the alternatives open to stabilization policy, particularly in periods of prosperity immediately before elections. Second, some monetary and fiscal actions impinge on particular groups in society, and governments may wish to avoid what appear to be discriminatory policies. Third, a policy designed to achieve one element of stabilization, such as full employment, may prevent the achievement of another.

The conflict between full employment and price stability seems to arise in two different sets of circumstances. Often wage increases that are made in the normal collective bargaining process are greater than the increases in labour productivity (or output per man-hour); such wage increases tend to increase the cost of production and to force prices upward. The government is then confronted with a choice between two unpleasant alternatives. One is to allow the general price level to rise approximately in proportion to the increase in production costs; the other alternative is to try to hold prices down by taking measures to restrict aggregate demand, thus making it difficult for firms to shift their increased costs to the consumer through higher prices. The latter alternative means increased unemployment. Many governments have been confronted with exactly this choice of alternatives. Wage gains made in collective bargaining have forced them to choose between allowing prices to move upward or attempting to hold prices stable at the cost of greater unemployment.

Another reason for the conflict between full employment and price stability is the tendency of wage increases to accelerate when the level of employment rises and the number of job vacancies increases. In other words, as the economy approaches full employment wages tend to rise at an increasing speed. As prices begin to rise, the conflict between full employment and price stability may be further exacerbated by the expectation that they will rise still further; this may, for example, induce employees and their organizations to press for greater wage increases than they otherwise would in order to compensate for the expected price increases.

Another conflict in policy may arise with respect to the balance of payments. When the economy is in a period of boom, there is a tendency for imports to increase, and sometimes for exports to decrease as well, with obvious difficulties for the balance of payments. The crisis may be heightened by short-term capital movements if buyers and sellers of foreign exchange expect that there may be a devaluation of the country's currency. This has caused much difficulty for many countries in the period since World War II. In Britain and Denmark, notably, periods of boom have usually been accompanied by balance-of-payments problems. When that occurs, the government must sooner or later take restrictive actions that slow the economy down and increase unemployment; if speculation in the currency is already under way, it may be necessary to pursue the restrictive policy far into the next recession. The problem is accentuated if there have been substantial price increases during the boom that have reduced the country's ability to compete with other countries. It is ironic that a temporary improvement in the employment situation may, if it leads to an accelerated increase in the price level, serve to create greater unemployment in the future, when restrictive actions become necessary for balance-of-payments reasons.

Attempts have been made to eliminate these conflicts of policy. One remedy is "incomes policy," direct efforts by the government to prevent employers and unions from raising prices and wages. Various methods have been tried. The most moderate is the so-called guideposts system, under which the government announces the need for restraints on wage increases and perhaps also sets targets to guide unions and management; this was attempted in the United States in the early 1960s. In Sweden, responsibility for limiting wage increases has been assigned to labour-management organizations where bargaining takes place in a centralized fashion. A more interventionist approach is for the government to enter the bargaining process and try to persuade unions to limit their wage demands. The government may go still further and announce a wage freeze, or even a system of wage and price control. In the Netherlands, the courts have occasionally been empowered to set wages, but the resulting decisions have often been uncoordinated with the rest of stabilization policy.

Incomes policies have sometimes succeeded for short periods. Generally, however, public refusal to accept the restraints has eventually led to their collapse. In the United States, the guideposts broke down during the boom of the mid-1960s, and attempts at incomes policy in Sweden and Britain have not been notable for their success. Even in the Netherlands later attempts to impose the system have failed to limit the rate of wage increase.

The Question of Governmental Competence

Governments have displayed serious deficiencies in their ability to handle stabilization policy. Political leaders often lack economic information and understanding, and their economic advisers find it difficult to explain the economic situation to them and to apprise them of the relevant tools. There are also a variety of political inhibitions against taking action. One consequence is that what is designed to be a countercyclical policy becomes a procyclical one; instead of stabilizing the economy it tends to destabilize it. The postwar experience in Britain is held by some to demonstrate the deficiencies of government in handling monetary and fiscal policy. In time of boom the government often followed an expansionary course; when a balance-of-payments crisis developed it then took restrictive action—too late—and pushed the economy into deeper recession than would otherwise have occurred. On the basis of this experience, some economists have argued that a policy that did not attempt to counter the short-run swings in the economy would have been more successful in achieving stabilization. They maintain that the authorities should concentrate on letting the volume of money and credit increase steadily at a rate dictated by the long-term growth trend of the economy. Those who hold this view believe that capitalist economies are inherently stable, that crises are usually the result of bad policies on the part of the public authorities. Most economists do not share their optimism as to the stability of the economy if left alone; they continue to believe that governments must seek better tools for the purpose of short-run stabilization.

Experience in Selected Countries

The application of full-employment policies after World War II was made more difficult by the fact that the postwar situation was radically different from that of the 1930s, when much of the policy thinking had been done. Most governments and their advisers expected a depression after the war, but it never materialized. One explanation is that the reallocation of resources from military to civilian uses proceeded more smoothly than expected. Another explanation is that the consumers spent a larger part of their disposable income than they had been observed to do in the 1930s, upsetting some of the statistical projections based on empirical data from those years. A third explanation, which applies perhaps to the years after 1948, was the Cold War between the United States and the Soviet Union, which raised defense spending in many countries.

The period of the late 1940s and early 1950s proved to be characterized by tendencies to inflation rather than to unemployment. Governments were slow to realize this and to shift their emphasis from employment-creating policies to anti-inflationary policies. The fact that governments had accepted, to a large extent, the belief that monetary policy was not very important made it difficult for them to combat the tendencies to inflation. In most countries a passive, even expansionary, monetary policy was in effect; interest rates were kept down and the supply of money was allowed to grow faster than would have been consistent with stable prices. Inflationary tendencies were further stimulated by the Korean War and the great increases in raw material prices that accompanied it.

During the 1950s several important developments influenced the attitudes of governments toward stabilization policy. Most of the economic controls engendered by the war were removed, particularly in international trade and finance. The western European countries were in a period of rapid economic growth. With the removal of direct controls on prices, imports, and building investment, governments began to develop and refine the tools of monetary and fiscal policy. In most countries the passive attitude toward monetary policy disappeared during the early 1950s; there was increased interest in more flexible monetary management. Interest also grew in developing a systematic fiscal policy that would offset the cyclical swings in production and employment. The most energetic attempts to devise a countercyclical fiscal policy were made in Britain and Sweden. Other European countries and the United States placed more reliance on monetary policy.

In the United States, a contributing factor in the revival of monetary policy was a theoretical reformulation that took place among monetary and banking experts. This was the so-called availability theory of credit; it held that monetary policy had its effect on spending not only directly through interest rates but also by restricting the general availability of credit and liquid funds. It was argued that even rather small changes in the rate of interest for government securities could have a considerable impact on the supply of private credit; if the supply diminished, this would induce banks and other financial institutions to stiffen their credit standards and ration credit to their customers; this in turn, it was argued, would tend to curb investment and thus have a braking effect on the economy. Similar ideas were at work in other countries, but with more emphasis on limiting the availability of credit through credit rationing, loan ceilings, control of private bond issues, regulation of installment credit for the purchase of durable consumer goods, and so on.

Serious attempts have been made to put a countercyclical monetary policy into practice in most advanced industrialized countries since the middle of the 1950s. In some, such as the United States, the emphasis has been, as suggested above, on changes in the interest rate and in the supply of money and credit; in others, such as France, Italy, and Japan, the emphasis has been on the rationing of credit by the central bank.

Fiscal policy has found less use than monetary policy in efforts to control cyclical fluctuations in the economy. It has been most favoured in Britain, the Scandinavian countries, and the Netherlands. There are specific situations in which fiscal measures have been used to stimulate the economy in other countries, as in Belgium and West Germany during the recessions of 1958 and 1962. Another example is the postponement of certain military expenditures in the United States as an anti-inflationary measure during the boom of the mid-1950s, and, most notably, the tax cuts passed by Congress in 1964 and 1981 as a stimulus to economic expansion. Several countries have taken restrictive fiscal actions to overcome balance-of-payments crises, including France and Finland on various occasions. During the later 20th century there was an increasing tendency to employ fiscal policies in the short run, partly in order to assist monetary policy in solving cyclical problems.

The Distributive Function

Virtually everything that a government does has some effect on the distribution of income or wealth at the various levels of society. Improvements in health care facilities benefit the sick, the old, and those about to have children. An increase in taxes on tobacco and beer affects the poor disproportionately, while an increase in capital taxes similarly affects the rich. Even regulatory and legislative activity benefits one group out of proportion to another. The redistributive consequences of the governmental budget can be reflected in a variety of ways; sometimes they are explicit and sometimes they are cited in the debate that follows the presentation of a budget. Usually, however, these consequences are hidden, unintended, and imperfectly understood.

Incidence of Taxation and Expenditure

The incidence of taxes is a subject that has generated much academic debate. It is usual to distinguish between the legal incidence of a tax and its effective, or final, incidence. The legal incidence is on the person or company who is legally obliged to pay the tax. Effective, or final, incidence refers to who actually ends up paying the tax; if, for example, the whole of a sales tax can be passed on in higher prices to the consumer, then consumers bear the final incidence of the tax.

Whether the final incidence of the tax is on those who actually pay it depends on their market power relative to the people with whom they trade. A payroll tax, for example, is likely to be reflected in lower wages if labour is mobile and in plentiful supply, but may be borne, at least in part, by the employer if there are labour shortages. Similarly, if a manufacturer is facing intense international competition, his ability to pass on any increase in a sales tax is limited; on the other hand, his ability to do so is much greater if he is the sole supplier of a good.

Arguments for Income Redistribution

Although governments do affect the distribution of resources in numerous ways, this is often a by-product of the other things they are trying to do. It has been long debated whether or not governments should seek explicitly to redistribute income from the rich to the poor and, if so, to what extent. More generosity to the poor, whether through higher benefits or through a more progressive tax system, means a higher tax burden on richer people, with, it is argued, consequent effects on work effort and on other behaviour. The appropriate degree of redistribution has been the subject of an extensive literature on optimal taxes, but economists generally agree that the final determination must be through the political process.

Economists point to a number of arguments favouring explicit as opposed to indirect methods of redistribution. The primary argument is that these would provide a more efficient means of eradicating severe hardship, suffering, or starvation. Left to itself, the market economy creates casualties among those who lack the skills to participate fully or those who have failed to generate sufficient resources to tide them over into old age. Countries have evolved programs for the prevention of severe need, although the definition of an acceptable minimum standard of living is typically more generous in European countries than in, for example, the United States, and this is reflected in the higher share of public expenditure in those countries. In most countries the definition of poverty, as measured by the level to which the state benefit system brings everyone's income, has moved from being "absolute" (determined by the minimum requirement of food, clothing, and shelter) to a more relative concept, which allows the poor to share in real rises in living standards.

The second argument for redistribution is that overall social welfare is thereby increased. An additional dollar makes more difference to the standard of living of someone earning $100 per week than to that of someone earning $1,000. Even if everyone has income above an agreed minimum level, there is a case for redistribution from the rich to the not-so-rich. The extent to which this should be pursued depends partly on the perceived distortions the redistribution would cause and partly on how much more value the far more numerous not-so-rich can squeeze out of each additional dollar.

Other arguments for redistribution occur where the market fails to allow individuals to redistribute between periods in their own lives. The classic example is that people tend to have their periods of highest expenditure (while bringing up children) at the points of minimum income (early in life). Those families with little or no access to credit markets can do very little about this, which has been used as one argument for redistribution toward those bringing up children. A second argument contends that children convey benefits to society as a whole, so that parents should be rewarded for creating a public good. This argument would, of course, have little strength in countries with serious problems of overpopulation.

A final group of arguments also concerns market failure. If particular areas or occupations have declined and the work force has not adjusted to this decline by moving to other areas or through retraining, then some subsidy to cushion the recessive effects might be considered appropriate. Most countries redistribute from better-off regions to those that have declined, or they allocate funds for specific programs designed to help particular groups.

Budget Surplus

A budget surplus is a period when income or receipts exceed outlays or expenditures. A budget surplus often refers to the financial states of governments; individuals prefer to use the term 'savings' instead of the term 'budget surplus.' A surplus is an indication that the government is being effectively managed.

A budget surplus might be spent to make a purchase, pay off debt or save for the future. A city government that has a surplus may use the money to render improvements to a local decaying park, for example.

When expenditures exceed income, the outcome is a budget deficit, which is funded by borrowing funds and paying interest on the borrowed money, similar to an individual spending more than he earns and carrying a balance on a credit card. A balanced budget exists once expenditures equal income.

The Clinton administration eliminated a large budget deficit, resulting in a surplus. A surplus is a positive value and is the sum by which government revenues are greater than government spending during a set period, usually a fiscal year. For example, June 2016 was a recent U.S. government budget surplus. The receipts for the year totaled $330 billion, while expenditures for the year were $323 billion. This resulted in a budget surplus of approximately $6 billion.

Economic and spending changes generate a surplus. A budget surplus is an indicator of a healthy economy. However, it is not necessary for a government to maintain a surplus. For instance, not having a budget surplus does not mean the economy is not being run efficiently.

A surplus implies the government has extra funds; these funds can be allocated to pay debts, which reduces the interest payable and helps the economy in the future. For example, a budget surplus can reduce taxes, start new programs and fund existing public programs, such as social security or Medicare.

In addition, a surplus can reduce the public debt, fund the military, infrastructure, energy, and public works, pay salaries, implement policy, or be saved to spend in the future once a deficit occurs. A budget surplus occurs after a reduction in costs and spending or both. An increase in taxes can also result in a surplus. A surplus decreases consumer demand, lowers consumer prices and slows down the economy.

Sources

When determining the best ways to utilize a budget surplus, it is essential to rank the potential uses, project the possible outcomes, project implementation costs and make decisions, which improves the overall financial health of the economy.

Budget surplus data appears in monthly statements, which summarizes whether the government is spending or collecting more money than expected. Data that appears in the monthly statements denotes transactions that have occurred during the month. In addition, the data records future collections or changes to the budget.

Fiscal Policy

Fiscal policy is the measure employed by governments to stabilize the economy, specifically by manipulating the levels and allocations of taxes and government expenditures. Fiscal measures are frequently used in tandem with monetary policy to achieve certain goals.

The usual goals of both fiscal and monetary policy are to achieve or maintain full employment, to achieve or maintain a high rate of economic growth, and to stabilize prices and wages. The establishment of these ends as proper goals of governmental economic policy and the development of tools with which to achieve them are products of the 20th century.

In taxes and expenditures, fiscal policy has for its field of action matters that are within government's immediate control. The consequences of such actions are generally predictable: a decrease in personal taxation, for example, will lead to an increase in consumption, which will in turn have a stimulating effect on the economy. Similarly, a reduction in the tax burden on the corporate sector will stimulate investment. Steps taken to increase government spending by public works have a similar expansionary effect. Conversely, a reduction in government expenditure or an increase in tax revenues, without compensatory action, has the effect of contracting the economy.

Fiscal policy relates to decisions that determine whether a government will spend more or less than it receives. Until Great Britain's unemployment crisis of the 1920s and the Great Depression of the 1930s, it was generally held that the appropriate fiscal policy for the government was to maintain a balanced budget. The severity of these disturbances gave rise to a new set of ideas, first given formal treatment by the economist John Maynard Keynes, revolving around the notion that fiscal policy should be used "countercyclically," that is, that the government should exercise its economic influence to offset the cycle of expansion and contraction in the economy. Keynes's rule, briefly, was that the budget should be in deficit when the economy was experiencing low levels of activity and in surplus when boom conditions (often accompanied by high inflation) were in force.

Under the balanced-budget regime, personal and business tax rates were raised during periods of declining economic activity to ensure that government revenues were not reduced. The effect of this was to reduce consumption still further, increase surplus industrial capacity, and depress investment, all of which exerted a downward pressure on the economy. Alternatively, if, in order to maintain a balanced budget, taxes remained level but government expenditures were cut back during such a period of declining economic activity, a similar downward pressure was exerted. The Keynesian theory showed that, under certain conditions, the operation of market forces would not automatically generate full employment, and that governments should abandon the balanced-budget concept and adopt active measures to stimulate the economy. Furthermore, to be really effective, these measures should be financed by government borrowing rather than by raising taxes or by cutting other government expenditures. Initial experiments with this new stabilizing technique in the United States during the first term of President Franklin D. Roosevelt's administration were somewhat disappointing, partly because the amount of deficit financing was not large enough and partly, perhaps, because the expectations of business had been dulled to such an extent by the Great Depression that it was slow to respond to opportunities. With the advent of World War II and soaring government spending, the unemployment problem in the United States virtually disappeared.

In the postwar period the use of fiscal policy changed somewhat. The problem was no longer massive unemployment but a persistent tendency to inflation against a backdrop of fairly rapid economic growth punctuated by short periods of shallow recession.

Since the days of Keynes, fiscal policy has been refined to smooth these cyclical movements. As a counterinflationary tool it has not been particularly effective, partly because of political constraints and partly because of the so-called automatic stabilizers at work. The political constraints arise from the fact that politicians have found it unpopular to raise taxes and cut government expenditure when the economy becomes overheated. The automatic stabilizers in the economy inhibited the use of discretionary fiscal policy. For example, during a recession personal incomes will be shrinking, but, owing to the highly progressive tax system (i.e., tax rates that rise disproportionately on higher incomes), the loss of purchasing power of the consumers is cushioned, leaving more spending money in the hands of the consumers than would otherwise have been the case. This will be accompanied by a decline in government tax revenues, and, so long as the government does not take steps to reduce expenditures to compensate for the loss of revenue, the net result will be to temper the decline in the level of economic activity. Conversely, during a boom a disproportionate share of the additional income flows into the treasury, keeping the rate of consumption expenditures below the rate that might have otherwise prevailed in the absence of a progressive tax system. Unemployment benefits produce a similar effect. During a recession unemployment benefits rise with the growing numbers of unemployed and prevent disposable incomes from falling by as much as would otherwise have been the case. This situation normally causes an increase in government expenditures and a decrease in tax revenue. When the economy begins to expand again and demand for labour picks up, the unemployment pay drops automatically, tax revenue increases, and expenditures decrease.

Monetary Policy

Monetary policy is an economic policy that manages the size and growth rate of the money supply in an economy. It is a powerful tool to regulate macroeconomic variables such as inflation and unemployment.

These policies are implemented through different tools, including the adjustment of the interest rates, purchase or sale of government securities, and changing the amount of cash circulating in the economy. The central bank or a similar regulatory organization is responsible for formulating these policies.

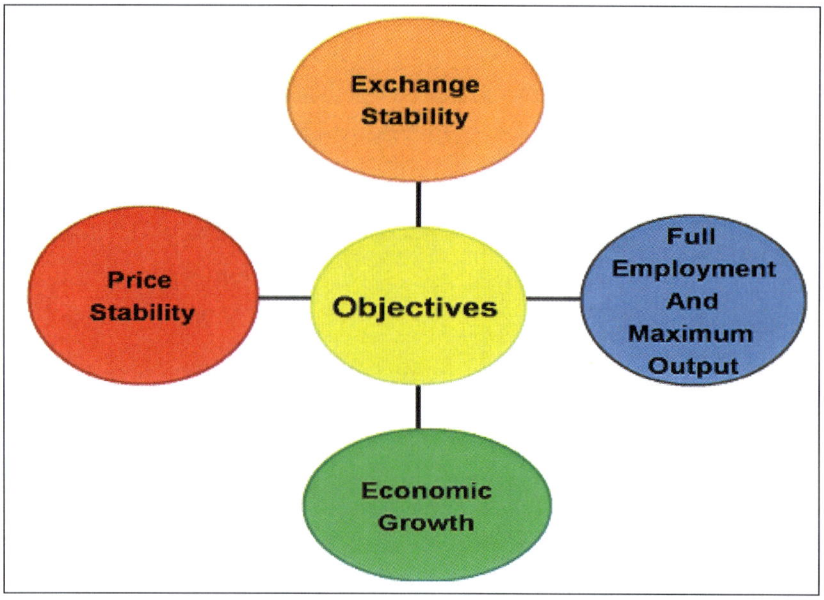

Objectives of Monetary Policy

The primary objectives of monetary policies are the management of inflation or unemployment, and maintenance of currency exchange rates.

Inflation

Monetary policies can target inflation levels. The low level of inflation is considered to be healthy for the economy. However, if inflation is high, the policy can address this issue.

Unemployment

Monetary policies can influence the level of unemployment in the economy. For example, an expansionary monetary policy generally decreases unemployment because the higher money supply stimulates business activities that lead to the expansion of the job market.

Currency Exchange Rates

Using its fiscal authority, a central bank can regulate the exchange rates between domestic and foreign currencies. For example, the central bank may increase the money supply by issuing more currency. In such a case, the domestic currency becomes cheaper relative to its foreign counterparts.

Tools of Monetary Policy

Central banks use various tools to implement monetary policies. The widely utilized policy tools include:

Interest Rate Adjustment

A central bank can influence interest rates by changing the discount rate. The discount rate (base rate) is an interest rate charged by a central bank to banks for short-term loans. For example, if a central bank increases the discount rate, the cost of borrowing for the banks increases. Subsequently, the banks will increase the interest rate they charge their customers. Thus, the cost of borrowing in the economy will increase, and the money supply will decrease.

Change Reserve Requirements

Central banks usually set up the minimum amount of reserves that must be held by a commercial bank. By changing the required amount, the central bank can influence the money supply in the economy. If monetary authorities increase the required reserve amount, commercial banks find less money available to lend to their clients and thus, money supply decreases.

Commercial banks can't use the reserves to make loans or fund investments into new businesses. Since it constitutes a lost opportunity for the commercial banks, central banks pay them interest on the reserves. The interest is known as IOR or IORR (interest on reserves or interest on required reserves).

Open Market Operations

The central bank can either purchase or sell securities issued by the government to affect the money supply. For example, central banks can purchase government bonds. As a result, banks will obtain more money to increase the lending and money supply in the economy.

Expansionary vs. Contractionary Monetary Policy

Depending on its objectives, monetary policies can be expansionary or contractionary.

Expansionary Monetary Policy

It is a monetary policy that aims to increase the money supply in the economy by decreasing interest rates, purchasing government securities by central banks, and lowering the reserve requirements for banks. An expansionary policy lowers unemployment and stimulates business activities and consumer spending. The overall goal of the expansionary monetary policy is to fuel economic growth. However, it can also possibly lead to higher inflation.

Contractionary Monetary Policy

The goal of a contractionary monetary policy is to decrease the money supply in the economy. It can be achieved by raising interest rates, selling government bonds, and increasing the reserve requirements for banks. The contractionary policy is utilized when the government wants to control inflation levels.

Supply Side Policies

Supply-side economics involves policies aimed at increasing aggregate supply (AS), a shift from left to right. They are based on the belief that higher rates of production will lead to higher rates of economic growth.

They are aimed at enhancing the productive capacities of an economy by fostering what they view as a better business climate via deregulation and tax cuts, which creates more jobs, thereby creating higher levels of demand and increasing economic growth. They focus on improving the quality and quantity of the four factors of production (i.e. labor, capital, land, and entrepreneurship).

Successful policies lower the natural rate of unemployment. Some economists also believe that successful supply-side policies can contribute to long-term economic growth without increasing the rate of inflation. It's important to note that supply-side policies are not perfect: they are difficult to implement, they are unpopular, and they take a great deal of time to take effect.

The Three Supply-side Pillars

Regulatory Policy

Advocates for supply-side economics prefer less government intervention in the free market (the typical laissez-faire, small government perspective of conservatives). This is because they don't believe that creating demand via government policy will actually create real economic growth.

Tax Policy

Supply-side economists advocate for decreased marginal tax rates as well as lower income tax that will spur workers to choose to work more. They also believe in lower capital gains taxes because they think this will encourage investors and entrepreneurs to apply their ample capital in a way that generates economic growth.

Monetary Policy

Monetary policy is the practice of increasing or decreasing the number of dollars circulating through the economy at a given time. The Federal Reserve can determine this quantity. Supply-side economists do not believe that monetary policy helps to manage the economy in a beneficial manner. Keynesian economists, by contrast, tend to argue for manipulating the money supply in order to improve growth and economic stability.

Examples of Supply Side Policies

Labor Market

Lowering wages frees up the labor market, which makes a lower-paid job more attractive. To lower wages, the government takes measures like abolishing minimum wage laws, decentralizing trade union power, reducing unemployment benefits, lowering income tax, and making hiring and firing easier and more affordable for firms. However, these policies are very politically unpopular, so they may not be implemented in many cases, especially in societies where there is a strong labor movement and high rates of union membership.

Capital Markets

The government needs to create money for banks to lend for investment. The government can do this by increasing competition between banks to make loans more attractive, reducing financial crowding out, and making savings more attractive.

Entrepreneurship

The government needs to encourage entrepreneurs to start new businesses by lowering the marginal tax rate and encouraging share ownership among employees. Another commonly employed policy is not requiring new businesses to pay corporate taxes during their first three years, or if they don't cross a minimum level of revenue during their initial years.

Competition and Efficiency

The government will need to increase competition between firms and increase the overall efficiency of the economy. They can do this by removing monopolies, by privatizing certain industries, by freeing up trade (through the reduction or even elimination of trade barriers), and by implementing inward investment policies.

Education

Better education and training to improve skills will improve labor productivity.

Impact of Successful Supply Side Policies

In the diagram below, we can see a shift in Aggregate Supply from S1 to S2, which demonstrates the impact of a successful supply-side policy.

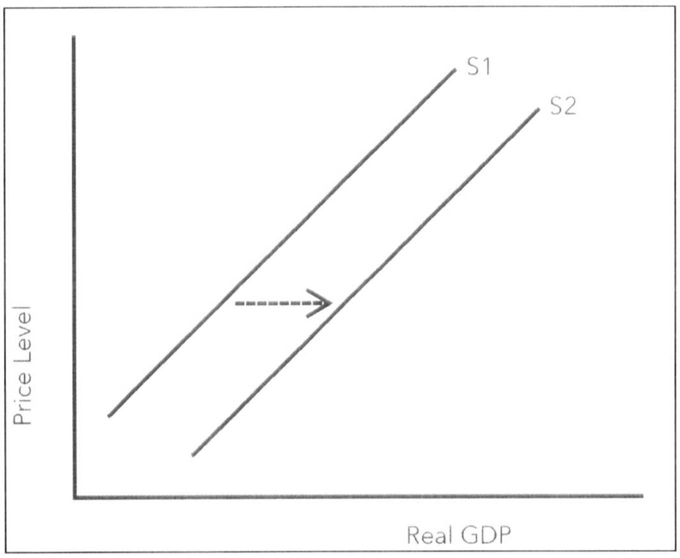

Lower Inflation

Shifting Aggregate Supply to the right will result in a lower price level. By making the economy more efficient, supply-side policies help reduce cost push inflation.

Lower Unemployment

Supply-side policies can help reduce structural, frictional and real wage unemployment and therefore help reduce the natural rate of unemployment.

Improved Economic Growth

Supply-side policies can increase the sustainable rate of economic growth by increasing Aggregate Supply.

Improved Trade and Balance of Payments

By making firms more productive and competitive, firms are able to export more goods and services.

Long Run Effects of Supply-side Policies

In the short run, supply-side policies will have an impact on the short-run aggregate supply (abbreviated as SRAS). They will cause a shift from SRAS1 to SRAS2 (an increase in aggregate supply). In the long run, this will result in an increase in aggregate supply from LRAS1 to LRAS2.

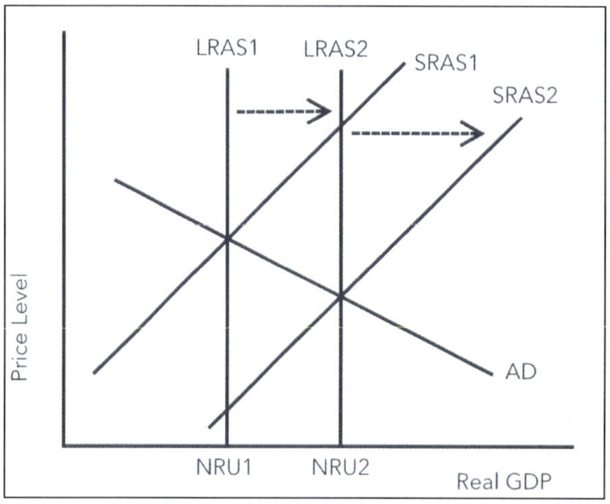

Production possibility curve with a successful supply side policy.

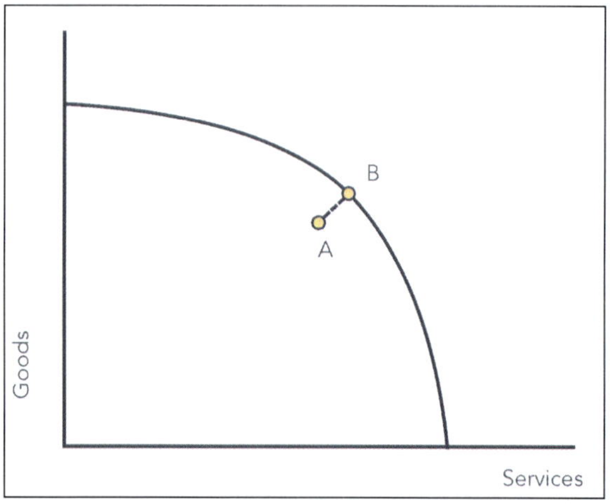

In terms of a production possibility curve, it would shift capabilities from "A" to "B". A production possibility curve represents a country's available resources along with the maximum amounts of two goods produced from those resources.

Supply-side Economics vs. Keynesian Economics

The central point of supply-side economics is that the most significant determinant element of economic growth is production (that is, the supply of products). This perspective is in opposition to Keynesian theory, which holds that if consumer demand drops and a recession occurs, then the government ought to intervene directly by creating monetary stimulus (increasing the money/credit supply) as well as fiscal stimulus (e.g. increasing government consumption).

Keynesian economists advocate for policies like government investment in infrastructure, such as constructing and maintaining roads and bridges, which creates many jobs. In addition, they push for more widespread education and for the provision of unemployment benefits.

While Keynesian economists believe that consumers and consumer demand are the most important source of economic growth, supply-side economists argue that producers are the most important contributors to economic growth. They even believe that, for the most part, demand doesn't matter. If there is a likely short-term instance of overproduction, argue supply-side economists, prices for that good or service will decrease and thus consumers will choose to purchase more of it.

Supply-side Economics and Reaganomics

Reaganomics—the laissez-faire economic policy furthered by U.S. President Ronald Reagan—espoused many supply-side policies. The most famous of these is probably "trickle-down" policy. This is the highly contentious, disputed idea that when you cut taxes for entrepreneurs and investors at the top tier of the economic strata, they are more motivated to invest their money, and the economic positives they create "trickle down" to the rest of the economic strata below them.

Disadvantages of Supply-side Policies

Time Lag

Most supply-side policies can take a long time to work and for the effects to be seen in the economy. For example, if the country wants to improve the quality of human capital through education and training, this will normally take years to complete and for the economy to reap tangible benefits, even if such investment is worthwhile.

Expensive

Supply-side policies can be costly to implement. For example, for the government to improve the quality of human capital, it will need to sponsor or subsidize education and training programs. These programs are highly labor intensive and therefore extremely costly.

Unpopular

Many supply-side policies are politically unpopular, which means that they are unlikely to be implemented. For example, unions wield significant political influence in many countries, and they will oppose any negative labor market changes like breaking up unions or abolishing minimum wages.

The aims of the supply-side policies are to positively affect the production side of the economy by improving the institutional framework and the capacity (quality and quantity of factors of production) to produce. Thus, supply-side policies shift the Long Run Aggregate Supply curve (or the vertical part of the supply curve in the Keynesian model) to the right.

There are two types of supply-side policies:

- Market based.
- Interventionist.

Interventionist Supply-side Policies

Investment in Human Capital

Governments might invest in education and training of people. Improve the level of schools or make education free. Also, provide various training schemes. In the short run, such policies increase aggregate demand, but importantly – shift the LRAS curve to the right. This happens because people's skills improve. Hence, productivity increases.

Investment in New Technology

Governments could invest in research and development of new technologies. Again, that would increase aggregate demand in the short run, however, in the long run LRAS would increase. That happens because new technology can increase productivity: e.g. 3D printers made modelling or even production of various products quicker than ever.

Investment in Infrastructure

Government expenditure might go towards infrastructure. Simple example – improving logistics could decrease transfer times and costs in turn increasing productivity and shifting the LRAS to the right. Remember the short term effect on AD.

Industrial Policies

Governments might target specific economic areas through tax cuts, tax allowances and subsidised borrowing which would promote growth of those areas. E.g. Useful startups which could improve the efficiency of other areas of the economy.

Market-based Supply-side Policies

Policies to Encourage Competition

- Deregulation.
- Privatisation.
- Trade liberalisation.
- Anti-monopoly regulation.

Labour Market Reforms

- Reducing the power of labour unions.
- Reducing unemployment benefits.
- Removing minimum wages.

All these reforms aim at making the labour market more flexible. E.g. When it is easier and cheaper for firms to hire and fire workers, they will be more likely to hire.

Incentive-related Policies

- Cutting the income tax – The idea is that your leisure becomes more expensive after the tax cut and so you start working more. Refer to the Laffer curve and Substitution vs Income effects.
- Cutting the business (corporate) tax – Firms get to keep more of their profit, that is an incentive to (take the risk) invest, find more efficient ways of production.

Evaluation of Supply-side Policies

All supply-side policies mentioned above can be evaluated in terms of:

- Time lags – Some supply-side policies can take years to take effect (e.g. investing in human capital), others – much shorter.
- Ability to create employment – Think whether a certain policy creates employment. E.g. investing in new technology can actually lead to technology substituting workers.
- Reducing inflationary pressure – Can a certain policy help deal with high inflation? Try not to make a rather unrealistic argument that "*governments could invest in better education and that would lead to higher productivity and eventually lower prices*". To see the effects of that investment on inflation can take up to 15 years, so does it really deal with inflation? Maybe in the very-very-long-run it does.
- Impact on economic growth – How certain policies can affect growth, which affect growth more than others and why.
- Impact on the government budget – Some policies may be very costly (investing in infrastructure). However, privatisation might lead to short-term budget improvements (but remember that possible long term benefits were given up).
- Effect on equity – How will a certain policy affect the distribution of income? Think about removing or changing the minimum wages, unemployment benefits.
- Effect on the environment – Could deregulation lead to higher pollution or overall quicker degradation of the natural environment? Think about policies which could lead to increasing negative externalities.

References

- Meaning-of-government-budget-and-its-objectives: vskills.in, Retrieved 22 March, 2019
- Measures-of-government-deficit, government-budget-and-the-economy: toppr.com, Retrieved 16 May, 2019
- Government-economic-policy: britannica.com, Retrieved 23 July, 2019
- Monetary-policy: corporatefinanceinstitute.com, Retrieved 19 June, 2019
- Supply-side-policies: intelligenteconomist.com, Retrieved 27 April, 2019

7

International Economics

International economics deals with the study of economic and political issues between international economies in relation with trade and finance. Some of its aspects include international monetary system, international trade, exchange rates, foreign exchange, foreign direct investment, etc. All these aspects of international economics have been carefully analyzed in this chapter.

International economics deals with the economic activities of various countries and their consequences.

In other words, international economics is a field concerned with economic interactions of countries and effect of international issues on the world economic activity.

It studies economic and political issues related to international trade and finance.

International trade involves the exchange of goods or services and other factors of production, such as labor and capital, across international borders.

On the other hand, international finance studies the flow of financial assets or investment across borders. International trade and finance became possible across nations only due to the emergence of globalization.

Globalization can be defined as an integration of economics all over the world. It involves an exchange of technological, economic, and political factors across nations due to advancement in communication, transportation, and infrastructure systems.

With the advent of globalization, there is a rapid increase in the free flow of goods and services, capital, labor and finance between nations. The consequences of globalization can be negative or positive.

For example, globalization has led to increase in employment opportunities and standardization of international economic laws and policies. In addition, it has also resulted in reduction in trade barriers, such as tariffs and quotas.

However, globalization has marked an increase in international competition, which results in decrease in the market share of organizations. Therefore, the repercussions of globalization are important for organizations, irrespective of whether they are indulged in international trade or not.

Apart from this, it describes the functioning of different international economic institutions, such as World Trade Organization (WTO), International Monetary Fund (IMF), and United Nations Conference on Trade and Development (UNCTAD).

International economics refers to a study of international forces that influence the domestic conditions of an economy and shape the economic relationship between countries. In other words, it studies the economic interdependence between countries and its effects on economy.

The scope of international economics is wide as it includes various concepts, such as globalization, gains from trade, pattern of trade, balance of payments, and FDI. Apart from this, international economics describes production, trade, and investment between countries.

International economics has emerged as one of the most essential concepts for countries. Over the years, the field of international economics has developed drastically with various theoretical, empirical, and descriptive contributions.

Generally, the economic activities between nations differ from activities within nations. For example, the factors of production are less mobile between countries due to various restrictions imposed by governments.

The impact of various government restrictions on production, trade, consumption, and distribution of income are covered in the study of internal economics. Thus, it is important to study the international economics as a special field of economics.

International economics is divided into two parts, namely, theoretical and descriptive.

These two parts are discussed as follows:

Theoretical International Economics

Deals with the explanation of international economic transactions as they take place in the institutional environment.

Theoretical international economics is further grouped into two categories, which are as follows:

Pure Theory of International Economics

Involves microeconomic part of international economics. The pure theory of international economics deals with trade patterns, impact of trade on production, rate of consumption, and income distribution. Apart from this, it also involves the study of effects of trade on prices of goods and services and rate of economic growth.

Monetary Theory of International Economics

Involves macroeconomic part of international economics. The monetary theory of international economics is concerned with issues related to balance of payments and international monetary system. It studies causes of disequilibrium between payments and international monetary system and international liquidity.

Descriptive International Economics

Deals with institutional environment in which international transactions take place between countries. Descriptive international economics also studies issues related to international flow of goods and services and financial and other resources. In addition, it covers the study of various international economic institutions, such as IMF, WTO, World Bank, and UNCTAD.

Among aforementioned concepts, such as globalization, gains from trade, pattern of trade, balance of payments, and FDI, globalization forms the major part to be learned in international economics.

Economic Globalization

Economic globalization refers to the mobility of people, capital, technology, goods and services internationally. It is also about how integrated countries are in the global economy. It refers to how interdependent different countries and regions have become across the world.

In the eighteen hundreds in the world economy generally, people and capital crossed borders with ease, but not goods. In this century, people do not cross borders easily, but technologies, capital and goods do.

Over the past two to three decades, under the framework of General Agreement on Tariffs and Trade (GATT) and World Trade Organization, economic globalization has been expanding at a much faster pace. Countries have rapidly been cutting down trade barriers and opening up their current accounts and capital accounts.

When you buy a car, its parts have probably been produced in several different countries.

This rapid increase in pace has occurred mainly with advanced economies integrating with emerging ones. They have done this by means of foreign direct investment and some cross-border immigration. They have also reduced trade barriers.

In some regions of the world, such as the European Union, a large area almost the size of a continent has opened up to the free movement of capital, labor, goods and services. The North American Free Trade Agreement (NAFTA) opened up the free movement of goods and services, but not labor.

Cuba and North Korea are among the most autarkic (self-sufficient) and isolated nations on the planet. The two countries are the last bastions of the Soviet economic model.

Economic Globalization Linked to Greater Wealth and Inequality

While becoming more integrated into the global economy tends to bring increased wealth to a nation, globalization is commonly linked to greater inequality.

According to the United Nations

"Economic globalization refers to the increasing interdependence of world economies as a result of the growing scale of cross-border trade of commodities and services, flow of international capital and wide and rapid spread of technologies. It reflects the continuing expansion and mutual integration of market frontiers, and is an irreversible trend for the economic development in the whole world at the turn of the millennium".

Economic development, apart from GDP growth, also includes improvements in literacy, life expectancy, and people's well-being.

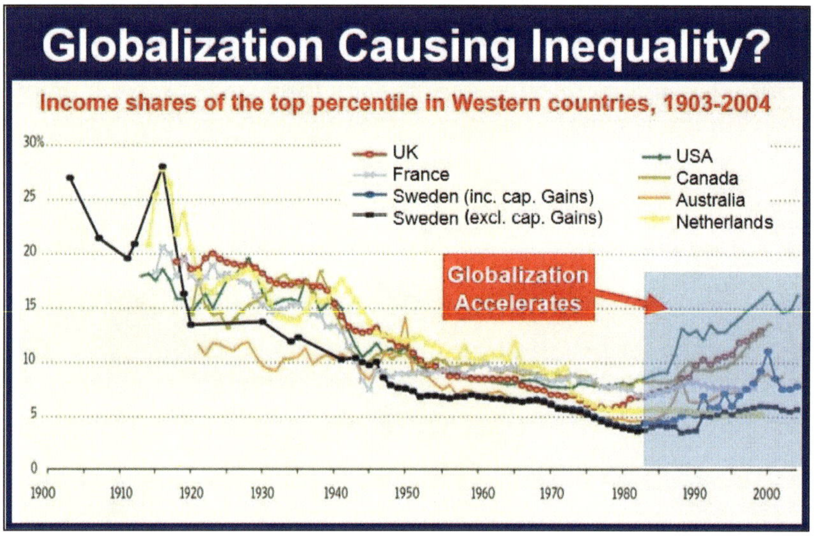

The big debate: 'Does globalization bring inequality, or is it just coincidence?'

Advances in Science and Technology

The United Nations says the fast globalization of the world's economies over recent decades is mainly due to the rapid development of science and technologies. They have created an environment in which the market economic system can spread across frontiers.

For example, the Internet and electronic communications today mean that businesses can employ workers from virtually anywhere in the world, and can trade in several countries at the same time without having to physically open up branches there.

Thanks to scientific and technological progress, transportation and communication costs today are just a fraction of what they used to be. Compared to 1930, current shipping costs are today about 50% cheaper, airfreight costs are now just 1/6 of what they were 85 years ago, while communication costs are just 1% of what they were.

With what it used to cost to buy a computer in 1960 (in today's dollars), you could buy 125 of them by 1990, and four times that number by 1998. All these advances in science, technology and communications have helped drive economic globalization.

The Internet and electronic communications have allowed advanced economies to outsource many of their jobs offshore. In the US, Canada, and EU, millions of jobs have been transferred abroad. Call center positions, especially, have gone overseas. These jobs have gone mainly to India, the Caribbean, and other English-speaking emerging economies.

The economic systems that exist in the world today are much more complex than in ancient times, when humans survived by hunting and subsistence farming.

Globalization of the Automotive Industry

Today, the automotive industry has companies producing vehicle parts and then assembling them in several countries. Most current parts production, assembly and vehicle sales take place in integrated regions.

These car production regions include MERCOSUR in Latin America, ASEAN in Asia, and NAFTA in North America. The also include the European Union and CIS for the former Soviet Bloc countries.

Within those regions, certain countries stand out – in China, Brazil, Mexico, Russia and India, car production and assembly have increased dramatically over the past 20 years.

The city of Detroit in the United States is still synonymous with auto manufacturing. America's 'Big Three,' i.e., Ford, General Motors and Chrysler, are still based there. However, the expansion in those three companies' operations have occurred outside the city, and mainly abroad.

"The 'Big Three' long ago moved some of the biggest chunks of their production, jobs and plants to places as near as Ohio and Ontario and as far away as China, Brazil and Russia. Without the plentiful factory jobs and incomes that once made Detroit a wealthy and teeming metropolis, the city steadily deteriorated into a hollow shell of vacant buildings and weed-covered lots. it became the largest American city ever to declare bankruptcy".

Does Globalization Bring more Inequality?

As the world has become more economically globalized, so has the income and wealth inequality within countries. Some people believe globalization is the cause – this has so far been difficult to prove.

They argue that if companies have access to the whole world market, and most of those companies are located in a few countries – the US, EU and Japan – they will suck money out of the whole world in much greater quantities than if they sold just within their own markets.

The counter-argument is that globalization brings well-paid jobs (compared to local pay rates) to emerging economies. A Ford factory worker in Mexico earns more and has better workplace conditions than he would as a farm laborer.

When looking at inequality between nations, however, globalization has coincided with more equality between the advanced and emerging economies. The rich countries today represent a smaller percentage of global GDP compared to twenty or thirty years ago.

Wealth inequality is not only a problem within emerging and low-income nations – it is also increasing in the advanced economies.

International Monetary System

International monetary system refers to a system that forms rules and standards for facilitating international trade among the nations.

It helps in reallocating the capital and investment from one nation to another.

It is the global network of the government and financial institutions that determine the exchange rate of different currencies for international trade. It is a governing body that sets rules and regulations by which different nations exchange currencies with each other.

With the growing complexity in the international trade and financial market, the international monetary system is necessary to assign a standard value of the international currencies. The rules and regulations set by the international monetary system to regulate and control the exchange value of the currencies are agreed upon by the respective governments of the nations. Thus, the government's stand may affect the decision making of the international monetary system. For example, change in the trade policy of a government may affect the international trade of goods and services.

International monetary system motivates and encourages the nations to participate in the international trade to improve their BOP and minimize the trade deficit. It has grown over the years as a single architectural body with a vision to integrate the global economy. Some of the important achievements of the international monetary system over the years have been the establishment of World Bank and International Monetary Fund in the year 1944.

The establishment of IMF and World Bank is the result of the agreement among nations to set a body, which promotes and supports the international trade. Now, let's discuss the evolution of international monetary system. Earlier in 1870 to 1914, trade was carried with the help of gold and silver without any institutional support. At that time, monetary system was decentralized and market based and money played a minor role as compared to gold in international trade.

The use of gold declined after World War I as war increased expenditure and inflation. In such a scenario, countries planned to revive the standard of gold but failed due to great depression. Thus, in 1944, 730 representatives of 44 nations met at Bretton Woods, New Hampshire, United States to create a new international monetary system.

This was called as the Bretton Woods system, which became a turning point in the history of international trade. The aim of new international monetary system is to create a stabilized international currency system and ensure a monetary stability for all the nations.

It was decided that since the United States held most of the world's gold, thus all the nations would determine the values of their currencies in terms of dollar. The central banks of nations were given the task of maintaining fixed exchange rates with respect to dollar for each currency.

The Bretton Woods system ended in 1971 as the trade deficit and growing inflation undermined the value of dollar in the whole world. In 1973, the floating exchange rate system, also known as flexible exchange rate system was developed that was market based.

International Trade

International trade allows countries to expand their markets for both goods and services that otherwise may not have been available domestically. As a result of international trade, the market contains greater competition, and therefore more competitive prices, which brings a cheaper product home to the consumer.

How International Trade Works

International trade gives rise to a world economy, in which supply and demand, and therefore prices, both affect and are affected by global events. Political change in Asia, for example, could result in an increase in the cost of labor, thereby increasing the manufacturing costs for an American sneaker company based in Malaysia, which would then result in an increase in the price charged at your local mall. A decrease in the cost of labor, on the other hand, would likely result in you having to pay less for your new shoes.

A product that is sold to the global market is called an export, and a product that is bought from the global market is an import. Imports and exports are accounted for in a country's current account in the balance of payments.

Comparative Advantage: Increased Efficiency of Trading Globally

Global trade allows wealthy countries to use their resources—whether labor, technology or capital—more efficiently. Because countries are endowed with different assets and natural resources (land, labor, capital, and technology), some countries may produce the same good more efficiently and therefore sell it more cheaply than other countries. If a country cannot efficiently produce an item, it can obtain it by trading with another country that can. This is known as specialization in international trade.

Let's take a simple example. Country A and Country B both produce cotton sweaters and wine. Country A produces ten sweaters and six bottles of wine a year while Country B produces six sweaters and ten bottles of wine a year. Both can produce a total of 16 units. Country A, however, takes three hours to produce the ten sweaters and two hours to produce the six bottles of wine (total of five hours). Country B, on the other hand, takes one hour to produce ten sweaters and three hours to produce six bottles of wine (a total of four hours).

But these two countries realize that they could produce more by focusing on those products with which they have a comparative advantage. Country A then begins to produce only wine, and Country B produces only cotton sweaters. Each country can now create a specialized output of 20 units per year and trade equal proportions of both products. As such, each country now has access to 20 units of both products.

We can see then that for both countries, the opportunity cost of producing both products is greater than the cost of specializing. More specifically, for each country, the opportunity cost of producing 16 units of both sweaters and wine is 20 units of both products (after trading). Specialization reduces their opportunity cost and therefore maximizes their efficiency in acquiring the goods they need. With the greater supply, the price of each product would decrease, thus giving an advantage to the end consumer as well.

Note that, in the example above, Country B could produce both wine and cotton more efficiently than Country A (less time). This is called an absolute advantage, and Country B may have it because of a higher level of technology.

According to the international trade theory, even if a country has an absolute advantage over another, it can still benefit from specialization.

Criticisms of Comparative Advantage

Why doesn't the world have open trading between countries? When there is free trade, why do some countries remain poor at the expense of others? There are many reasons, but the most influential is something that economists call rent-seeking. Rent-seeking occurs when one group organizes and lobbies the government to protect its interests.

Say, for example, the producers of American shoes understand and agree with the free-trade argument—but they also know that their narrow interests would be negatively impacted by cheaper foreign shoes. Even if laborers would be most productive by switching from making shoes to making computers, nobody in the shoe industry wants to lose his or her job or see profits decrease in the short run.

This desire could lead the shoemakers to lobby for special tax breaks for their products and extra duties (or even outright bans) on foreign footwear. Appeals to save American jobs and preserve a time-honored American craft abound—even though, in the long run, American laborers would be made relatively less productive and American consumers relatively poorer by such protectionist tactics.

Other Possible Benefits of Trading Globally

International trade not only results in increased efficiency but also allows countries to participate in a global economy, encouraging the opportunity for foreign direct investment (FDI), which is the amount of money that individuals invest into foreign companies and assets. In theory, economies can therefore grow more efficiently and can more easily become competitive economic participants.

For the receiving government, FDI is a means by which foreign currency and expertise can enter the country. It raises employment levels, and theoretically, leads to a growth in gross domestic product. For the investor, FDI offers company expansion and growth, which means higher revenues.

Free Trade vs. Protectionism

As with all theories, there are opposing views. International trade has two contrasting views regarding the level of control placed on trade: free trade and protectionism. Free trade is the simpler of the two theories: a laissez-faire approach, with no restrictions on trade. The main idea is that supply and demand factors, operating on a global scale, will ensure that production happens efficiently. Therefore, nothing needs to be done to protect or promote trade and growth, because market forces will do so automatically.

In contrast, protectionism holds that regulation of international trade is important to ensure that markets function properly. Advocates of this theory believe that market inefficiencies may hamper the benefits of international trade, and they aim to guide the market accordingly. Protectionism exists in many different forms, but the most common are tariffs, subsidies, and quotas. These strategies attempt to correct any inefficiency in the international market.

As it opens up the opportunity for specialization, and therefore more efficient use of resources, international trade has the potential to maximize a country's capacity to produce and acquire goods. Opponents of global free trade have argued, however, that international trade still allows for inefficiencies that leave developing nations compromised. What is certain is that the global economy is in a state of continual change, and, as it develops, so too must its participants.

Fixed and Flexible Exchange Rates

Under inconvertible paper money standard, there can be two types of exchange rates -fixed and flexible. Under the present monetary system of the International Monetary Fund (IMF), fixed or stable exchange rates are known as pegged exchange rates or par values.

In fact, IMF was established with the object of stabilising the rates of exchange, with proper safeguards for adjustments whenever necessary. On the other hand, free or flexible exchange rates are left uninterrupted by the monetary authorities to be determined by the forces of demand and supply in the foreign exchange market.

Thus, flexible exchange rates are determined by the conditions of demand for and supply of foreign exchange and are perfectly free to fluctuate according to the changes in the demand or supply forces, if there are no restrictions on buying and selling in the foreign exchange market.

The free or floating rate is allowed to seek its own level, as no par of exchange is fixed. Sometimes when a currency is floated a former fixed par no longer applies, and the government also does not care to enforce it.

Under the system of fixed pars, as adopted by the IMF member nations, the exchange rate is determined by the government and enforced either by pegging operation, or by resorting to some form of exchange control and sometimes by a healthy combination of both these methods.

Under the pegging operation, the government fixes an official par of exchange and tries to enforce it through central bank or a kind of exchange stabilisation fund which enters foreign exchange market and purchase its currency when the market rate falls below the specified level and sell it when the rate rises above a particular mark.

This system of pegged rates of exchange is government propped up. There is, however, one major defect in this system that if the market rate of exchange has a consistent tendency to decline, pegging operations would be very expensive, as it would lead to a heavy reduction in the exchange reserves of the country concerned.

Recently, therefore, it has been held by many that the IMF's system of adjustable stable exchange rates is not desirable and that free or fluctuating exchange rates would be more helpful in adjusting prevailing rates of exchange to their true value.

It is a highly debatable question as to whether the fixed exchange rate system is good or the fluctuating exchange rate is better.

Free Trade in Economic Theories

According to the World Bank global trade in goods (merchandise) amounted to roughly 19 trillion US $ (2016 US $) in exports and about the same sum in imports in 2014. The sum of these two divided by World GDP, which in 2014 stood at around 78 trillion US $ gives a figure of around 49,8% trade share of GDP. If services are included it amounts to 59.2%.

In comparison in 1960 world trade stood at 629 billion US $ (in 1995 US $) only. This means that the world now is trading more goods in absolute $ values than ever before. However, as a historical observation reveals, in relative terms, international trade has experienced its ups and downs from a high tide at the end of the 19th century through relatively modest levels for most time of the 20th century and then again rising to high levels over the last 40 to 50 years. While international trade had been a topic already in ancient societies, it was one of the most pressing concerns for the first economists in Europe in the era of industrialization. In 18th century Europe figures such as Adam Smith, David Ricardo, Friedrich List and Jean Baptiste Colbert developed theories regarding international trade, which either embraced free trade seeing it as a positive sum game or recommended more cautious and strategic approaches to trade seeing it as a potential danger and a rivalry and often as a zero-sum game.

Theory

Classical and Neoclassical

Classical Political Economy, as well as Neoclassical theory, embraces free trade. This is mostly because of the theory of comparative advantage first developed by David Ricardo. Broadly speaking, Ricardo's theory postulates that free trade is advantageous as it allows nations to specialize in production that requires relatively fewer factor inputs. This reasoning is based on the concept of opportunity cost and postulates that even nations that are worse in producing any good stand to gain something from trade. As a consequence of trade, nations would be able to reach consumption (and thereby utility) that goes beyond the possibilities that could be reached by producing all required goods in an autarch manner. The neoclassical theory later refined Ricardo's assumptions by introducing increasing marginal costs when shifting production factors from one good to another, thereby explaining why there is no complete specialization in countries.

A theory that seeks to explain why different countries specialize in different goods is the Heckscher-Ohlin theory. This theory says that countries will tend to export goods that require more inputs from a production factor (capital, land, labour) they have in abundance and vice versa import goods that require more input from a production factor that is scarce. Also, due to trade both the prices of goods as well as the returns to production factors will reach an equilibrium or a world price.

The political implications of these insights are to repeal restrictions on trade such as quotas, tariffs or national subsidies wherever possible, since they reduce the overall welfare of the world and lead to inefficient production. Historically, free trade proponents' first great victory was the mobilization against the "Corn Laws" in 19th century Britain. Contemporarily the different rounds of the GATT and the WTO are promoting trade by reducing tariffs as well as non-tariff barriers (such as regulations and bans on certain goods).

Institutionalist

Institutionalists have a more ambiguous stance about free trade. This is mostly because they embrace a more active role for state management of economic development and fear that opening up national economies to world trade (too soon) might interfere with those plans. Also, most of the times a different normative metric for welfare or goodness is applied. Friedrich List, in particular, eschewed the classicals' preoccupation with the utility of individuals or welfare of the world as a whole. Instead, he places an emphasis on the nation as the locus of collective identity. Consequently, national indicators like, for example, the balance of payment, the share of the manufacturing (or any other nationally relevant) industry or the exchange rate of the nation's currency would become more important issues than consumers' welfare gains. Another prominent contribution of List is the "kicking away the ladder" metaphor. He argued that the British economy had actually relied on protectionist tariffs and interventionist policies before embracing free trade and that prescribing other nations to go directly from underdevelopment to free trade would be the equivalent of kicking away the ladder. Contemporary institutionalists might not necessarily share List's strong attachment to economic nationalism. Still, institutionalists are wary of the consequences for political and cultural consequences that might arise due to free trade i.e. when production patterns are shifted.

Marxian and Developmentalist

Marx did stress the necessity of international trade for the sake of capital accumulation in his analysis. Others working in the Marxian tradition such as Karl Kautsky, Rosa Luxemburg, J.A. Hobson and V.I. Lenin subsequently developed theories of imperialism whereby the conquest of new markets was a function of the capitalist mode of production in the industrialized economies. Consequently, capital needed to expand ruthlessly and violently in order to realize its surplus value and therefore bring all parts of the world not yet subjected to capitalist production under its aegis. It is noteworthy that free trade here is seen as a zero sum game, where value is transferred from the powerless to the powerful, often under the use of (physical) force i.e. in the form of colonial armies, foreign backed dictators or economic and financial pressure.

A variant of imperialist theorizing is World Systems Theory developed by Immanuel Wallerstein, in which a "core" set of nations exploits the "periphery". In this model, the core imports cheap raw materials from the periphery and sells expensive manufactured goods back to the periphery market. As a consequence of this structure, the core is able to maintain its wealth by keeping the most profitable sectors of economic production within its boundaries, while the periphery is unable to move out of impoverishment (even though transitions towards a semi-periphery are possible).

Somewhat connected to this strand of thinking is the developmentalist school. Developmentalists, however, instead of embracing revolution against capitalism as a policy prescription are closer to the early institutionalists in the sense that they advocate for national strategies such as infant industry protection or the development of import substitution industries that are seen to be able to increase their power in the world trade system in the long term. The political implications from this theory were, for example, the proposal of the New International Economic Organization (NIEO) in the UN in the 1970s, which however failed, and national economic strategies pursued by various states in Latin America roughly from the 1930s until the 1970s.

Ecological

Ecological economists take issue with free trade for a variety of reasons. Firstly, they contend that the negative externalities from the shipping of goods around the globe are not sufficiently accounted for (i.e. CO_2 emissions from transport, environmental damages from shipwrecks, destruction of the biosphere for transport routes). So from an environmentalist view, it might actually be preferably to produce and consume locally sidestepping global production chains, which have a high and often not even clearly measurable impact on the environment. Secondly, free trade agreements are criticized as a means to break local or national environmental protection laws. This concern is related to the reduction of non-tariff barriers, which might include environmental protection laws and also the inclusion of international trade arbitration courts, which could fine states for introducing future protection laws. Yet another concern related to trade is that states might "green" their economies not by altering production and consumption patterns but by outsourcing environmentally harmful production to other parts of the world and then import goods, whose production entails, for example, high levels of CO_2.

Balance of Payment

Balance Of Payment (BOP) is a statement which records all the monetary transactions made between residents of a country and the rest of the world during any given period. This statement includes all the transactions made by/to individuals, corporates and the government and helps in monitoring the flow of funds to develop the economy. When all the elements are correctly included in the BOP, it should sum up to zero in a perfect scenario. This means the inflows and outflows of funds should balance out. However, this does not ideally happen in most cases.

BOP statement of a country indicates whether the country has a surplus or a deficit of funds i.e when a country's export is more than its import, its BOP is said to be in surplus. On the other hand, BOP deficit indicates that a country's imports are more than its exports. Tracking the transactions under BOP is something similar to the double entry system of accounting. This means, all the transaction will have a debit entry and a corresponding credit entry.

Vitality of Balance of Payment for a Country

A country's BOP is vital for the following reasons:

- BOP of a country reveals its financial and economic status.
- BOP statement can be used as an indicator to determine whether the country's currency value is appreciating or depreciating.
- BOP statement helps the Government to decide on fiscal and trade policies.
- It provides important information to analyze and understand the economic dealings of a country with other countries.

By studying its BOP statement and its components closely, one would be able to identify trends that may be beneficial or harmful to the economy of the county and thus, then take appropriate measures.

Elements of Balance of Payment

There are three components of balance of payment viz current account, capital account, and financial account. The total of the current account must balance with the total of capital and financial accounts in ideal situations.

Current Account

The current account is used to monitor the inflow and outflow of goods and services between countries. This account covers all the receipts and payments made with respect to raw materials and manufactured goods. It also includes receipts from engineering, tourism, transportation, business services, stocks, and royalties from patents and copyrights. When all the goods and services are combined, together they make up to a country's Balance Of Trade (BOT).

There are various categories of trade and transfers which happen across countries. It could be visible or invisible trading, unilateral transfers or other payments/receipts. Trading in goods between countries are referred to as visible items and import/export of services (banking, information technology etc) are referred to as invisible items. Unilateral transfers refer to money sent as gifts or donations to residents of foreign countries. This can also be personal transfers like – money sent by relatives to their family located in another country.

Capital Account

All capital transactions between the countries are monitored through the capital account. Capital transactions include the purchase and sale of assets (non-financial) like land and properties. The capital account also includes the flow of taxes, purchase and sale of fixed assets etc by migrants moving out/in to a different country. The deficit or surplus in the current account is managed through the finance from capital account and vice versa.

There are 3 major elements of capital account:

- Loans & borrowings – It includes all types of loans from both the private and public sectors located in foreign countries.
- Investments – These are funds invested in the corporate stocks by non-residents.
- Foreign exchange reserves – Foreign exchange reserves held by the central bank of a country to monitor and control the exchange rate does impact the capital account.

Financial Account

The flow of funds from and to foreign countries through various investments in real estates, business ventures, foreign direct investments, etc., is monitored through the financial account. This account measures the changes in the foreign ownership of domestic assets and domestic ownership of foreign assets. On analyzing these changes, it can be understood if the country is selling or acquiring more assets (like gold, stocks, equity etc).

Foreign Exchange

Foreign exchange, or forex, is the conversion of one country's currency into another. In a free economy, a country's currency is valued according to the laws of supply and demand. In other words, a currency's value can be pegged to another country's currency, such as the U.S. dollar, or even to a basket of currencies. A country's currency value may also be set by the country›s government.

However, most countries float their currencies freely against those of other countries, which keeps them in constant fluctuation.

Factors Affecting Currency Value

The value of any particular currency is determined by market forces based on trade, investment, tourism, and geo-political risk. Every time a tourist visits a country, for example, they must pay for goods and services using the currency of the host country. Therefore, a tourist must exchange the currency of his or her home country for the local currency. Currency exchange of this kind is one of the demand factors for a particular currency.

Another important factor of demand occurs when a foreign company seeks to do business with another in a specific country. Usually, the foreign company will have to pay in the local company's currency. At other times, it may be desirable for an investor from one country to invest in another, and that investment would have to be made in the local currency as well. All of these requirements produce a need for foreign exchange and contribute to the vast size of foreign exchange markets.

Foreign exchange is handled globally between banks and all transactions fall under the auspice of the Bank for International Settlements (BIS).

How Inflation Affects Foreign Exchange Rates

Inflation can have a major effect on the value of a country's currency and its foreign exchange rates with other currencies. While it is just one factor among many, inflation is more likely to have a significant negative effect on a currency's value and foreign exchange rate. A very low rate of inflation does not guarantee a favorable exchange rate, but an extremely high inflation rate is very likely to have a negative impact.

Inflation is also closely related to interest rates, which can influence exchange rates. The interrelationship between interest rates and inflation is complex and often difficult for currency-issuing countries to manage. Low interest rates spur consumer spending and economic growth, and generally positive influences on currency value. If consumer spending increases and demand grows to exceed supply, inflation may ensue, which is not necessarily a bad outcome. However, low interest rates don't usually attract foreign investment the way higher interest rates can. Higher interest rates attract foreign investment, which is likely to increase demand for a country's currency.

Foreign Exchange Rate

Foreign exchange rate is the price at which one currency can be converted into another. It represents the rate at which a firm may exchange one currency for another. Thus, the exchange rate is simply the amount of a nation's currency that can be bought at a given time for a specified amount of the currency of another country.

The actual amount received in conversion or the effective exchange rate, usually differs from the stated rate because it takes into account all taxes, commissions and other costs that the public must pay to complete the transaction and actually receive the foreign funds.

Types of Foreign Exchange Rate

Fixed and Floating Rates:

When Government of a country fixes the rate of exchange for its own currency, it is termed as 'Fixed Exchange Rate'. This is also known as official rate of exchange. Fixed exchange rates are fixed by the respective Governments from time to time for the betterment of their economy.

In contrast exchange rates move, as in any other market place, depending on the demand and supply pressure and are further influenced by the market forces and economic conditions of the respective countries. Floating exchange rate may be free floating or a managed floating.

A currency is freely floating if there does not exist a system of fixed exchange rates and if the Central Bank of the country in question does not attempt to influence the value of the currency. However, in reality this kind of situation does not exist.

In most of the countries Governments attempt to influence movements of exchange rate either through direct intervention in the exchange market or through a mix of fiscal and monetary policies. Under such circumstances, floating is called as 'managed' or 'dirty float'.

A number of countries use a pegged float as a system of exchange rates. The value of one currency is pegged to the value of another currency that itself floats. In a joint float, currencies in a particular group have a fixed exchange value in terms of each other, but the group of currencies floats in relation to other currencies outside the group.

The fixed exchange rate system has inbuilt advantage of simplifying exchange transactions. It imbibes self-discipline for economic policies by participating countries.

Spot and Forward Rates:

Spot rates refer to those rates which are applicable on the day of transaction in which physical delivery is made within two working days after the date of transaction the spot exchange between two currencies should be the same across the various banks engaged in rendering foreign exchange services.

In case of large discrepancy customers or other banks would buy large amounts of a currency from whatever banks quoting relatively low price and sell the same immediately to a bank quoting a relatively high price. This will cause adjustments in the exchange rate quotations that would offset the existing discrepancy.

In Forward rates, exchange rates are fixed in advance for a transaction which matures at some specified future date. The exchange at the date in future will be at the price agreed upon now. Foreign exchange rates are function of forward demand and forward supply of various currencies.

A foreign currency is said to be at a forward premium if its future value exceeds its present value in terms of domestic currency and it is said to be at discount if the reverse is true.

Forward exchange rates are quoted on most major currencies for different maturities. Standard maturities quoted by banks are of 1, 3, 6, 9 and 12 months. Maturities beyond one year are now becoming more common. Maturity extending to 5 and beyond 5 years is also possible for good bank customers.

Foreign Exchange Markets

The foreign exchange market (also known as forex, FX or the currency market) is an over-the-counter (OTC) global marketplace that determines the exchange rate for currencies around the world. Participants are able to buy, sell, exchange and speculate on currencies. Foreign exchange markets are made up of banks, forex dealers, commercial companies, central banks, investment management firms, hedge funds, retail forex dealers and investors.

The foreign exchange market – also called forex, FX, or currency market – was one of the original financial markets formed to bring structure to the burgeoning global economy. In terms of trading volume it is, by far, the largest financial market in the world. Aside from providing a venue for the buying, selling, exchanging and speculation of currencies, the forex market also enables currency conversion for international trade settlements and investments. According to the Bank for International Settlements (BIS), which is owned by central banks, trading in foreign exchange markets averaged $5.1 trillion per day in April 2016.

Currencies are always traded in pairs, so the "value" of one of the currencies in that pair is relative to the value of the other. This determines how much of country A's currency country B can buy, and vice versa. Establishing this relationship (price) for the global markets is the main function of the foreign exchange market. This also greatly enhances liquidity in all other financial markets, which is key to overall stability.

The value of a country's currency depends on whether it is a "free float" or "fixed float". Free floating currencies are those whose relative value is determined by free market forces, such as supply/demand relationships. A fixed float is where a country's governing body sets its currency's relative value to other currencies, often by pegging it to some standard. Free floating currencies include the U.S. Dollar, Japanese Yen and British Pound, while examples of fixed floating currencies include the Chinese Yuan and the Indian Rupee.

One of the most unique features of the forex market is that it is comprised of a global network of financial centers that transact 24 hours a day, closing only on the weekends. As one major forex hub closes, another hub in a different part of the world remains open for business. This increases the liquidity available in currency markets, which adds to its appeal as the largest asset class available to investors.

The most liquid trading pairs are, in descending order of liquidity:

- EUR/USD.
- USD/JPY.
- GBP/USD.

Forex Leverage

The leverage available in FX markets is one of the highest that traders and investors can find anywhere. Leverage is a loan given to an investor by their broker. With this loan, investors are able to increase their trade size, which could translate to greater profitability. A word of caution, though: losses are also amplified.

For example, investors who have a $1,000 forex market account can trade $100,000 worth of currency with a margin of 1 percent. This is referred to as having a 100:1 leverage. Their profit or loss will be based on the $100,000 notional amount.

Benefits of using the Forex Market

There are some key factors that differentiate the forex market from others, like the stock market.

- There are fewer rules, which means investors aren't held to the strict standards or regulations found in other markets.
- There are no clearing houses and no central bodies that oversee the forex market.
- Most investors won't have to pay the traditional fees or commissions that you would on another market.

- Because the market is open 24 hours a day, you can trade at any time of day, which means there's no cut-off time to be able to participate in the market.
- Finally, if you're worried about risk and reward, you can get in and out whenever you want and you can buy as much currency as you can afford.

International Capital Market

A capital market is basically a system in which people, companies, and governments with an excess of funds transfer those funds to people, companies, and governments that have a shortage of funds. This transfer mechanism provides an efficient way for those who wish to borrow or invest money to do so. For example, every time someone takes out a loan to buy a car or a house, they are accessing the capital markets. Capital markets carry out the desirable economic function of directing capital to productive uses.

There are two main ways that someone accesses the capital markets—either as debt or equity. While there are many forms of each, very simply, debt is money that's borrowed and must be repaid, and equity is money that is invested in return for a percentage of ownership but is not guaranteed in terms of repayment.

In essence, governments, businesses, and people that save some portion of their income invest their money in capital markets such as stocks and bonds. The borrowers (governments, businesses, and people who spend more than their income) borrow the savers' investments through the capital markets. When savers make investments, they convert risk-free assets such as cash or savings into risky assets with the hopes of receiving a future benefit. Since all investments are risky, the only reason a saver would put cash at risk is if returns on the investment are greater than returns on holding risk-free assets. Basically, a higher rate of return means a higher risk.

For example, let's imagine a beverage company that makes $1 million in gross sales. If the company spends $900,000, including taxes and all expenses, then it has $100,000 in profits. The company can invest the $100,000 in a mutual fund (which are pools of money managed by an investment company), investing in stocks and bonds all over the world. Making such an investment is riskier than keeping the $100,000 in a savings account. The financial officer hopes that over the long term the investment will yield greater returns than cash holdings or interest on a savings account. This is an example of a form of direct finance. In other words, the beverage company bought a security issued by another company through the capital markets. In contrast, indirect finance involves a financial intermediary between the borrower and the saver. For example, if the company deposited the money in a savings account, and then the savings bank lends the money to a company (or a person), the bank is an intermediary. Financial intermediaries are very important in the capital marketplace. Banks lend money to many people, and in so doing create economies of scale. This is one of the primary purposes of the capital markets.

Capital markets promote economic efficiency. In the example, the beverage company wants to invest its $100,000 productively. There might be a number of firms around the world eager to borrow funds by issuing a debt security or an equity security so that it can implement a great business idea. Without issuing the security, the borrowing firm has no funds to implement its plans. By shifting the funds from the beverage company to other firms through the capital markets, the funds are employed to their maximum extent. If there were no capital markets, the beverage company might have kept its $100,000 in cash or in a low-yield savings account. The other firms would also have had to put off or cancel their business plans.

International capital markets are the same mechanism but in the global sphere, in which governments, companies, and people borrow and invest across national boundaries. In addition to the benefits and purposes of a domestic capital market, international capital markets provide the following benefits:

- Higher returns and cheaper borrowing costs: These allow companies and governments to tap into foreign markets and access new sources of funds. Many domestic markets are too small or too costly for companies to borrow in. By using the international capital markets, companies, governments, and even individuals can borrow or invest in other countries for either higher rates of return or lower borrowing costs.
- Diversifying risk: The international capital markets allow individuals, companies, and governments to access more opportunities in different countries to borrow or invest, which in turn reduces risk. The theory is that not all markets will experience contractions at the same time.

The structure of the capital markets falls into two components—primary and secondary. The primary market is where new securities (stocks and bonds are the most common) are issued. If a corporation or government agency needs funds, it issues (sells) securities to purchasers in the primary market. Big investment banks assist in this issuing process as intermediaries. Since the primary market is limited to issuing only new securities, it is valuable but less important than the secondary market.

The vast majority of capital transactions take place in the secondary market. The secondary market includes stock exchanges (the New York Stock Exchange, the London Stock Exchange, and the Tokyo Nikkei), bond markets, and futures and options markets, among others. All these secondary markets deal in the trade of securities. The term securities includes a wide range of financial instruments. You're probably most familiar with stocks and bonds. Investors have essentially two broad categories of securities available to them: equity securities, which represent ownership of a part of a company, and debt securities, which represent a loan from the investor to a company or government entity.

Creditors, or debt holders, purchase debt securities and receive future income or assets in return for their investment. The most common example of a debt instrument is the bond. When investors buy bonds, they are lending the issuers of the bonds their money. In return, they will receive interest payments usually at a fixed rate for the life of the bond and receive the principal when the bond expires. All types of organizations can issue bonds.

Stocks are the type of equity security with which most people are familiar. When investors buy stock, they become owners of a share of a company's assets and earnings. If a company is successful, the price that investors are willing to pay for its stock will often rise; shareholders who bought stock at a lower price then stand to make a profit. If a company does not do well, however, its stock may decrease in value and shareholders can lose money. Stock prices are also subject to both general economic and industry-specific market factors.

The key to remember with either debt or equity securities is that the issuing entity, a company or government, only receives the cash in the primary market issuance. Once the security is issued, it is traded; but the company receives no more financial benefit from that security. Companies are motivated to maintain the value of their equity securities or to repay their bonds in a timely manner so that when they want to borrow funds from or sell more shares in the market, they have the credibility to do so.

For companies, the global financial, including the currency, markets (1) provide stability and predictability, (2) help reduce risk, and (3) provide access to more resources. One of the fundamental purposes of the capital markets, both domestic and international, is the concept of liquidity, which basically means being able to convert a noncash asset into cash without losing any of the principal value. In the case of global capital markets, liquidity refers to the ease and speed by which shareholders and bondholders can buy and sell their securities and convert their investment into cash when necessary. Liquidity is also essential for foreign exchange, as companies don't want their profits locked into an illiquid currency.

Major Components of the International Capital Markets

International Equity Markets

Companies sell their stock in the equity markets. International equity markets consists of all the stock traded outside the issuing company's home country. Many large global companies seek to take advantage of the global financial centers and issue stock in major markets to support local and regional operations.

For example, ArcelorMittal is a global steel company headquartered in Luxembourg; it is listed on the stock exchanges of New York, Amsterdam, Paris, Brussels, Luxembourg, Madrid, Barcelona, Bilbao, and Valencia. While the daily value of the global markets changes, in the past decade the international equity markets have expanded considerably, offering global firms increased options for financing their global operations. The key factors for the increased growth in the international equity markets are the following:

- Growth of developing markets: As developing countries experience growth, their domestic firms seek to expand into global markets and take advantage of cheaper and more flexible financial markets.
- Drive to privatize: In the past two decades, the general trend in developing and emerging markets has been to privatize formerly state-owned enterprises. These entities tend to be large, and when they sell some or all of their shares, it infuses billions of dollars of new equity into local and global markets. Domestic and global investors, eager to participate in the growth of the local economy, buy these shares.
- Investment banks: With the increased opportunities in new emerging markets and the need to simply expand their own businesses, investment banks often lead the way in the expansion of global equity markets. These specialized banks seek to be retained by large

companies in developing countries or the governments pursuing privatization to issue and sell the stocks to investors with deep pockets outside the local country.

- Technology advancements: The expansion of technology into global finance has opened new opportunities to investors and companies around the world. Technology and the Internet have provided more efficient and cheaper means of trading stocks and, in some cases, issuing shares by smaller companies.

International Bond Markets

Bonds are the most common form of debt instrument, which is basically a loan from the holder to the issuer of the bond. The international bond market consists of all the bonds sold by an issuing company, government, or entity outside their home country. Companies that do not want to issue more equity shares and dilute the ownership interests of existing shareholders prefer using bonds or debt to raise capital (i.e., money). Companies might access the international bond markets for a variety of reasons, including funding a new production facility or expanding its operations in one or more countries.

Foreign Bond

A foreign bond is a bond sold by a company, government, or entity in another country and issued in the currency of the country in which it is being sold. There are foreign exchange, economic, and political risks associated with foreign bonds, and many sophisticated buyers and issuers of these bonds use complex hedging strategies to reduce the risks. For example, the bonds issued by global companies in Japan denominated in yen are called *samurai bonds*. As you might expect, there are other names for similar bond structures. Foreign bonds sold in the United States and denominated in US dollars are called *Yankee bonds*. In the United Kingdom, these foreign bonds are called *bulldog bonds*. Foreign bonds issued and traded throughout Asia except Japan, are called *dragon bonds*, which are typically denominated in US dollars. Foreign bonds are typically subject to the same rules and guidelines as domestic bonds in the country in which they are issued. There are also regulatory and reporting requirements, which make them a slightly more expensive bond than the Eurobond. The requirements add small costs that can add up given the size of the bond issues by many companies.

Eurobond

A Eurobond is a bond issued outside the country in whose currency it is denominated. Eurobonds are not regulated by the governments of the countries in which they are sold, and as a result, Eurobonds are the most popular form of international bond. A bond issued by a Japanese company, denominated in US dollars, and sold only in the United Kingdom and France is an example of a Eurobond.

Global Bond

A global bond is a bond that is sold simultaneously in several global financial centers. It is denominated in one currency, usually US dollars or Euros. By offering the bond in several markets at the same time, the company can reduce its issuing costs. This option is usually reserved for higher rated, creditworthy, and typically very large firms.

Eurocurrency Markets

The Eurocurrency markets originated in the 1950s when communist governments in Eastern Europe became concerned that any deposits of their dollars in US banks might be confiscated or blocked for political reasons by the US government. These communist governments addressed their concerns by depositing their dollars into European banks, which were willing to maintain dollar accounts for them. This created what is known as the Eurodollar—US dollars deposited in European banks. Over the years, banks in other countries, including Japan and Canada, also began to hold US dollar deposits and now Eurodollars are any dollar deposits in a bank outside the United States. (The prefix *Euro-* is now only a historical reference to its early days). An extension of the Eurodollar is the Eurocurrency, which is a currency on deposit outside its country of issue. While Eurocurrencies can be in any denominations, almost half of world deposits are in the form of Eurodollars.

The Euroloan market is also a growing part of the Eurocurrency market. The Euroloan market is one of the least costly for large, creditworthy borrowers, including governments and large global firms. Euroloans are quoted on the basis of LIBOR, the London Interbank Offer Rate, which is the interest rate at which banks in London charge each other for short-term Eurocurrency loans.

The primary appeal of the Eurocurrency market is that there are no regulations, which results in lower costs. The participants in the Eurocurrency markets are very large global firms, banks, governments, and extremely wealthy individuals. As a result, the transaction sizes tend to be large, which provides an economy of scale and nets overall lower transaction costs. The Eurocurrency markets are relatively cheap, short-term financing options for Eurocurrency loans; they are also a short-term investing option for entities with excess funds in the form of Eurocurrency deposits.

Offshore Centers

The first tier of centers in the world are the world financial centers, which are in essence central points for business and finance. They are usually home to major corporations and banks or at least regional headquarters for global firms. They all have at least one globally active stock exchange. While their actual order of importance may differ both on the ranking format and the year, the following cities rank as global financial centers: New York, London, Tokyo, Hong Kong, Singapore, Chicago, Zurich, Geneva, and Sydney.

In addition to the global financial centers are a group of countries and territories that constitute offshore financial centers. An offshore financial center is a country or territory where there are few rules governing the financial sector as a whole and low overall taxes. As a result, many offshore centers are called tax havens. Most of these countries or territories are politically and economically stable, and in most cases, the local government has determined that becoming an offshore financial center is its main industry. As a result, they invest in the technology and infrastructure to remain globally linked and competitive in the global finance marketplace.

Examples of well-known offshore financial centers include Anguilla, the Bahamas, the Cayman Islands, Bermuda, the Netherlands, the Antilles, Bahrain, and Singapore. They tend to be small countries or territories, and while global businesses may not locate any of their operations in these locations, they sometimes incorporate in these offshore centers to escape the higher taxes they would have to pay in their home countries and to take advantage of the efficiencies of these financial centers. Many global firms may house financing subsidiaries in offshore centers for the same benefits. For example, Bacardi, the spirits manufacturer, has $6 billion in revenues, more than 6,000 employees worldwide, and twenty-seven global production facilities. The firm is headquartered in Bermuda, enabling it to take advantage of the lower tax rates and financial efficiencies for managing its global operations.

As a result of the size of financial transactions that flow through these offshore centers, they have been increasingly important in the global capital markets.

The Role of International Banks, Investment Banks, Securities Firms and Global Financial Firms

The role of international banks, investment banks, and securities firms has evolved in the past few decades. Let's take a look at the primary purpose of each of these institutions and how it has changed, as many have merged to become global financial powerhouses.

Traditionally, international banks extended their domestic role to the global arena by servicing the needs of multinational corporations (MNC). These banks not only received deposits and made loans but also provided tools to finance exports and imports and offered sophisticated cash-management tools, including foreign exchange. For example, a company purchasing products from another country may need short-term financing of the purchase; electronic funds transfers (also called wires); and foreign exchange transactions. International banks provide all these services and more.

In broad strokes, there are different types of banks, and they may be divided into several groups on the basis of their activities. Retail banks deal directly with consumers and usually focus on mass-market products such as checking and savings accounts, mortgages and other loans, and credit cards. By contrast, private banks normally provide wealth-management services to families and individuals of high net worth. Business banks provide services to businesses and other organizations that are medium sized, whereas the clients of corporate banks are usually major business entities. Lastly, investment banks provide services related to financial markets, such as mergers and acquisitions. Investment banks also focused primarily on the creation and sale of securities (e.g., debt and equity) to help companies, governments, and large institutions achieve their financing objectives. Retail, private, business, corporate, and investment banks have traditionally been separate entities. All can operate on the global level. In many cases, these separate institutions have recently merged, or were acquired by another institution, to create global financial powerhouses that now have all types of banks under one giant, global corporate umbrella.

However the merger of all of these types of banking firms has created global economic challenges. In the United States, for example, these two types—retail and investment banks—were barred from being under the same corporate umbrella by the Glass-Steagall Act. Enacted in 1932 during the Great Depression, the Glass-Steagall Act, officially called the Banking Reform Act of 1933, created the Federal Deposit Insurance Corporations (FDIC) and implemented bank reforms, begining in 1932 and continuing through 1933. These reforms are credited with providing stability and reduced risk in the banking industry for decades. Among other things, it prohibited bank-holding companies from owning other financial companies. This served to ensure that investment banks and banks would remain separate—until 1999, when Glass-Steagall was repealed. Some analysts have criticized the repeal of Glass-Steagall as one cause of the 2007–8 financial crisis.

Because of the size, scope, and reach of US financial firms, this historical reference point is important in understanding the impact of US firms on global businesses. In 1999, once bank-holding companies were able to own other financial services firms, the trend toward creating global financial powerhouses increased, blurring the line between which services were conducted on behalf of clients and which business was being managed for the benefit of the financial company itself. Global businesses were also part of this trend, as they sought the largest and strongest financial players in multiple markets to service their global financial needs. If a company has operations in twenty countries, it prefers two or three large, global banking relationships for a more cost-effective and lower-risk approach. For example, one large bank can provide services more cheaply and better manage the company's currency exposure across multiple markets. One large financial company can offer more sophisticated risk-management options and products. The challenge has become that in some cases, the party on the opposite side of the transaction from the global firm has turned out to be the global financial powerhouse itself, creating a conflict of interest that many feel would not exist if Glass-Steagall had not been repealed. The issue remains a point of ongoing discussion between companies, financial firms, and policymakers around the world. Meanwhile, global businesses have benefited from the expanded services and capabilities of the global financial powerhouses.

For example, US-based Citigroup is the world's largest financial services network, with 16,000 offices in 160 countries and jurisdictions, holding 200 million customer accounts. It's a financial powerhouse with operations in retail, private, business, and investment banking, as well as asset management. Citibank's global reach make it a good banking partner for large global firms that want to be able to manage the financial needs of their employees and the company's operations around the world.

International Banking

International banking is just like any other banking service, but it takes place across different nations or internationally. To put in another way, international banking is an arrangement of financial service by a residential bank of one country to the residents of another country. Mostly multinational companies and individuals use this banking facility for transacting.

Example of International Banking

Suppose Microsoft, an American company is functioning in London. It is in need of funds to meet its working capital requirements. In such scenario, Microsoft can avail the banking services in form of loans, overdraft or any other financial service through banks in London. Here, the residential bank of London shall be giving its services to an American company. Therefore, the transaction between them can be said to be part of international banking facility.

Let us have a look at features and benefits of international banking.

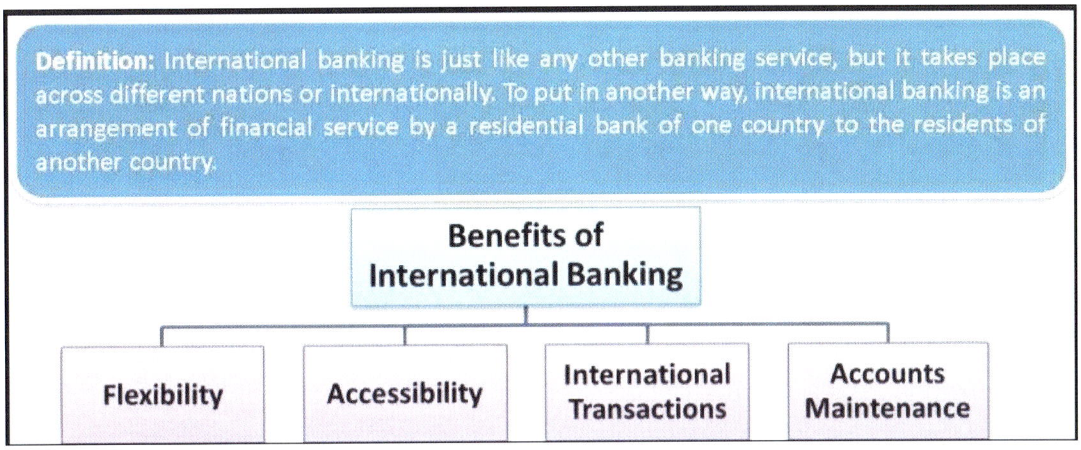

Features and Benefits of International Banking

Flexibility

International banking facility provides flexibility to the multinational companies to deal in multiple currencies. The major currencies that multinational companies or individuals can deal with include euro, dollar, pounds, sterling, and rupee. The companies having headquarters in other countries can manage their bank accounts and avail financial services in other countries through international banking without any hassle.

Accessibility

International banking provides accessibility and ease of doing business to the companies from different countries. An individual or MNC can use their money anywhere around the world. This gives them a freedom to transact and use their money to meet any requirement of funds in any part of the world.

International Transactions

International banking allows the business to make international bill payments. The currency conversion facility allows the companies to pay and receive money easily. Also, the benefits like overdraft facility, loans, deposits, etc. are available every time for overseas transactions.

Accounts Maintenance

A multinational company can maintain the records of global accounts in a fair manner with the help of international banking. All the transactions of the company are recorded in the books of the banks across the globe. By compiling the data and figures, the accounts of the company can be maintained.

Globalization and growing economies around the world have led to the development of international banking facility. The world is now a marketplace and each business wants to exploit it. Geographical boundaries are no more a concern. With access to technology, banking facilities have grown vastly. One prime example of it is international banking. In the years to come, such banks would see higher growth and higher profitability. Big business houses are expanding themselves at a rapid pace. To maintain the growth, these businesses will need the financial services of international banking. Therefore, the demand for international banking facilities will increase.

Foreign Direct Investment

Foreign Direct Investment (FDI) is an investment from a party in one country into a business or corporation in another country with the intention of establishing a lasting interest. Lasting interest differentiates FDI from foreign portfolio investments, where investors passively hold securities from a foreign country. A foreign direct investment can be made by obtaining a lasting interest or by expanding one's business into a foreign country.

Lasting Interest and the Element of Control

An investment into a foreign firm is considered an FDI if it establishes a lasting interest. A lasting interest is established when an investor obtains at least 10% of the voting power in a firm.

The key to foreign direct investment is the element of control. Control represents the intent to actively manage and influence a foreign firm's operations. This is the major differentiating factor between FDI and a passive foreign portfolio investment.

For this reason, a 10% stake in the foreign company's voting stock is necessary to define FDI. However, there are cases where this criterion is not always applied. For example, it is possible to exert control over more widely traded firms despite owning a smaller percentage of voting stock.

Methods of Foreign Direct Investment

As mentioned above, an investor can make a foreign direct investment by expanding their business in a foreign country. Amazon opening a new headquarters in Vancouver, Canada would be an example of this.

Reinvesting profits from overseas operations, as well as intracompany loans to overseas subsidiaries, are also considered foreign direct investments.

Finally, there are multiple methods for a domestic investor to acquire voting power in a foreign company. Below are some examples:

- Acquiring voting stock in a foreign company.
- Mergers and acquisitions.
- Joint ventures with foreign corporations.
- Starting a subsidiary of a domestic firm in a foreign country.

Benefits of Foreign Direct Investment

Foreign direct investment offers advantages to both the investor and the foreign host country. These incentives encourage both parties to engage in and allow FDI.

Below are some of the benefits for businesses:

- Market diversification.
- Tax incentives.
- Lower labor costs.
- Preferential tariffs.
- Subsidies.

The following are some of the benefits for the host country:

- Economic stimulation.
- Development of human capital.
- Increase in employment.
- Access to management expertise, skills, and technology.

For businesses, most of these benefits are based on cost-cutting and lowering risk. For host countries, the benefits are mainly economic.

Disadvantages of Foreign Direct Investment

Despite many benefits, there are still two main disadvantages to FDI, such as:

- Displacement of local businesses.
- Profit repatriation.

The entry of large firms, such as Walmart, may displace local businesses. Walmart is often criticized for driving out local businesses that cannot compete with its lower prices.

In the case of profit repatriation, the primary concern is that firms will not reinvest profits back into the host country. This leads to large capital outflows from the host country.

As a result, many countries have regulations limiting foreign direct investment.

Types and Examples of Foreign Direct Investment

Typically, there are two main types of FDI: horizontal and vertical FDI.

Horizontal: a business expands its domestic operations to a foreign country. In this case, the business conducts the same activities but in a foreign country. For example, McDonald's opening restaurants in Japan would be considered horizontal FDI.

Vertical: a business expands into a foreign country by moving to a different level of the supply chain. In other words, a firm conducts different activities abroad but these activities are still related to the main business. Using the same example, McDonald's could purchase a large-scale farm in Canada to produce meat for their restaurants.

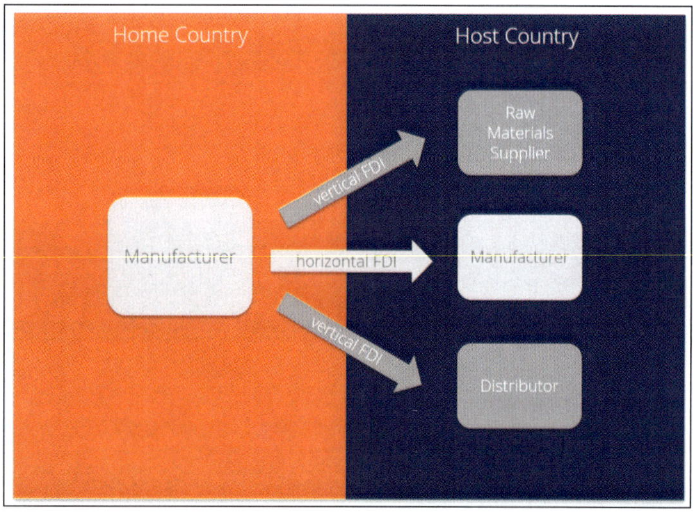

However, two other forms of FDI have also been observed: Conglomerate and platform FDI.

Conglomerate: A business acquires an unrelated business in a foreign country. This is uncommon, as it requires overcoming two barriers to entry: Entering a foreign country and entering a new industry or market. An example of this would be if Virgin Group, which is based in the United Kingdom, acquired a clothing line in France.

Platform: A business expands into a foreign country but the output from the foreign operations is exported to a third country. This is also referred to as export-platform FDI. Platform FDI commonly happens in low-cost locations inside free-trade areas. For example, if Ford purchased manufacturing plants in Ireland with the primary purpose of exporting cars to other countries in the EU.

References

- International-economics-its-concept-parts, international-economics- 4205: economicsdiscussion.net, Retrieved 23 April, 2019
- Economic-globalization, financial-glossary: marketbusinessnews.com, Retrieved 27 June, 2019
- International-monetary-system- 4256: economicsdiscussion.net, Retrieved 19 May, 2019
- Fixed-and-flexible-exchange-rates-international-trade, international-trade- 26046: yourarticlelibrary.com, Retrieved 28 March, 2019
- Free-trade-economic-theories: exploring-economics.org, Retrieved 30 January, 2019
- Foreign-exchange-rate-concept-and-types, foreign-exchange- 72309: yourarticlelibrary.com, Retrieved 18 August, 2019

Permissions

All chapters in this book are published with permission under the Creative Commons Attribution Share Alike License or equivalent. Every chapter published in this book has been scrutinized by our experts. Their significance has been extensively debated. The topics covered herein carry significant information for a comprehensive understanding. They may even be implemented as practical applications or may be referred to as a beginning point for further studies.

We would like to thank the editorial team for lending their expertise to make the book truly unique. They have played a crucial role in the development of this book. Without their invaluable contributions this book wouldn't have been possible. They have made vital efforts to compile up to date information on the varied aspects of this subject to make this book a valuable addition to the collection of many professionals and students.

This book was conceptualized with the vision of imparting up-to-date and integrated information in this field. To ensure the same, a matchless editorial board was set up. Every individual on the board went through rigorous rounds of assessment to prove their worth. After which they invested a large part of their time researching and compiling the most relevant data for our readers.

The editorial board has been involved in producing this book since its inception. They have spent rigorous hours researching and exploring the diverse topics which have resulted in the successful publishing of this book. They have passed on their knowledge of decades through this book. To expedite this challenging task, the publisher supported the team at every step. A small team of assistant editors was also appointed to further simplify the editing procedure and attain best results for the readers.

Apart from the editorial board, the designing team has also invested a significant amount of their time in understanding the subject and creating the most relevant covers. They scrutinized every image to scout for the most suitable representation of the subject and create an appropriate cover for the book.

The publishing team has been an ardent support to the editorial, designing and production team. Their endless efforts to recruit the best for this project, has resulted in the accomplishment of this book. They are a veteran in the field of academics and their pool of knowledge is as vast as their experience in printing. Their expertise and guidance has proved useful at every step. Their uncompromising quality standards have made this book an exceptional effort. Their encouragement from time to time has been an inspiration for everyone.

The publisher and the editorial board hope that this book will prove to be a valuable piece of knowledge for students, practitioners and scholars across the globe.

Index